D0185417

The aim of the Overcoming series is to enable people with a range of common problems and disorders to take control of their own recovery programme.

Each title, with its specially tailored programme, is devised by a practising clinician using the latest techniques of cognitive behavioural therapy – techniques that have been shown to be highly effective in changing the way patients think about themselves and their problems.

The series was initiated in 1993 by Peter Cooper, Professor of Psychology at Reading University and Research Fellow at the University of Cambridge in the UK, whose original volume on overcoming bulimia nervosa and binge-eating continues to help many people in the USA, the UK and Europe.

Titles in the series include:

OVERCOMING ANXIETY

*A self-help guide to using
Cognitive Behavioral Techniques*

Helen Kennerley

ROBINSON

ROBINSON

First published in Great Britain in 1997 by Robinson Publishing Ltd

This edition published in 2014 by Robinson

Copyright © Helen Kennerley, 1997, 2014

7 9 10 8

A CIP catalogue record for this book
is available from the British Library.

Important Note
This book is not intended as a substitute for medical advice or treatment.
Any person with a condition requiring medical attention should consult
a qualified medical practitioner or suitable therapist.

ISBN 978-1-84901-878-4

Printed and bound in Great Britain by CPI Group (UK) Ltd, Croydon CR0 4YY

Papers used by Robinson are from well-managed forests and other responsible sources

Robinson
An imprint of
Little, Brown Book Group
Carmelite House
50 Victoria Embankment
London EC4Y 0DZ

An Hachette UK Company
www.hachette.co.uk

www.littlebrown.co.uk

Dedicated to the memory of Liz Campbell (1954–2010)

Contents

Contents

Acknowledgements

In 1980 I arrived in Oxford and met the two psychologists who influenced this book. The first was Peter Cooper, the series editor of the 'Overcoming' series, and the second was Liz Campbell. They introduced me to cognitive therapy and helped me appreciate its potential – they got me hooked on CBT. I suspect they used it in helping me overcome my own anxieties about settling in Oxford, and I remain very grateful for their generous conversations, their encouragement and support.

Sadly, Liz Campbell died recently and I want to dedicate this second edition of the book to her – if anyone managed stress well and helped others to deal with it, it was Liz. She was a remarkable woman: warm, witty, determined to enjoy life and to help others enjoy life. Anyone who has met Liz will have stories to tell about how she inspired them. I can't imagine that anyone would fail to say that she was extraordinary. Dr Campbell was a champion: she was an excellent clinician, she pioneered psychology courses, was president of the British Psychological Society, and wrote texts that changed the face of stress management in the police force. She was also a brave woman who always did what she thought was right, and I'll never forget being in Asia with her doing charity work. For the most part I sought the safety of the British Council build-ings and adopted the approach of never upsetting anyone and staying where it was safe. She took on officials, slipped out at night to attend forbidden meetings, got involved in the poli-tics and continued to support these causes from the UK. That was Liz – brave, principled, an example to us all.

Liz was an inspiration, as are each of the people with whom I've been fortunate enough to work clinically. I am indebted to the patients who have bravely shared their difficulties and their recoveries, and I am indebted to outstanding colleagues such as Joan Kirk, Gillian Butler, Melanie Fennel, Christine Padesky and the late David Westbrook who have shared their wisdom over the years.

Writing a book like this takes time away from loved ones and I am grateful, too, for the indulgence of my children and husband. Thank you.

Preface to the Second Edition

In the fifteen years since this book was first published, some things in the world of anxiety management remain unchanged. In particular, it is still a fact that we need worries, fear and anxieties to survive and that we are in the business of *managing* unhelpful anxieties not getting rid of them. This, as you will see, remains a theme throughout this new book.

However, there have been some key developments in the last decade and a half that are reflected in this second edition. We know so much more about the brain and stress, about the problems caused by worry, about the importance of compassion in recovering from psychological problems, about the role of exercise in coping. I've tried to embrace these developments in this second edition and so you'll notice familiar messages and some new ones, too.

Something else that has happened since 1997, when the first edition of this book was published, is that there has been increasing research on very particular anxiety disorders, and the 'Overcoming' range reflects this: Constable & Robinson now offer self-help books that focus on Panic, Worry, Social Anxiety, Obsessive Compulsive Disorder, Health Anxiety and Post-traumatic Stress. I'm really pleased to be able to say that you now have so much more to guide you in overcoming different forms of anxiety – but I also hope that you will still find that this single volume makes a difference.

Introduction

Why a cognitive behavioural approach?

The approach this book takes in attempting to help you over-come your problems with anxiety is a cognitive behavioural one. A brief account of the history of this form of intervention might be useful and encouraging. In the 1950s and 1960s a set of thera-peutic techniques was developed, collectively termed 'behaviour therapy'. These techniques shared two basic features. First, they aimed to remove symptoms (such as anxiety) by dealing with those symptoms themselves, rather than their deep-seated under-lying historical causes (traditionally the focus of psychoanalysis, the approach developed by Sigmund Freud and his associates). Second, they were scientifically based, in the sense that they used techniques derived from what laboratory psychologists were finding out about the mechanisms of learning, and they put these techniques to scientific test. The area where behaviour therapy initially proved to be of most value was in the treatment of anxiety disorders, especially specific phobias (such as extreme fear of animals or heights) and agoraphobia, both notoriously difficult to treat using conventional psychotherapies.

After an initial flush of enthusiasm, discontent with behav-iour therapy grew. There were a number of reasons for this, an important one of which was the fact that behaviour therapy did not deal with the internal thoughts which were so obviously central to the distress that many people were experiencing. In particular, behaviour therapy proved inadequate when it came to the treatment of depression. In the late 1960s and early 1970s a treatment for depression was developed called 'cognitive therapy'. The pioneer in this enterprise was an American psychiatrist, Professor Aaron T. Beck. He developed a theory of depression which emphasized the importance of people's depressed styles of thinking, and, on the basis of this theory, he specified a new form of therapy. It would not be an exaggeration to say that Beck's work has changed the nature of psychotherapy, not just for depression but for a range of psychological problems, including anxiety.

The techniques introduced by Beck have been merged with the techniques developed earlier by the behaviour therapists to produce a therapeutic approach which has come to be known as 'cognitive behavioural therapy' (or CBT). This therapy was originally investigated for the treatment of depression. It was subjected to the strictest scientific testing and was found to be highly successful for a significant proportion of cases. Furthermore, it has now become clear that there are specific patterns of disturbed thinking associated with a wide range of psychological problems, not just depression, and that the CBT treatments which deal with these are highly effective. So, effective cognitive behavioural treatments have been developed for a range of anxiety disorders, such as panic disorder, generalized anxiety disorder, specific phobias, social phobia, obsessive compulsive disorders, and hypochondriasis (health anxiety), as well as for other conditions such as drug addictions, and eating disorders like bulimia nervosa. Indeed, cognitive behavioural techniques have been found to have an application beyond the narrow categories of psychological disorders. They have been applied effectively, for example, to helping people with weight problems, couples with marital difficulties, as well as those who wish to give up smoking or deal with drinking problems; and they have also been successfully applied to dealing with low self-esteem and perfectionism.

The current book is concerned with the treatment of anxiety disorders. This is the area where the most research into the effectiveness of CBT has been done and where there is the most evidence for the success of this approach. Importantly, there is a core of therapeutic techniques that have applicability across a wide range of anxiety disorders, as well as specific strategies of use in particular forms of anxiety. These techniques, both general and specific, are described in this book, in a particularly engaging and accessible manner.

The starting-point for CBT is the realization that the way we think, feel and behave are all intimately linked, and changing the way we think about ourselves, our experiences, and the world around us changes the way we feel and what we are able to do. So, for example, by helping an anxious person identify and challenge their automatic thoughts about danger, a route out of the cycle of anxious thoughts and feelings can be found. Similarly, habitual responses, like avoidance of potential threat, are driven by a complex set of thoughts and feelings, and CBT, as you will discover from this book, by providing a means for the behaviour, thoughts and feelings to be brought under control, enables these responses to be undermined and a different kind of life to be possible.

Although effective CBT treatments have been developed

for a wide range of disorders and problems, these treatments are not currently widely available; and, when people try to help themselves on their own, they often, inadvertently, do things which make matters worse. In recent years the community of cognitive behavioural therapists has responded to this situation. What they have done is to take the principles and techniques of specific cognitive behavioural therapies for particular problems and present them in manuals which people can read and apply themselves. These manuals specify a systematic programme of treatment which the person works through to overcome their difficulties. In this way, CBT techniques of proven value are being made available on the widest possible basis.

The use of self-help manuals is never going to replace the need for therapists. Many people with emotional and behavioural problems will need the help of a qualified therapist. It is also the case that, despite the widespread success of CBT, some people will not respond to it and will need one of the other treatments available. Nevertheless, although research on the use of these self-help manuals is at an early stage, the work done to date indicates that for a great many people such a manual is sufficient for them to overcome their problems without professional help. Sadly, many people suffer on their own for years. Sometimes they feel reluctant to seek help without first making a serious effort to manage on their own. Sometimes they feel too awkward or even ashamed to ask for help. Sometimes appropriate help is not forthcoming despite their efforts to find it. For many of these people the cognitive behavioural self-help manual will provide a lifeline to a better future.

Peter J. Cooper
The University of Reading, 2013

Part One

Understanding Worry, Fear and Anxiety

1

Worries, fears and anxieties

Some things are just fact, and it is a fact that we need worries, fears and anxieties to survive. But we do need to make our anxiety work for us, not against us, and that's what this book will help you to do.

Worries, fear and anxieties are not usually physically or mentally damaging. We've evolved to have anxious feelings and our minds and bodies have evolved to recover from them. On the whole they are understandable and they are often vital to survival. You might find that you cope better just by reassuring yourself that you have normal reactions to stress or danger.

Not long ago I experienced the normal response to threat. Walking across a field, I heard an aggressive 'mooing' behind me. I felt fear – it could be an unfriendly bull – and I felt the sensations of anxiety: my heart raced and my muscles tensed. This was perfectly normal and it turned out to be vital as there was indeed a bull behind me. I needed muscle tension and a pumping heart to give me the energy to get out of the way quickly. Much to onlookers' amusement, I raced to the edge of the field and leapt over a fence – inelegant but effective! I hadn't done this sort of physical activity since my schooldays and I simply would not have managed if I hadn't been so primed for action and full of fear.

Clearly, anxiety, worry and fear are necessary responses if we are in danger. They only become a problem when they are exaggerated or when there is no need to worry or be afraid. If you were in an open field and heard angry 'mooing', fear would be reasonable – but your anxiety would be misplaced if you were simply walking through the countryside and felt fearful of every noise in case it meant a nearby bull, or if you were watching a farming programme on TV and felt anxious when you heard the sound of a bull or when you saw a bull on the screen. This is not at all helpful and this type of anxiety might even be handicapping you because it stops you from watching nature programmes or simply taking a walk in the countryside. This is the sort of problem anxiety that this book will help you master.

So what we are saying is that anxiety only becomes a problem when it is exaggerated or you experience it when there is no need to worry or be afraid. Keep it under control and it's an important ally, as we will see later.

The normal responses to stress

We couldn't have been more relaxed. We were holidaying, driving through the hills – the scenery was beautiful, the weather was great. Suddenly something large leapt out in front of us – it was a deer but I didn't really notice just what it was at the time; I simply felt a whoosh of adrenalin and my heart jumped into my throat. The hairs on the back of my neck bristled, my body tensed and all I could think of was our safety. I gripped the steering wheel, turning the car away from the animal but

4

trying to keep us on the road. That was all I could think of: keep the car on the road, keep everyone safe. We went into a skid – I didn't hear my passengers' questions or comments; I just concentrated on using my strength to keep us safe and keep the van away from the trees. It was a heavy vehicle – I don't know where the strength came from but I managed to steer us clear of danger. Afterwards, I felt jittery and exhausted but this eased off with time.

From this brief account you can, again, see how anxiety is crucial to survival because it prepares us for coping with stress or danger:

- First, we sense danger (this is the trigger for the stress response);
- Next, fear triggers the release of hormones that cause physical and mental changes. These prepare us for *fight* (taking on a challenge) or *flight* (getting out of a dangerous situation) or *freeze* (cautious watchfulness);
- Now our bodies are primed for action (we find the energy and strength for fight or flight or we find the stamina to remain still and watchful) and our thinking is focused;
- Once the stress or danger has passed, these temporary changes subside and our minds and bodies return to a calmer state.

Our ancestors were faced with very tangible threats to their safety, such as wild animals or hostile neighbours, so for them this repertoire of *fight-flight-freeze* responses was very necessary.

The stresses we face today might be more subtle – delays, ongoing domestic problems, deadlines, job loss – but we still experience the same bodily, mental and behavioural changes as did our forebears.

It starts in your brain

It all begins in the brain: we are 'hard-wired' to react. A structure in the brain (the thalamus) is very sensitive to information that could be important to our survival and it immediately activates another part of the brain that determines how we should react (the amygdala). The amygdala then triggers very basic emotional reactions – namely fear, disgust, anger, sadness and joy – but it is particularly sensitive to threat, and it responds to danger by switching on a number of reactions in our bodies and minds (see below). This happens very rapidly and without our awareness; we 'react to danger rather than think about it', as neuroscientist James le Doux has said. This is a crucial observation – it explains why we just can't stop our fear responses, why we can feel so helpless in our reactions: *we are simply programmed that way.*

It is very important that we react so automatically because rapid and unquestioned responses can sometimes be life-saving – the van driver in the example above just reacted, she didn't *think* about the situation, she didn't try to identify the animal before she took action to avoid it and keep the vehicle on the road – and this is just as well because it would have lost her valuable time. So the next time you have that 'whoosh' of emotion the van driver described, remember that it's your brain doing what it's supposed to do – reacting to danger rather than wasting valuable time reflecting on it.

The thalamus also sends an ever so slightly slower message to the brain's cortex. The cortex stores memories and information that allows us to check out our emotional responses against previous experiences – again we do this automatically. For example, the van driver had seen 'something' that could have been dangerous – her amygdala would have reacted and she would have had the 'whoosh'. However, suppose it was not a deer but a shadow suddenly falling across the road. A fraction of a second after the amygdala had responded, the information in the cortex would have enabled her to recognize that it was just a shadow and the feelings would have subsided. Perhaps you've had that experience – that 'Agh . . . oh, it's OK actually'. This is another quite normal reaction to perceived danger, and something that happens without our having consciously to think about it. We first react to danger and then we put on the emotional brakes if necessary – if it's just a shadow and not a deer.

Sometimes the trigger for the fear reaction is *a thought or an image* crossing our mind rather than something tangible, something external like the deer or the bull in my examples. Our brain is so sensitive to threat that sometimes if we simply think about something frightening, the amygdala will do its job and get the fear response going.

A shy man who is asked to a party might have the thought: 'I can't do that, I'll embarrass myself, it would be awful.' Or he might have a mental image of being embarrassed at the party.

Either way, something will go through his mind that heralds threat and his amygdala will kick in swiftly. Once it does, he will experience a powerful mental and bodily response, even though he's not in immediate danger.

A woman with a snake phobia would feel a powerful sense of fear just on seeing a picture of a snake, or if she mistakenly *believed* that she had seen a snake or if she *believed* that she was likely to come into contact with one.

Just thinking about the thing you fear can make you feel afraid – your brain is set up to do this really quickly, and again it's normal for this to happen. Your mind and your body will respond to try to keep you safe – and this means that it will sometimes do this *even if the threat is not real.*

So let's look more closely at these responses to fear, starting with the bodily changes that you can expect.

The bodily changes

. . . I felt a whoosh of adrenalin and my heart jumped into my throat. The hairs on the back of my neck bristled, my body tensed . . .

The physical responses that we are likely to experience include:

- tensing of muscles
- increased breathing
- raised blood pressure
- perspiration
- digestive changes

8

All of these reactions increase our readiness for action and explain many of the bodily sensations that we associate with anxiety, such as tight muscles (even to the point of getting muscle tremor), panting, racing heart, sweating, 'butterflies'. This is the ideal state for someone who has to react with a burst of energy: the athlete who is about to run an important race, the child who needs to escape bullies, the driver who has to manage a dangerous skid, or the middle-aged mum who has to get out of the way of a bull, for example. Without these physical changes, we are sluggish rather than primed for action.

These changes are usually short-lived and disappear once we sense that danger has passed. They are not harmful in themselves as our bodies are well evolved to cope with these sudden changes.

In addition to priming our bodies for action, fear also primes our minds to deal with threat, so we experience psychological changes, too.

The psychological changes

. . . all I could think of was our safety . . . That was all I could think of: keep the car on the road . . . I didn't hear my passengers' questions or comments . . .

The psychological changes linked with stress include shifts in the way we think (mental changes), and sometimes in the way we feel (emotional changes). These, again, help us to cope under stress. If we face danger or stress, our thinking becomes more focused and our ability to concentrate and problem-solve gets better. We are in an ideal state of mind to face serious challenges – a surgeon carrying out an operation, a stockbroker making a swift decision about an investment, a parent restraining a child who is about to walk into the road. Without this mental stress response our reactions might be too careless.

We can also experience a range of emotions, such as an increased irritability or even a sense of well-being. We've all seen the stressed father becoming short-tempered with his children or heard of the executive who becomes exhilarated as she gets closer to meeting her stressful deadlines, or witnessed the excited teenager watching a horror film. We can also feel emotionally numb during or after a stressful or traumatic experience. The van driver in the earlier example felt no emotion during the skid, and this was a good thing – she wasn't distracted by strong feelings. It is also common to feel emotionally numb or 'flat' following a shock – after an accident, for example, people often report feeling nothing or even feeling a bit serene. I can recall crashing my car and feeling almost 'dream-like' afterwards. I knew intellectually that I'd just escaped a life-threatening experience, but I felt detached and calm. I had no trouble getting out of the wreckage, organizing help, giving a clear account to the police and the hospital workers. I even took an exam the next day and did rather well. Two days later my emotions caught up with reality and I was distressed, but by that time I had been able to deal with the aftermath of the crash. Once more, we see that the brain's response to stress can be really helpful.

In essence, the natural bodily and psychological changes that happen in the face of a threat increase our chances of survival.

The behavioural changes

. . . It was a heavy vehicle — I don't know where the strength came from but I managed to steer us clear of danger. . .

The behavioural responses to stress or danger are usually forms of:

- escape (flight)
- combat (fight)
- cautious watchfulness

If I see a tree branch falling towards me, I get a burst of energy and jump out of the way in order to escape (flight). If I am driving and go into a skid, I find the strength to hold on to the steering wheel (fight). If a colleague criticizes me unfairly, I argue my case (fight). If I sense that the dark street could conceal a mugger, I don't run but I am cautious and keep my eyes and ears open for signs of danger (freeze), or if I sense that I could be challenged in a meeting, I keep a watchful eye on my colleagues so that I am prepared (freeze). By now, you know that I am going to remind you that these are vital reactions: without such changes in behaviour I would find myself trapped under a branch or caught up in an uncontrolled skid or ill-prepared for threat.

In summary then, the bodily, mental and behavioural responses to stress that I've described so far are absolutely normal, helpful,

11

and they can be vital. You should also be aware that, up to a point, our ability to cope with stress actually improves as we experience more stress. This might sound counter-intuitive, but the fact is that if we are too calm or relaxed we simply cannot get our minds and bodies into action. We need stress to activate us. Imagine the concert pianist or the professional footballer who is very relaxed – this is not a good state for their performance; they will not be as mentally alert or as physically prepared as the performer who feels some stress, whose thinking has become focused and whose body is ready to give that extra surge of energy if necessary. This is shown in Figure 1. At the bottom of the graph, we are relaxed but physically and mentally ill-equipped to deal with danger because we are not primed for action. As our tension rises, our body and mind become increasingly able to confront stress.

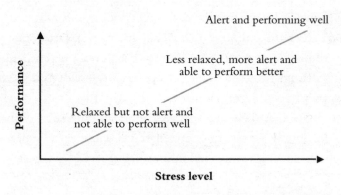

Figure 1: Stress and performance

It is so important to appreciate that the bodily and mental experience of stress is normal and helpful because our *interpretation* of what is happening colours our emotional response. That, in turn, determines how well we cope. Some years ago I was listening to the British radio programme *Desert Island Discs*. The guest that day was the singer Carly Simon who still suffers from pre-performance nerves, despite many years performing in front of large audiences. She described an interesting conversation she had with Bruce Springsteen. Just before a concert she reflected that it was strange, after all these years, that she still felt her heart race, her breathing change and she became tense and edgy. Apparently, Springsteen nodded in agreement: 'Yeah – great, isn't it!' For him it was a welcome (and exhilarating) sign of being prepared and this helped his performance, while for her it was an unwelcome sign that she was feeling very nervous. One set of normal responses, two interpretations, two different outlooks.

So far we have looked at the short-term impact of stress, but many of you will be concerned about the effects of long-term anxiety and long-term stresses. So let's turn our attention to that.

Long-term and excessive stress

I used to feel good about my life and about my part-time work. I enjoyed things, felt I had a good relationship and, I think, I did well at my job. Then the cutbacks started and we were

13

all under stress. At first it wasn't too bad because we 'pulled together' and supported each other. But as time has gone on the stress has increased. People I know have been made redundant so there is a constant threat of losing my job and we support each other less now because we are all struggling and we don't have the emotional energy to give to each other. Emotionally it is taking quite a toll on me: I wake up feeling nervous and I can't concentrate as well as I used to. I've started to simply get through the working day rather than being able to enjoy it. I'm much more tired than I used to be and I am sorry to say much more irritable. I try not to let it affect our home life but I do find it harder to find the enthusiasm and energy to do things with my partner and I know I'm more 'snappy' with those around me.

We've seen that stress responses are helpful in the short term because they prepare us for physical action and focus our minds on the immediate problem. However, they evolved as an immediate and temporary response to stress – a reaction that was switched off as soon as the danger had passed. If these reactions are not switched off – if the stress response becomes chronic – then we pass our peak. After that point our performance, our ability to cope, begins to deteriorate. You can see this in Figure 2 opposite: the stress–performance curve. This is a pattern that was established over a hundred years ago by two researchers, Yerkes and Dodson. Although their initial research was on mice, it was quickly established that the same pattern is seen in humans.

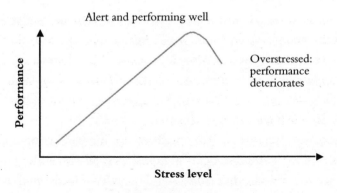

Figure 2: The stress–performance curve

In short, what Yerkes and Dodson's findings tell us is that we can have too much of a good thing. Up to a point the stress response works well for us, but if it goes on too long we become overstressed and we cope less well. It is not just chronic (long-term) stress that sends us 'over the edge' as it were, but excessive stress will do this, too. Excessive stress can be caused by external circumstances (such as having to sit many exams in a short period, or if a great deal depends on the outcome of an exam) or by internal triggers (such as long-standing health fears exaggerating our worries about illnesses). So the exhausted and nervous student taking an exam might become *so* worried that his mind goes blank; the anxious mum who is *so* frightened that her baby might have meningitis can't think straight and is rather incoherent in telling the doctor about her fears; the nervous musician might be *so* worried about her performance that her hands become shaky and she can't play her guitar. In each of these instances, the stress response is no longer working *for* the person but has started to work *against* them.

15

The good news is that it is possible to 'rein in' the stress response and get it working for you again – and the techniques in this book will help you to do just this – but before we go on to managing long-term or excessive stress, let's look more closely at the bodily and mental changes you might expect if your stresses have become chronic.

This next section is not intended to increase your anxieties – you won't necessarily experience all the difficulties that are described – but understanding what can happen as a result of being under excessive strain might help you to gain a different perspective when you are anxious about the way you feel.

The bodily changes

When we are under long-term stress, the bodily sensations become more persistent and sometimes unpleasant. Although the following lists of symptoms might sound alarming, remember:

- they are reversible
- they are normal responses to more extreme stress
- you can look forward to being able to manage these symptoms

Muscular tension, so important for fight and flight, can develop into muscular discomfort throughout the body and be experienced as:

- headaches
- difficulty in swallowing
- shoulder, neck and chest pain

- stomach cramps
- trembling
- weak legs

With prolonged or extreme stress, you can become aware of your heart pounding and, as your blood pressure rises, begin to experience:

- light-headedness
- blurred vision
- ringing in your ears

As your breathing rate increases you might feel:

- dizzy
- nauseous
- short of breath

If your digestive system is affected by prolonged stress then you might suffer from:

- sickness
- diarrhoea
- stomach pain

Finally, sweating can become excessive and, although this is not harmful, it can cause embarrassment.

Clearly, these sensations and reactions can be alarming in themselves; but remind yourself that they are common responses to extreme stress and that there is an explanation for them. This then might help you feel a little calmer.

By now, it will be obvious that the stress response is a very physical reaction and, if it is prolonged, it can become really uncomfortable. However, these physical reactions are sometimes the first indication that we are overstressed. So, if you get aches, pains, high blood pressure and so on, ask yourself: *Is my body telling me I'm overstressed?* These symptoms can be an invaluable 'stress-thermometer' reminding us to take it easy.

The psychological changes

The psychological reactions to extreme stress tend to show themselves in our thinking and our emotions.

With regard to the thoughts (or the images) that run through our minds, we worry, we anticipate the worst; we predict that a problem can't be solved and generally think negatively. If you are reading this book, you have probably experienced this sort of thinking:

> *This is all going to go badly! I can't cope! It's never going to be OK!*

This negative outlook makes us even more afraid and then the physical symptoms of fear kick in and these can be alarming enough to drive more negative thinking.

> *Pains in my chest. There's something wrong with my heart! This feeling is unbearable and there's nothing I can do about it.*

Therefore we can get caught up in a most unhelpful vicious cycle, with negative thoughts and bodily changes fuelling each other during stressful times – a perfect recipe for keeping stress levels high and prolonging the physical discomfort and worry.

18

It is also more difficult to stay tuned in to what is going on around us and to think quickly and to remember things when we are under extreme stress. At such times, we tend to suffer from:

- poor concentration
- less creative thinking
- memory problems
- worrying

We tend to be preoccupied with our fears and this takes its toll in another way – we find that we have:

- poor problem-solving abilities

All in all, this means that it gets harder to think ourselves out of a difficult situation. We might tell ourselves to 'calm down' or 'be sensible', but this is very difficult to do when we are under stress.

The emotional changes linked with onoing worry and anxiety are typically those of:

- irritability
- constant fearfulness
- demoralization

As you can imagine, when any of us is feeling like this we are bound to find it much more difficult to cope, and then stress is much more likely to get on top of us.

It's no wonder that managing stress and anxiety can be really hard, so don't berate yourself if you find it difficult.

The behavioural changes

Now to the changes in our behaviour: these, if they go on for a long time, can also cause more difficulties. We can become exhausted by:

- constant fidgeting
- rushing around
- sleep problems

Stress might cause unhealthy changes in our appetite:

- increased comfort eating, smoking or drinking
- under-eating

These physical reactions can take a toll on our sense of well-being and further handicap us in dealing with difficulties.

The most common response to fear, though, is running away:

- avoidance

This is part of the hard-wired 'flight' response we learnt about earlier. Unfortunately, the relief we get from avoidance is often only temporary and, worse still, it can start to eat away at our self-confidence so that certain situations become even more difficult to face. So it starts to work against us rather than for us as a coping strategy.

You might remember that we also have a 'fight' response, and this often represents our best attempt at coping. We try to tackle our fear head-on. Although this can be helpful, sometimes we overdo things, or we take on too much too soon, and our coping strategy makes things worse:

- coping gone wrong

Elissa thought that she could cope with her health fears by constantly going to her GP for reassurance, but she just got 'hooked' on hearing his reassuring words and the anxieties would come back soon after each consultation.

Fabio seemed to worry about everything and he tried to manage this by carrying out a simple ritual each morning. This gave him the confidence to start the day, but (because this didn't really make him safe) things still went wrong from time to time and so he kept making his ritual more elaborate until it had become a problem in itself.

Clara was afraid of travelling on public transport but she believed that the way to overcome fear was to face it head on – so she bravely tried to use the train during the rush hour. This was far too much for her and so she felt terrible and even less confident that she could cope.

You can see that anxiety-related problems can actually be driven by *our best efforts to cope*. There is a logic to what we do: if we are afraid and believe that there is nothing we can do about it, we avoid; and if we think that we can do something, we'll give it a try even though our coping strategy might backfire. So give yourself credit for doing your best to manage your fears and worries and make a commitment to improving your coping strategies so that they start to work for you and not against you. This book will help you find new ways of coping.

From all you have now read, it will be clear that despite our best efforts, our response to anxieties and stress can itself become distressing. This might be because the physical changes are alarming, or because the worrying and the emotional changes impair our ability to cope, or because a loss of self-confidence makes it difficult to face fears and overcome them. Whatever the reason, when the natural stress response causes more distress, a cycle has been created that is difficult to control. This cycle, which maintains the stress response after it has been triggered, is the common factor in all forms of *problem* worry, fear and anxiety.

Whatever the trigger, the keys to persistent problems are the *maintaining cycles* or the *vicious cycles* of worry, fear and anxiety, and the key to overcoming anxiety is breaking these cycles – this is what we will explore in the next chapter.

Summary

- Worries, fears and anxieties are not just normal, they are vital to survival

- They trigger changes in the way we feel in our bodies and emotions, and changes in the way that we think and behave

- When stress and anxiety go on for lengthy periods of time, or when they are out of proportion to the situation, they can cause problems

- Vicious cycles keep these problems alive, and the key to overcoming anxiety is breaking them

2

The cycles that maintain anxieties

Once I start to worry, I don't seem to be able to stop. Something enters my head and just seems to take over. I get upset and tense when this happens and then I begin to worry that I am doing myself physical harm by being so tense. This sets off another chain of fears and then I get scared that I am losing my mind. I try to avoid things that might set off my anxieties but then I get concerned that I am getting more and more withdrawn. There doesn't seem to be a way out.

The answer to the questions: 'Why doesn't my anxiety get better?' and 'Why does my anxiety get worse?' is usually: 'Because you are caught up in a *vicious cycle*.' Vicious cycles are very effective in that they are good at keeping stress and fear going. The example above shows us how a perfectly healthy or normal response to stress can develop into a problem when we get caught up in a pattern that creates more stress. The cycle can be driven by bodily sensations, by a psychological reaction, by certain behaviour or by social circumstances, and sometimes it is driven by a combination of these factors. The first step in breaking the pattern is identifying the cycles that drive your distress.

Below we explore the different ways that anxieties are maintained. Don't get disheartened when you see just how many forms this 'vicious cycle' can take – the more examples we look at, the more likely it is that you will recognize the unhelpful cycles that fit your experiences. Then you'll be able to appreciate that it's no wonder that you are struggling. Better still, you will be able to see a way out. The key to managing anxieties is breaking these cycles – each time you spot one, you will have moved a step further in overcoming your anxieties. The techniques in Part Three of this book will give you lots of ideas and skills for breaking patterns and even turning them into 'virtuous cycles' that can work to your advantage.

Bodily maintaining cycles

Bodily responses to stress can trigger cycles of distress. Although strong physical experiences are common when we worry and we are scared, they can be very alarming and can then cause even more tension and worry – especially if we misinterpret what's happening to us or if our physical reactions are rather excessive. When this happens, what are essentially normal responses can lead to alarming consequences:

- Muscular tension can be misinterpreted: 'Chest pain: this is a heart attack!'; 'Tight throat: I'll choke!'; 'Pain in my head: I have a tumour!'; 'Stomach pains: cancer!'
- Changes in breathing rates can be misconstrued: 'I can't breathe: I'll suffocate!'

- Light-headedness might be misunderstood: 'I'm getting dizzy. I'll collapse!'; 'I'm having a stroke!'

Alternatively, the reaction might simply be: 'I can't cope!' It is easy to see that reaching any of these alarming conclusions would increase anyone's distress. This is illustrated in Figure 3, below.

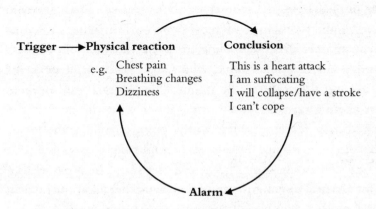

Figure 3: How our physical reactions can maintain stress

Sometimes we actually recognize that the muscular pain, the difficulties in breathing, and so on, are simply responses to stress. However, if our bodily reactions are extreme the experience can be really uncomfortable and frightening enough to create a fear of the symptoms of anxiety: *a fear of fear.*

> *I had an anxiety attack last year. I know that it was anxiety, nothing life-threatening, but the way I felt was so awful that I'm now scared of getting anxious.*

Once this happens, even the anticipation of the awful experience of feeling afraid can set off anxiety: the fear of fear triggers fear. This can be a terrible bind to get into, but, as you will see later, it is possible to break free of it.

Bodily reactions to stress can keep problems going in other ways, too. Physical symptoms like shaking, sweating, nausea and faltering voice can impair our performance, particularly in public. Being self-conscious about this can easily increase worry and worsen the physical symptoms. Imagine a nervous man who is afraid of spilling tea as he carries a cup across a room, or an anxious child who has to recite a poem to his class and is scared that he might falter. In each case the fear of making mistakes could bring about what the man or the child most fears: trembling to the point of spilling the tea or becoming inarticulate. Another example might be a child who is stressed at school and because of her stress she is nauseous – this physical discomfort could then cause her additional worry and worsen her stress. Or a man might discover that he has developed high blood pressure and be so concerned by this that his anxiety levels increase and further elevate his blood pressure.

Another way that longer-term stress can affect us is by disrupting our sleep:

It's all very well for my doctor to say, 'Just relax and then you'll find that you sleep better,' but she's not the one who is tossing and turning for hours, worrying that another night of poor sleep is going to make the next day hell. I'm a teacher and I find it impossible to control a classroom full of children if I am feeling exhausted, and that's how I feel every day. I do avoid coffee now, but it doesn't help much because I have reached the point where I am on edge all of the time. I dread going to bed because I know I won't sleep properly and then I can predict that I won't be able to cope well the next day at school. Knowing this winds me up so much that the last thing I'm able to do is relax.

In this example you can appreciate that the sleeplessness causes new difficulties and, sadly, stress responses often do just this.

Sometimes the way that we cope with the new difficulties just adds to the problem:

I get so irritated with my sister who keeps saying: 'It's all in your mind.' When I go on a car journey, I assure you that it's all in my stomach! While I'm at home I feel fine – unless I know that I have to go out later and then I can get into a bit of a state and have to go to the loo two or three times – but, as a rule, I am only ill on journeys. That's why I rarely go anywhere now. I stopped using public transport ages ago because I can't get out when I want to. I don't visit my sister, who lives thirty miles away, and I rely on the telephone much more now. Luckily, most of my family members live close by and they seem happy to drop in on me. If I have to make a trip, I will take some calming tablets that the doctor gave me. They make it possible for me to get to and from the clinic. I'm losing my confidence and my relationship with my sister is getting strained, and I think that's causing me more stress, which can't be good for me.

Psychological maintaining cycles: biased thinking

Problem anxieties are also driven by mental and emotional processes (psychological processes). Our thinking and our feelings can become more extreme as our fear levels increase – this happens to all of us. Sometimes our thoughts get quite distorted and we call this *biased thinking* (we will look at this in more detail later).

When we come face to face with a frightening or threatening situation, we tend to do a quick calculation – we estimate the danger and we estimate our ability to manage the situation. Imagine that I want to cross the road and I see a car travelling towards me – I quickly judge how likely it is to hit me if I step out now (estimating the danger) and I take into consideration how quickly I can move (coping ability). If the car is close, and if I'm weighed down by shopping, I decide to wait; if it isn't so close (less danger), and if I'm wearing sensible shoes and am free of baggage (good ability to cope), I might decide that it's safe for me to cross. It's a useful calculation and we do it automatically each time we face a potential threat. However, those of us with problem anxieties tend to:

- overestimate the danger and / or
- underestimate our ability to manage the situation or to cope

For example, people with a fear of driving tend to overestimate the dangers of driving and underestimate their driving skill; exam nerves are made worse by overestimating the likelihood

28

of failing an examination and underestimating one's ability; people with health anxieties overestimate the likelihood of disease and underestimate their ability to cope with it.

As you might predict, this is often the beginning of a vicious cycle: this unbalanced view exaggerates the fear and this then makes thinking more distorted or biased. Then it gets even harder to maintain a realistic view and to keep in mind our ability to cope, and we tend to manage the situation less and less well.

Imagine that you can't immediately spot your car keys on the kitchen table. You would simply scan the room in case you had put them somewhere else, and if you did not see them you would begin to think of all the other places where you might have left them. Now imagine that you are under pressure – you are late for a meeting and in a state of stress, the importance of the meeting increases:

- 'This is the one meeting this week that I can't afford to miss!' (overestimating the danger)
- 'I'll never find them in time and then I don't know what I'll do!' (underestimating ability to manage)

You become more anxious and your mind goes blank. You can't think where the keys might be. You begin to predict that you will miss the appointment and your position in the firm will be at risk. The worry makes you careless as you pick up bowls and cushions at random, unable to organize your search. Your tension levels rise further and all you can think about are the disastrous consequences of missing this now *very* important meeting. You are so focused on your escalating fears that you miss the obvious – your partner points out that the keys are in your pocket.

In this example, it is clear that an anxious mind can be a distorting mind, biased towards negative thoughts such as: 'I'll *never* find them!' This sort of biased thinking is common when we are stressed, and from time to time we all do it and we can get caught up in a simple and yet very powerful unhelpful cycle of increasing anxiety, worry and stress shown in Figure 4.

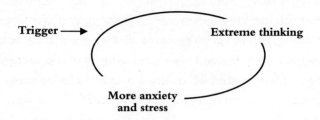

Figure 4: How the way we think can maintain anxieties

Thinking biases tend to fall into five areas:

- extreme thinking
- selective attention
- relying on intuition
- self-reproach
- worrying

It's a good idea to become familiar with this sort of 'skewed thinking' because if you can recognize it early you can often stop a vicious cycle from taking hold. The more familiar you are with your 'skewed thinking' the more easily you will catch it. There are many, many thinking biases, but some are more common than others, particularly when we get anxious, and the common ones are described in more detail below.

While you are reading through them, consider how many are typical of you and also when you are more likely to think like this – because different situations cause us to think differently. Also bear in mind that thinking biases can coexist, which means that you can experience more than one type of biased thinking. You will probably notice that some of these thinking styles are very similar, perhaps confusingly so: all-or-nothing thinking often overlaps with exaggeration and over-generalizing, while catastrophizing and worry can sometimes be similar. . . and so on. Don't get hung up on defining your thinking precisely; simply use the examples below to help you recognize how and when your thinking might be skewed. Try to get a feel for your particular 'Achilles heels' when it comes to thinking.

1 Extreme thinking: stretching a point

Catastrophizing

I'm worried that my report wasn't good enough – no, it was rubbish. The client will be disappointed and word will get out and people will know how useless I am and there will be repercussions. I'll be paying for it for a long time.

This wonderful word 'catastrophizing' simply means anticipating disaster as the only outcome, always assuming the worst.

Anyone with this outlook would be anxious. 'Catastrophizers' automatically assume that an official envelope must contain a tax demand or a speeding fine; that a scowl on a colleague's face means that he has a personal dislike of you; that a tremor in the aircraft is a sign of engine failure; that minor surgery will result in death. Sounds familiar?

Catastrophizing is common amongst people with health worries, and if your anxieties focus on health concerns, you might recognize some of the following: a headache heralds a stroke; chest pain means heart attack; skin tingling or numbness is a sign of multiple sclerosis; a lump below the skin surface is cancer; a sore throat is the beginning of a bout of flu that will stop you from completing the work you have lined up and that will mean that you never catch up with yourself and your reputation will be damaged for good . . . !

Catastrophizing can involve words and images. Sometimes it is a series of fleeting mental pictures that causes the distress rather than a series of thoughts. Although the thoughts and images are dramatic, the process of catastrophizing usually takes only a moment – and it is a powerful engine driving anxiety. Are there times and situations when you find yourself falling into this pattern?

All-or-nothing thinking

I have completely wrecked things. It couldn't be worse.

This means seeing everything in absolute terms rather than experiencing more moderate responses. Someone might declare 'I will *always* feel this badly', rather than considering 'I feel bad at the moment but I could get better with help', or '*Everyone always* picks on me', rather than 'Sometimes I'm criticized and sometimes it isn't fair'. Does this sound familiar?

Another common form of all-or-nothing thinking is expecting perfection in oneself: 'If it isn't perfect, it isn't acceptable'; 'This is not quite right: I have failed'. None of us is perfect, certainly not all of the time, and if we expect this of ourselves there's a good chance that we will be disappointed – and that might create further stress.

Unrealistic standards

I should have done this perfectly. I shouldn't have made a single mistake.

If you find that you frequently use 'should' and 'ought' and 'must', you are probably putting yourself under a lot of pressure. Sometimes we do this because teachers or parents impressed rules upon us, sometimes we do this because we don't feel good about ourselves and we try to compensate by performing well in all we do. While there is nothing wrong in trying our best, holding unrealistic expectations tends to cause disappointment and exhaustion – no one can please all the people all of the time. If I believe: 'I shouldn't make a single mistake', there is a chance that I'll be more nervous (and perhaps less able) than if I consider that I'll do my best and give myself credit for that. If I look back and think: 'I should have done better, I should have been perfect!' then I will feel bad about my performance and my self-confidence will suffer. This will make it harder for me next time and so I might not do so well. Can you recognize yet another example of a vicious cycle?'

2 Selective attention: looking on the bleak side

Exaggerating

Just my luck! Everything goes wrong for me – always.

This describes those times when we magnify the negative or worrying things in our lives. So if my boss pointed out that I'd forgotten to do something, I might exaggerate the meaning of this and think: 'I really am rubbish', rather than simply accepting that I had overlooked one thing amongst many things that I'd remembered. Another example would be if I hear a radio presenter saying that there is a link between drinking alcohol and getting cancer and I immediately conclude: 'I'm at risk! I drink alcohol – I'll get cancer!' I forget that the presenter has said moderate to high levels of alcohol and I only drink a little, and I forget that the presenter said that this is only in some cases. Instead, I immediately exaggerate the personal risk and this triggers real fear and panic. Do you ever find yourself doing this?

Overgeneralizing

Story of my life. I mess up everything and everyone knows it.

This is similar to exaggerating and the two often go together. *Overgeneralizing* means that we make too much of a single incident. For example, Ruth walked in to the office and one of her colleagues ignored her – she felt terrible because she immediately concluded that no one liked her. In fact, her colleague had his own worries and was preoccupied – but Ruth had fallen into the trap of assuming something far too quickly and then jumping to an alarming conclusion. She's not alone in doing this – we all do it from time to time, particularly when we are worried or stressed. A different example is Stefan who was concerned about being made redundant and so he had become more nervous at work. In this state, he became particularly aware of his mistakes – however small – and he exaggerated any errors he made. So, a really minor mistake could trigger a dramatic chain of thought: 'I'll never be able to complete this or any other task [all-or-nothing thinking, overgeneralization] and the manager will see me as incompetent [jumping to conclusions] and I'll lose my job [catastrophizing].' Of course, this would increase the poor man's stress and then it would be even more likely that his thinking became biased. Without wishing to be too catastrophic in writing this – the situation could get worse because the increased stress might also impair his work performance and further fuel his fears. Can you see how vicious, unhelpful cycles can build up all because our outlook is biased? The good news is that biased thinking can be addressed and vicious cycles can be broken – and we will get to that later.

Ignoring the positive

I can't do anything right.

Another common trap is mentally filtering out good and reassuring facts and events. If I were caught in this trap I wouldn't notice compliments or acknowledge achievements; I wouldn't recognize my strengths or good fortune; friends would hear me dismiss kind words and I would go home thinking that I'd achieved nothing. It's a thinking style that sucks the reward out of life. Other examples include: the student who ignores a range of good grades and focuses on a single poor result; the nurse who does not notice the many 'Thank-you's from his patients and dwells on the fact that one patient has criticized his work; the teenager who forgets compliments on her appearance because she is unhappy with the way her hair looks. These people are all ignoring the positive and sometimes combining it with exaggerating or overgeneralizing. Again, vicious cycles can emerge because anyone who fails to recognize achievements and personal strengths will lack self-confidence and therefore cope less well with stress. And when we are stressed we are more likely to fall into the trap of ignoring the positive.

Scanning

Nothing escapes my eagle eye.

Scanning, or searching for the thing we fear, can also drive problem anxiety, and this is for two reasons.

First, it simply increases the likelihood of seeing, feeling or hearing something scary. Someone who doesn't fear spiders might walk into a room without noticing cobwebs, dusty corners or even spiders. However, someone who is scared of spiders is on the lookout for danger and notices every single web, corner or crawling creature. Nothing that could suggest the presence of a spider would go unobserved, and this may make the fear worse. Similarly, someone who doesn't worry about their health usually tolerates aches, pains and minor discomforts without giving them too much notice, while the person with health fears notices exactly the same physical sensations, dwells on them and starts to worry about serious illness.

Second, when scanning, it is all too possible to experience false alarms. A false alarm for someone with a spider phobia might be mistaking fluff on the carpet for a spider or a crack in the wall for a web, while a frightening misinterpretation for a person with health fears would be finding a perfectly innocent swelling and presuming it's cancer. In either case, the worried person will become more scared.

Think about it for a moment – are there things you scan for? An unfriendly face, perhaps? Signs of poor hygiene? Curious noises on the plane?

3 Relying on intuition: having a gut feeling

Jumping to conclusions

That's the end of my job. My boss is going to think I'm totally incompetent.

This happens when we don't weigh up facts before we make up our mind – we simply respond to a gut feeling: 'That went really badly, everyone thought I was rubbish, I'll never be taken seriously!' We can jump to conclusions about the past ('That went really badly') or we can make predictions about the future ('I'll never be taken seriously'), and a particularly common form of jumping to conclusions involves mind-reading ('Everyone thought I was rubbish'). If we can't back up our conclusions then it's not really fair that we let them upset us – but that's what tends to happen. Once one of these thoughts comes to mind and we feel scared or depressed by it, then it is even harder to cope. Sometimes we simply feel jittery or scared and we jump to the conclusion that we must

37

be under threat – 'I feel it so it must be true' (more about this below, under emotional reasoning). How often do you find yourself accepting your conclusion rather than asking yourself if it's backed up by fact?

Emotional reasoning

I feel jittery – I must be shaking and everyone can see.

I feel jittery – I must be scared.

I feel scared – I must be under threat.

I feel like an idiot so I must be an idiot!

I feel self-conscious so everyone must be looking at me now.

This is the I-feel-it-so-it-must-be-true trap, and there are different triggers: physical (I feel jittery . . .'); emotional ('I feel scared . . .'); cognitive ('I feel like an idiot . . .'). Take the first of these – feeling shaky or jittery. Is it really the case that everyone would notice? Does it automatically follow that these sensations are fear? Away from a challenging situation it is possible to entertain other possibilities – perhaps I feel jittery, but no one can see it; perhaps I feel jittery because I'm hungry or I've had too much coffee or I'm cross. Any of these things could make me a bit shaky.

What about the conclusion that feeling scared must mean that there is something to be frightened about? Well, sometimes the sensation of fear is unfounded – a feeling is a feeling, not a fact. We've all probably had the experience of a *false* alarm – feeling scared when there is no need to, discovering that our alarm was unfounded – and it is important to hold onto that possibility.

Finally, there is the thought or image that triggers worry and fear: 'I feel like an idiot' or 'I feel as if everyone is looking at me'. Feeling something – even if we feel it quite strongly – doesn't make it so. At some point in your life you might well have had the conviction that Father Christmas was real, but that didn't make it true.

The point here is that we can sometimes misinterpret our thoughts and our feelings, and we need to think through the options before drawing a conclusion that could make our anxiety worse. For example, a teacher might feel like an idiot for all sorts of reasons (perhaps he was frequently told this by a cruel parent, perhaps he has low self-esteem and he's overly hard on himself), but the reality is he's a perfectly able person who makes an understandable mistake now and then. The best guideline you can follow is to review the evidence before drawing a conclusion based on intuition.

4 Self-reproach: the inner critic

Self-blame and criticism

I've only got myself to blame. It's all my fault.

A child accidentally breaks something. He's upset and afraid of what his mother might say. His older brother stands by his side and says: 'Look what you've done – that was so stupid!' How does he feel? Better? Worse? Less afraid? More frightened? Can he think straight now or is he less able to work out what to do? There's a good chance he feels bad and not very able to deal with the problem because, on the whole, a telling-off is undermining rather than inspiring. It reduces rather than builds confidence.

It makes it harder to cope. It is so easy to slip into the trap of self-reproach and criticism and it usually makes things worse.

If you catch yourself doing this, try to pause for a moment and ask yourself if you would be so hard on a good friend or on your child. Ask yourself what you would say to them if they were upset. You'd probably be much more understanding and constructive which would help them. Use the same standards for yourself.

Name calling

What an idiot I am!

It's so easy to carry around a really harsh and unforgiving inner voice. And just like the self-blaming voice it tends to make things worse. I know that sometimes we think that being tough will spur us on – and perhaps it does *sometimes* – but research shows us that on the whole encouragement works better. Throughout this book you will probably notice a theme of being compassionate towards yourself. It's an increasingly popular perspective in the world of Cognitive Behavioural Therapy (CBT) and for a good reason – people find that it helps them deal with quite a variety of difficulties. I appreciate that it's really difficult to adopt this attitude if you are used to being harsh towards yourself, but it will help you to become stronger and more resilient in the longer term.

Taking things personally

This is my fault. I must be to blame.

Some years ago I worked with a woman who tended to blame herself when something bad happened, but she argued that this was realistic and she was actually to blame – that is, until she found herself feeling guilty at a bus stop in the rain because a fellow passenger was complaining of feeling cold and uncomfortable. As she stood there feeling responsible, she realized that she took things personally even to the point of assuming personal blame for bad weather. As she thought more about it, she saw just how often she did this – at a social gathering she would feel that it was her fault if there was a lull in the conversation or if someone seemed awkward; if her boss was unhappy she assumed that he must be disappointed with her work; if a colleague was critical of the department in general she assumed that he was really getting at her. Does this sound at all familiar? Interestingly, she didn't take things personally if a colleague praised the department or her boss looked pleased. It was a no-win outlook – she got no pleasure from pleasant events and always took unpleasant things personally. This brought down her mood and her self-confidence and she was increasingly anxious. Just like the rest of us, the more anxious she got, the more skewed her thinking became and she was quickly caught in a vicious cycle.

5 Worrying: getting nowhere fast – and slow

What if my boss finds out? What if he fires me? What if . . . ?

Worrying is very common amongst anxious people. It describes a particular type of thinking style that, up to a point, can serve us well. I'm going to Sweden tomorrow and it's my worry about forgetting my passport and about being stranded without cash that prompted me to check that my passport is in my bag and to find time to go to the bank to get some Swedish currency. When I'm driving, my worry about having an accident keeps me alert to dangers on the road, and when I'm giving a presentation, it's my worry the night before that motivates me to prepare properly. So why worry about worry if it is so helpful? Well, if we worry too much, it tends to work against us, we become less able to make decisions, to stay focused, to plan ahead and, most importantly, it stops us from problem-solving effectively. Also, if it goes on, it can disturb our sleep, create tension and leave us feeling exhausted. Once more we see the disadvantage of having too much of a good thing.

Worrying describes a way of thinking, not an emotion. It's my worrying [my thinking style] that makes me anxious [my emotion]. This might sound like a 'nit-picking' distinction, but it is an important one because it's much easier to change our style of thinking than to change our emotions directly. If we can stop the worrying process, the anxiety will take care of itself.

Worrying is characterized by the 'What if . . . ?' question. This can make us anticipate the future with fear: What if it all goes wrong? What if I lose my ticket? What if I'm seriously ill?

Sometimes a similar form of thinking – *rumination* – kicks in. Rather than looking to the future, this looks to the past and is recognizable by a different premise: 'If only . . .'. 'If only I had prepared better . . .'; 'If only I had said the right thing at the right time . . .'; 'If only I'd been more careful . . .'. Just like worry, this can be helpful up to a point. As long as I use my ruminations to develop hindsight, a wisdom that will guide me, it's of benefit – perhaps next time I will prepare better, say something more timely, be more careful, and so on. But if I just get caught up in thinking 'If only . . .' then I will get demoralized and it will be more difficult to prepare and to cope.

Worrying often comes as a series of thoughts: 'My tooth aches – I'm worried that there's something wrong . . . that I'll have to have a filling . . . Oh no, that could be really painful. I could even lose my tooth . . . What would I do then? What if it costs a lot to have a replacement?' A chain of alarming possibilities – no wonder worry is really distressing once it takes hold. The more uncertain we are the more we tend to speculate and worry. Once we know what an outcome will be we can often get on with problem-solving our way through it, but the unknown is so much harder to deal with.

Unpleasant as worrying can be, sometimes it's hard to let go of it because we believe that it might be helpful. For example, it is not unusual to hear: 'If I worry about it at least I'm pre-pared.' Now there is some truth in this because a bit of worry will direct my attention to things that ought to concern me: 'Have I got enough petrol in the car?'; 'What if we lose our luggage – have I got travel insurance?' This is very helpful as long as my initial worry spurs me to taking action and dealing with potential problems. If, however, I just get locked in a string of worries then I'll get less and less capable of dealing with difficulties. Sometimes the belief that keeps worry going is more like a superstition: 'If I worry about it, it might never happen.' This falls into that category of relying on intuition and, as we saw in the earlier section, the arguments for relying on 'gut feelings' are weak.

For some people, the major part of their anxiety problem is worry, and there is an excellent book called *Overcoming Worry* (see 'Further Reading' for details), which can help you if your problems revolve around excessive worrying.

Biased thinking isn't all bad

I don't want to be extreme in telling you about thinking biases, so I have to stress that they aren't all bad; remember that they can stand us in good stead for coping with danger. Gerry, in the example below, is quickly caught up in all-or-nothing and catastrophic thinking, and it's a good thing.

Gerry is driving along a dark road and sees a human-like shape move in front of the car. He thinks: 'A child! I'll kill him!' and he brakes. No collision, no one hurt, it's a good response. If there is a child then a life has been saved, if it's just a shadow there's no harm done – better safe than sorry.

Now meet Ian who doesn't engage in 'skewed thinking'. He sees the shape and considers: 'Mmm, I wonder if this is a child, or a shadow, or maybe something else . . .' He is *not* using all-or-nothing thinking. He then goes on to think: 'If it is a child, I might or I might not be travelling fast enough to knock him over [*not* catastrophizing]. When I think about it, I have been in situations like this before and it's turned out to be a shadow [*not* overgeneralizing]. And when I look back, I realize that I have had very few accidents [*not* ignoring the positive] so on the basis of probability I won't have an accident this evening [*not* jumping to conclusions].' If the spectre was shadow this is fine, but if it had been a child, that child would have been knocked over by now. You might remember from the earlier chapter that our brains are set up to be 'better safe than sorry' so we are all more likely to have Gerry's response and there is essentially nothing wrong with that.

Another example of useful biased thinking is scanning when we could be in danger because it increases the likelihood of spotting something harmful: the frightened soldier who scans for the enemy as he moves through a war zone is more likely to survive than the soldier who does not bother to check for danger; the schoolboy who looks out for traffic before he crosses the road will be safer than the unobservant child.

However, it's all about getting the balance right; and although biased thinking can be helpful under certain circumstances, it is unhelpful if it is a persistent way of viewing things or if it is triggered too readily. Later, I will ask you to keep logs or diaries of your thoughts, and one of the things you will be able to see is the amount of skewed thinking that you get caught up in, which will give you a sense of whether it's in proportion.

Powerful as they are, though, our thoughts aren't the only psychological driver of vicious cycles. Sometimes our mood or our behaviours or even other people can fuel the problem. So let's have a look at these other areas – the more you can understand what drives your anxiety the stronger a position you will be in to manage your fears.

Emotional maintaining patterns: mood matters

Our mood affects our stress and anxiety levels – almost everyone will have had periods (however brief) when their mood was good and they felt they could take on challenges – being in a good mood does this. However, many of us have probably gone through bad patches where things seemed like so much more of a challenge and it was too easy to become anxious and worried.

Unfortunately, the mood changes that are sometimes associated with stress can stop us from coping with stress. Being constantly anxious can be demoralizing and make us feel both hopeless and miserable – which of course makes it harder to cope and so we get even more stressed: another vicious cycle. So you can see that it's important to learn how to catch problem worry, fear and anxiety as early as possible and to beat the cycles.

Irritability, which is often linked with stress, can also drive anxiety because in this emotional state we often find it difficult to concentrate and to think beyond ourselves – so we tend to make mistakes and then the worry and the self-criticism can set in: 'What if I've done that wrong?'; 'I could get in trouble for forgetting to do that'; 'What is she going to think of me? If only I hadn't blurted that out'; 'I'm so careless!' These sorts of thoughts get in the way of dealing with anxieties and the cycle closes.

Behavioural maintaining cycles: the search for comfort

Behavioural problems are largely accounted for by the fact that when we are upset we seek relief – simple as that. It is not always a bad thing to seek relief, but sometimes what we do backfires and makes things worse.

Avoidance and escape

A natural reaction when we believe we are in danger is to flee from, or avoid, it. This is comforting in the short term and helpful if it removes us from real danger, but *avoidance* of, and *escape* from, situations that are not really dangerous simply maintains our fear because it stops us from learning that we can cope. A child who fears going to school and is therefore taught at home never learns that school can be a safe place; a man who avoids flying because he predicts that he will not cope with being in a confined space never has the opportunity to learn how to cope; a woman who avoids driving on major roadways never discovers that she has the necessary driving skills to tackle main roads. . . You probably get the picture.

Avoidance and escape can take very obvious or subtle forms:

- **Obvious avoidance and escape**: these are easy to see – the person who never goes into a frightening shopping mall or who walks in only to race out again.
- **Subtle avoidance**: this is more difficult to spot because it appears that a person is facing their fears – but they are only doing so with the help of a 'crutch', which stops them from ever learning how to cope. For example, Steve uses shopping malls but only when accompanied by a friend or when he's taken a shopping trolley for physical support or after he's had a glass of wine to give him 'Dutch courage'. So you can see that Steve never learns that it is possible to face his fear without help, and so his confidence remains low.

Stimulants and alcohol

Another common behaviour that can worsen the sensations of anxiety is turning to alcohol and *stimulants* in response to stress, particularly those containing caffeine. Lighting up a cigarette, drinking a cup of coffee or tea, or eating a chocolate bar for comfort will encourage the release of adrenalin rather than reduce it. This can then make the stress symptoms worse. In turn, this can cause more discomfort and worrying thoughts – so it really isn't a good strategy. Using alcohol is also counterproductive. Although it is a sedative in the short term, and it will tend to calm us, it too becomes a stimulant as it is metabolized. Thus, while the immediate effect might be to help you relax, this is short-lived and using alcohol can actually heighten the feelings of stress. You might have already experienced this on those evenings when you have unwound with a drink or two, only to find that you woke in the night and were unable to get back to sleep.

If using food, drugs or alcohol develops into a longer-term coping strategy, physical changes can result (such as overweight, ill-health, addiction). It is easy to see that these consequences can then worsen stress levels and anxiety. Often, using these substances is also a subtle form of avoidance. If you are avoiding in this way, then you are not learning to face your fears and you are not learning how to meet the challenge of difficult situations. You saw Steve using alcohol as a 'crutch', and as a result he didn't overcome his fear of shopping in busy areas.

Seeking reassurance

Reassurance seeking also fuels problem worries, fears and anxieties. It is very natural to try to find comfort in the words of others or by looking up information – and getting assurance is helpful if we use it to work out better ways to deal with our concerns. However, constantly seeking *re*assurance isn't such a good idea. If you don't use assurances and information gathering as a basis for reviewing the situation and finding new ways of coping, the relief is only temporary. Soon it feels necessary to seek assurance again and a really unhelpful pattern of *re*assurance seeking develops. The worried father who takes his daughter to the doctor each time she gets a rash never learns to discriminate between what is dangerous and what is harmless; the panicky wife who repeatedly asks her husband if she is really OK will not learn to calm herself. Both these people will ultimately feel more scared than they need to because they can't assure themselves when things are really all right.

Reassurance seeking is understandable because in the very short term it gives relief without any pressure to deal with worries oneself – it's a quick fix, but a fix that leaves a person increasingly dependent on reassurance and less able to face and tackle challenges. You can probably see how this sets up a vicious cycle.

To make matters worse, friends, family and professionals can grow tired of being asked for reassurance, and this can strain relationships, and of course this can then cause more stress. Remember, ongoing problems of stress and anxiety can go beyond an individual: there can be more to it than just us.

Our relationships or our surroundings often affect our levels of fear and worry so we need to look at the social maintaining traps we can fall into.

Social maintaining cycles: unhelpful circumstances

Stress and anxiety-related problems can be triggered (or maintained) by circumstances or by other people. That's not to say that there is nothing we can do about it because something else or someone else is involved – there's a lot we can do to change our circumstances and our relationships with others, but first we have to understand the part they play.

Stressful situations

Stress and worries can all be made worse by all sorts of situations. Some common ones are:

- difficult work environments (particularly if it is a place where you are bored or bullied or criticized)
- ongoing domestic difficulties – problem relationships, worries about family members
- ongoing social difficulties – being lonely or not getting along with friends or being worried about friends
- long-term unemployment
- financial pressures
- lingering health problems

Do any of these ring bells for you?

It's really understandable that these sorts of situations would make life difficult, and it is important to recognize them – if there are external reasons behind your stress or anxieties you need to acknowledge them. If you don't, you run the risk of:

- blaming yourself 100 per cent for your difficulties – which is likely to bring down your self-esteem and make matters worse
- missing opportunities for managing your distress, failing to see what might be in your power to change

Clearly, changing a difficult situation can improve things, but we all know that it isn't always possible and so we need to build up a range of stress- and anxiety-management skills to help deal with the pressure and keep it to a minimum. Fortunately, this is what this book will show you – a range of 'tools' to bring into play when the going gets tough.

Relationships that cause stress

Obviously, chronic stress at work and at home can keep on fuelling anxieties, but there are other ways in which people, in particular, can feed into maintaining cycles, and you need to consider if any of your relationships is causing you stress. Sometimes stressful relationships are very obvious – having a critical or bullying partner or boss would be an example of that. But sometimes the cause of stress is quite subtle and often the motives of key people are well meaning, so it never occurs to us that the relationship is one that gives us stress. It is the latter, because it goes unnoticed, that can really undermine our ability to cope.

Ralph had health worries: his difficulties and loss of confidence were maintained because his caring wife always responded to her husband's pleas for reassurance about his health. She soothed him with reassuring words and in the short term he felt better. In the longer term he became reliant on her comforting him and he never learnt to assure himself that his health anxieties were unfounded.

Violet had agoraphobia – she feared leaving her home. She felt lucky having a kindly friend who thoughtfully dropped off some shopping every few days. This meant that she was able to stay at home, which, in turn, meant that she never overcame her fear of going out.

In these examples, both the wife and the friend unwittingly contributed to maintaining the problems. Their motives were generous, but the outcome unhelpful. Is anyone in your circle of friends or family helping you in a way that actually undermines your confidence?

Understanding the cycles

To sum up, once the stress response has been triggered it can be maintained by a cycle that develops because of bodily, psychological, behavioural or social factors, or a mixture of different elements. You need to reflect on all these areas in order to begin to understand what keeps *your* problem going. Your foundation for overcoming your anxiety is an understanding of what causes it and what keeps it going. That's why we are spending so much time discussing maintaining cycles. When you can recognize the cycles that maintain *your* worries, fears and anxieties, you can start to think about the best *personalized* approach for breaking them. Part Two of this book covers practical ways of doing this, but the rest of Part One will be devoted to understanding more about how different kinds of problems can develop.

Why me?

Possibly the most common question that I am asked in my clinic is: 'Why do I have these difficulties?' You've probably asked the very same question. Be assured that there will be understandable reasons why you developed your difficulties, and just knowing this can take some of the distress out of having the problem. But knowing what made you vulnerable in the first place can also help in your long-term planning: if you know your vulnerabilities you can start 'stress-proofing' yourself. This is crucial to your long-term management of anxiety, so the next thing that we need to look at is the possible origins of your difficulties.

Summary

- Problem worries, fears and anxieties are maintained by unhelpful cycles

- Cycles can be driven by the way we feel, the way we think, the way we behave and by our environment

- You need to know just what your problem cycles look like – and then you can plan to take charge of them, to break unhelpful patterns

3

Why me?

I have always been a worrier. My mother would warn me about the dangers of germs and we had to almost 'scrub up' when we went into her kitchen. Grandfather was just as bad because he predicted doom and gloom and made us quite frightened. Now I'm just like them! I always see and fear the worst and I'm just as concerned about contamination as Mum. I have a stressful job and I don't suppose that helps. I cope by restricting the things I do because so much worries me. This means that I don't have much of a social life and this often gets me down.

Worries, fears and anxieties affect us all differently: some of us are very sensitive to them, while others seem tougher. Anyone who experiences anxiety-related problems will ask 'Why me?', and this is an important question. The answer will help you better understand your difficulties and this will put you in a stronger position when it comes to taking charge of your fears. Understanding 'Why me?' can put problems in perspective and also show you where changes need to be made in your lifestyle, outlook and attitudes. The prevention and management of worries, fears and anxieties depends, in part, on understanding the aspects of your life that might make you prone to such problems – your 'risk factors'.

Broadly speaking, risk factors for anxiety-related problems can be linked with:

- Personality type, genes and family
- Environment, life stresses and social support
- Psychological and coping style

Personality type, genes and family

I have always been a worrier.

Some people just seem to have a character or personality that is more prone to worry or anxiety, and although the significance of personality type remains rather controversial, many researchers would agree that certain characteristics seem to be linked with a tendency towards anxiety. In the early 1960s cardiologists identified a 'Type A' personality that seemed to be associated with higher blood pressure and some stress-related problems. 'Type A' individuals were quite driven, with a tendency to ignore stress symptoms. Around the same time, the term 'neurotic' was used to distinguish those whose stress response was easily triggered but who had a slow rate of recovery. This group of people were vulnerable to developing anxieties.

However, being a particular 'personality type' does not mean that you are condemned to being anxious. A very hopeful finding has been that 'Type A' individuals are able to change their behaviour and outlook, and can benefit from this by becoming calmer. They can learn to reduce their competitive drive and increase their stress awareness and their ability to relax. They then reduce their stress and any associated health problems.

Perhaps even more hopeful is the track record of Cognitive Behavioural Therapy for anxiety problems – study after study has shown that CBT can help anxious people learn to manage their anxiety. So even if you feel that you are 'the worrying type' or have 'always been a worrier', you can look forward to being able to change your outlook and the way you feel in yourself.

Our genes have also long been one of the 'usual suspects' for anxiety problems. We know that our genes 'hard-wire' early fears that are there to keep us safe. We are all born with certain 'phobias': we all have a fear of strangers, heights, snake-like objects, novelty, 'creepy-crawlies' and separation at some point in our childhood. In evolutionary terms this is excellent because the infant who recoils from a stranger or a precipice, or who cries for help as a snake or a tarantula crawls towards him, will alert an adult and will therefore survive. In time, with the assurances of adults, children learn not to overreact to these triggers. However, some of us will carry some of these fears into adulthood and that is why it is not always possible to identify the trigger for a phobia – there might never have been a trigger, just the absence of unlearning a fear. All this suggests that fears can be encoded in our genes, and there is the possibility that fears can be passed on in families.

Sure enough, studies have shown that anxiety disorders can run in families, although it is difficult to know whether this is because of a pure genetic influence or if it is the result of family members observing each other's behaviour and heeding each other's warnings.

My mother would always warn me about the dangers of germs and we had to almost 'scrub up' when we went into her kitchen. Grandfather was just as bad because he predicted doom and gloom and made us quite frightened.

A fearful mother can easily communicate her health anxieties to her young daughter; an over-concerned father's constant warning that dogs bite can make his son afraid of dogs – so it's not always about 'hard-wiring'. Again, this is good news, because even though there might be strong trends in families, it is possible to overcome fears or tendencies to worry – even long-standing fears and worries. If you had grown up in a French-speaking family and had only learnt to communicate in French, you would still expect to be able to learn another language if you had to – and in a similar way, you can learn a new response to feared things and situations.

Environment, life stresses and social support

I have a stressful job and I don't suppose that helps.

Since the 1970s we have known that our environment can shape our emotional states – trauma, stresses, relationship difficulties all play a part in the onset of anxieties and depression, too. Whereas 'loss events' (such as the ending of a relationship or job loss) tend to be linked with the onset of depression, and hope with the lifting of depression, 'threat events' (such as a diagnosis of illness or an impending examination) are associated with the beginnings of anxiety disorders, and events promoting security are linked with recovery from them. For example, a student would have higher stress levels before and during an examination (the threat event), but a lowering of stress levels when she heard that she had passed them (the security event); or a mother would have heightened anxiety while she waited for her child's X-ray results (threat), but this would ease when she learnt the child had only a minor fracture (security).

Significant events can be 'one-off' (such as accidents, job loss) or continuous stresses (such as long-term physical illness, chronic financial problems or fears of redundancy), and an event does not have to be unpleasant in order to cause stress: adjusting to any change causes stress. This means that welcome happenings like marriages, house moves or the birth of a child can be just as stressful as unhappy occasions such as personal injury and job loss. So, if you were estimating your personal risk of stress-related problems, you would need to reflect on both positive and negative events. You would also need to bear in mind that the effect of life stresses is cumulative – the more you have the more likely you are to get stressed and anxious. Unfortunately, life events often cluster (marriage is likely to be linked with a house move, redundancy with financial crisis, for example) and this means more vulnerability to problems.

Even life events in the past count. Childhood experiences of danger and insecurity tend to predispose us to overestimate danger and underestimate our ability to cope. It is as if threat in our early years puts us on 'red alert'. Studies of brain development actually show that the 'fear networks' in stressed and traumatized children are more developed than in other children and that these children tend to grow into adults who are more sensitive to threat. Their threatening past has made them more efficient at responding to perceived danger – in evolutionary terms this is an understandable development, but, as we've seen already, you can have too much of a good thing. Sometimes this sensitivity is overdeveloped and causes problems. So if you had a challenging childhood, you could now be more vulnerable to getting stressed – but please remember that this does not doom you for life: you can take charge of your anxieties.

Before we leave life events and life stresses it is worth noting that someone stressed in childhood will probably be particularly sensitive to similar stresses as an adult. For example, a man who had been involved in a serious road accident as a boy would react more strongly to witnessing a car crash than would a person who had not experienced a car accident; a child who was bitten by a dog would be more wary of one as an adult; a girl who had grown up in a family that suffered severe illness might be more sensitive to health fears as an adult. There are often patterns to our fears and anxieties.

It is useful to understand the impact of life events and stresses on your own difficulties as this can help you put them into perspective:

- Jonathon had a panic attack after his daughter's wedding – he wasn't 'losing the plot', as he feared; the attack was quite understandable, considering how many stresses are involved in preparing for a wedding and the 'loss' of a daughter.

- Jasmine was struck by extreme worry when her husband was told that he might have mild angina. This apparent overreaction made sense, given that both her parents had died of coronary problems when she was young.

The same researchers who looked at the impact of stressful events also discovered what they called a 'protective factor', namely, social support. It was very clear that the more friends we have, especially those in whom we can confide, the less affected we are by life's stresses. Quite simply, our vulnerability to emotional problems decreases with increased levels of social support. This is good news because many of us can do things to improve our social contacts.

Social support can take many forms: close and confiding relationships, less intense friendships or a wide network of supportive contacts, such as workmates, other mothers at playgroup, and so on. All of these help to 'stress-proof' us, but we are most protected if we have a confiding relationship. It really does help to talk. The more social support we have, the more protected we are, so it is particularly important to turn to friends when we are facing major life events and life crises. Ideally we would all have a combination of non-intimate friendships and close friends, although this is not always possible. But remember that simply having one friend in whom you confide will help to protect you in the face of stress.

Being socially active or simply maintaining a friendship can of course be a huge challenge for someone who is anxious, particularly if shyness and social fears are part of the problem. Nonetheless, if you are socially isolated, it is worth beginning to consider how you might improve your social support. There are strategies in this book for helping you if you are shy and socially anxious – after you have learnt these you will be much more confident about rising to the challenge, and the research tells us that it is worth it.

Psychological and coping style

I always see and fear the worst . . . I cope by restricting the things I do . . . this often gets me down.

The final category in the 'Why me?' trilogy concerns the way we think and the way we tend to cope with stresses and challenges. Earlier, we saw how thinking biases, such as catastrophizing, jumping to conclusions and ignoring the positive, contribute to worry, fear and anxiety, but there are other ways in which our thinking can affect our outlook and it is worth being aware of these.

For over thirty years now, research has shown that our current mood state colours the way we view situations and filter our memories. If I am in a confident, good mood then I will tend to see 'the glass as half full' and be optimistic about taking on challenges. Furthermore, when I reflect on my past experiences, I tend to recall the happier events and my memories have something of a positive slant. This is all very well, but if I am feeling down or anxious then the 'glass' seems 'half empty' and my memories are skewed towards the unhappy or frightening ones. Therefore, not only do I feel rather hopeless, but it also seems as though it's always like this for me. This phenomenon is well borne out by research, and you have probably experienced it yourself – it's normal. However, normal as it is, if any of us is in low spirits for any length of time, this negative outlook can really take a hold and fuel the biased thinking we talked about on pages 28–45. The point of introducing you to this particular psychological factor isn't to scare you but to help you understand why it can be so difficult to shake off the negative thinking – you are not being weak or silly if you struggle, so don't be harder on yourself than you need be. Once again, the good news is that we can still use anxiety-management strategies to break out of this pattern – but it is only fair to recognize that this is hard work.

Back to some different and reassuring research – it has been shown that the majority of the general population has good coping strategies for managing psychological problems. It appears that we tend to have a good 'sense' of how to cope. So you have probably developed some very good ways of coping yourself and you can now build on them and refine them. The most common coping methods are:

- trying to keep busy and other forms of distraction
- facing the worry and trying to problem-solve

The least popular methods are using drugs and alcohol – which is good news.

Activity, distraction, facing fears and problem-solving are all helpful, though that cliché that you can have too much of a good thing is relevant again. Too much distraction and we can fall into the trap of avoidance; facing the fear too vigorously without proper preparation and we can find ourselves ill-equipped to cope. Of course, overusing drugs or alcohol (or comfort eating) not only becomes a means of avoidance but substance misuse carries its own risks to our physical health.

So you need to review your coping style and identify where it is working against you rather than for you. You might discover that actually you are doing things that are basically OK but you're just relying on them too much or using them without sufficient planning. This is good because it means that you've got a foundation for coping, something that comes naturally that you can build on and adapt to make it more effective. As a general rule, we stand a better chance of learning new skills if we build on what we are drawn to and what we are good at. Personally, I am not drawn to sport and I'm not good at it – I worry about letting down my team (yes, I know I should try to overcome that!), I can't catch a ball to save my life, I dislike remembering rules and I'm not naturally competitive. So when I reached a stage in my life when I really could no longer avoid exercise I had to think hard about what I should do. I did try squash and spent most of the time picking up the ball and frustrating my partner; I tried modern dance, but having to remember moves and sequences did me in; I tried rock climbing, but my appalling spatial sense made it very risky. So, I wasn't learning new skills and I had to rethink the situation from the standpoint of what I am good at and what I tend to do naturally. I prefer to be able to take exercise when I like and not be tied to a gym, I love walking and I respond to rewards – so I started to jog (albeit gently) and kept myself going by making sure that there was a reward at the end of the run – a Sunday newspaper, an extra-special take-away coffee, an indulgent DVD. I have had my lapses, but twenty years on I'm still taking this sort of exercise – because it fits my preferences and abilities. Now it's part of my lifestyle. The reason I'm telling you this is because, in a similar way, you will need to personalize your approach to anxiety management so that it becomes part of your lifestyle.

In working your way through this book you will find lots of ideas for curbing the coping strategies that you overuse and adding other useful ones to your repertoire, strategies that you will find appealing.

Summing up

Our vulnerability to anxiety-related problems tends to be the result of a combination of things rather than a single factor. For example:

- Worrying and checking ran in Zoe's family and she developed an obsessive disorder when she was under extreme strain and without a best friend to confide in. Under other circumstances Zoe might never have suffered from this problem but unfortunately things came together and her biology and environment contributed to her difficulties.

- Adam had a minor road accident and, much to his girl-friend's surprise, he developed a driving phobia. What she did not appreciate was that he was under a great deal of stress taking out his first mortgage, and he had also spent his childhood hearing his mother's frantic warn-ings about the dangers of driving. The combination of this history, his ongoing stress and the trauma of the accident was enough to sap his confidence and cause a phobia.

Perhaps by now you are able to answer the question: 'Why me?' It is worth giving it some thought as the answer will help you gain a perspective that makes your difficulties understand-able. If you can understand your difficulties then it is easier to be less self-critical and to get a sense of what needs to change in order to overcome those difficulties. Figure 5 shows you some of the factors to consider, and you can read Frank and Jan's stories to help you get an idea. If you have one or two difficulties then you can simply do this exercise for each of them, as Jan does in the example below.

Understand how the problem arose in the first place by looking at your personal risk factors and your social / environ-mental risk factors. Then consider why your problems are not going away by looking at your coping style and ongoing pres-sures. You will see how your current difficulties originated and understand why they are so hard to shake off.

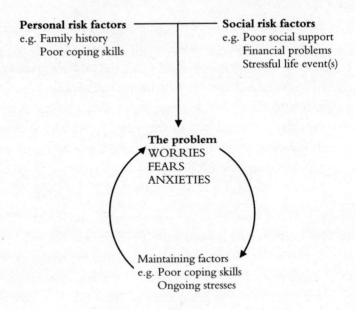

Figure 5: Assessing your problem

Frank's story

Frank saw himself as a 'solid reliable bloke', a no-nonsense man. Others turned to him for practical help. He prided himself on being like his father and his grandfather who used to say: 'Don't get upset, get on!' Now he felt like a wreck and he didn't know what to do – he thought he was letting himself down and everyone around him. Since his retirement he had felt a bit 'empty' and he realized that work had filled quite a gap in his life since the children had left home and he missed his colleagues. He also discovered that he and his wife, Diane, didn't get on as well as he'd hoped now he was at home more – she had her own domestic routines and he seemed to get in the way. Then he had his health scare. His GP had taken it very seriously and made sure that Frank had extensive tests and luckily all was well – except in Frank's mind. It came as a shock that he might have cancer – his view of himself shifted from 'healthy' to 'vulnerable' and he began to look out for signs of illness, checking his skin for moles and lumps, noting his bowel movements, wondering if headaches indicated a brain tumour. He became so worried about his health that he could find himself panicking – which was a first for Frank. He turned to his wife who always reassured him that there was nothing to worry about, and he would feel OK for a while but the worries came back. There came a point when Frank decided to take stock of his situation and to try to understand what was going on. He identified the following:

Personal risk factors:

- a family background of not expressing worries and therefore not learning how to deal with them
- the fact that he is sixty-five and might be more prone to serious illnesses

Social / environmental risk factors:

- adjusting to retirement – the loss of purpose and the frictions with his wife
- sudden loss of his work friends and colleagues

Maintaining factors:

- ongoing stress between Frank and Diane
- Diane's reassurances about his health
- his harsh attitude towards himself and his sense of letting himself (and others) down
- continued lack of purpose and social contact
- coping by checking and reassurance seeking rather than by calming and assuring himself
- time on his hands to worry – no pleasurable distractions

When Frank had taken the time to stand back and review things, he was able to come up with a new take on the situation – one that was compassionate and understanding.

'I can see why I'm feeling so wretched – I've actually been through quite a lot. Retirement was a bigger stress than I'd anticipated: I wasn't expecting to miss people so much or feel so lost without a working role. I also thought that Diane and I would be very active together and I hadn't considered that she's built up her own lifestyle. I wished we'd talked about it beforehand – but that was never my style. My style was to ignore worries and get on with life. What an irony that I can't ignore my worries now! I can understand why I might worry about my health at my age, but I think I've got it all out of proportion because I am dealing with so much. There's this adjustment to retirement, Diane and I still argue and I turn to her too much for reassurance, and that doesn't help me in the long term.'

Frank actually went one step further by considering what he would now do differently: 'I'm going to think and talk about problems from now on so that I can prepare myself and learn to cope better, but I'm going to keep it in proportion. No more relying on Diane to reassure me – I need to do that for myself and I need to get myself a new "retirement-life" so that I don't dwell on things so much, so that I have more company and so that I don't get in Diane's hair. I'm going to do a couple of things that I've always wanted to do – learn Italian and join a Jazz class. I might even start taking a daily walk so that I look after myself both physically and mentally.'

Jan's story

Jan had worries and fears stretching back into her childhood – it was hard for her to pinpoint a time when they began. As a child she had always been shy, just like her mother, and always scared of things and very self-conscious. At school she tried not to be noticed so that she wouldn't have to speak in class, and she never volunteered to take part in school productions or join clubs. Sometimes other children would tease her about this but she was never bullied, thank goodness. Her dad would laugh at her and also tease her. This made her feel stupid for being so afraid of things, but she thinks that he was only trying to help, trying to toughen her up. Once he gently tapped her on the shoulder and when she turned he was wearing a clown mask and he shouted, 'Boo!' She became hysterical and developed a really strong fear of clowns. In contrast, her mother was protective: if Jan was nervous about going somewhere, her mother went too, if Jan was afraid of doing something her mother would try to do it for her, if there was a picture of a clown in the newspaper or a magazine, her mother would get rid of it as quietly as possible hoping that Jan had not seen it.

Now as an adult she led a very quiet life, avoiding a whole range of things that scared her and still turning to her mother for support. She rejected social invitations, attended doctor and dentist appointments with her mother, she kept a low profile at work so that she wouldn't be noticed (and this had limited her career opportunities), and she steadfastly avoided going anywhere where she might see a clown's face. She felt lonely and limited, but the prospect of being laughed at or of having to cope with the image of a clown was too daunting, so she accepted her lot in life – until a work colleague insisted on befriending her and helping her see how her difficulties arose. Together they identified two main problems:

1. Social anxieties

Personal risk factors:

- a shy mother, and a father who teased her and left her feeling embarrassed
- a life history of avoiding socially challenging situations

Social / environmental risk factors:

- a mother who was so supportive that Jan never faced her fears
- very few friends and activities to build her confidence

Maintaining factors:

- mother's excessive support
- avoidance of social situations as her only coping strategy
- no social life: loneliness, which sapped her confidence

2. Clown phobia

Personal risk factors:

- a father who scared her with a clown mask
- an avoidant coping style: a life history of avoiding anywhere where she might see a clown

Social / environmental risk factors:

- a mother who was so supportive that Jan never faced her fears

Maintaining factors:

- a mother's excessive support
- avoidance of clowns as her only coping strategy

This exercise really opened Jan's eyes: she could see that she wasn't just born afraid; other things had played a part in building up her anxieties, and the main reason for her current fears was avoidance. 'I might have a bit of a genetic predisposition because Mum is a nervous person but the clown phobia came later – I wasn't born with it, I only developed it because Dad gave me such a fright. I can see now that a lifetime of avoiding the things that scare me has only made the problems worse over the years and it's left me feeling vulnerable and lonely.' With the help of her friend, Jan made plans: 'Hard as it will be, I have to tell Mum not to help me so much – it's time I stood on my own two feet and faced these things – but not Dad's way, not so quickly that I scare myself.'

Everyone experiences worry, fear and anxiety differently and it is very important that you reflect on and understand what they mean to you personally. Both Frank and Jan were able to develop a personal understanding of their problems by doing this exercise – an important starting point for overcoming difficulties. In both these instances, understanding 'Why me?' led to ideas about managing the problems.

If you seek help with stress-related problems, you might find your difficulties being labelled or diagnosed by professionals. This is simply the way in which emotional or psychological problems are classified, and diagnoses (labels) often enable professionals to develop ideas about the best way to help. However, diagnosis is only part of the understanding you need in order to overcome anxiety, and not everyone will have a problem that fits a diagnosis, so don't skimp on doing the exercise that Frank and Jan did. A diagnosis can help you say 'This is what I'm suffering from', but it will not answer the question 'Why me?'

In the next section we will look at the most commonly used diagnoses, so that if your doctor or another professional uses those labels you will know what they mean.

Summary

- We all want to know 'Why me?' and it is a very good question to ask because it gives us an explanation and also points to our vulnerabilities

- Each of us will be vulnerable in different ways – there is no single reason why people develop anxiety and stress problems

- The main factors that shape our vulnerability are: our character and family history, environmental stress and our own personal coping style

- Knowing more about our vulnerability can help us appreciate how to stress-proof ourselves in the future

4

Fears and anxieties: the labels

Clearly, the experience of fear and anxiety can be a very individual one, but professionals have recognized that some fears and anxieties share features, and this has made it possible to classify them using specific labels. You may already have come across some of these: phobias, panic disorder, social anxiety, hypochondriasis, generalized anxiety disorder (GAD), obsessive-compulsive disorder (OCD), post-traumatic stress disorder (PTSD) and burn-out.

Phobias

Fears are common, but they become a 'phobia' when they are out of proportion – when they are inappropriately intense. They also become a problem when they lead to avoidance, which spoils our quality of life. In Jan's case you saw this – her fears stopped her from having a social life and really restricted her. Although she originally had no fear of clowns, her brain had linked clowns with feelings of fear and she had learnt to be afraid. Over time it simply got worse and worse. In fact, her fear had become so extreme that pictures of clowns and even the word itself distressed her, so she avoided a certain part of town because of a restaurant that used a clown to advertise children's food and she crossed the road to avoid posters just in case one was promoting a circus, and she never went near the children's sections of department stores — not even the same floor. Jan is not unusual; many people find that the scope of their phobia increases over time and, as you can imagine, it restricts life more and more.

However, not all intense fears are inappropriate — some are very healthy: fear of being burnt by fire, fear of aggressive-looking dogs, and so on, are pretty vital to survival. Also, some intense fears don't impair the quality of our lives and we needn't fret about them. For example, a phobia of climbing ladders might never trouble a person who does not have to climb a ladder — but the very same fear would be a major problem for an exterior decorator.

A common question is: 'Why don't these fears just disappear?' Well, some do. You already know that we are born with several life-saving phobias. So as an infant you will have been fearful of strangers, of snakes and of heights, for example. Many of us will unlearn the fear because our parents and carers will have comforted us and built up our confidence. Some of you will still have your phobia because you never unlearnt these 'built-in' fears — so if you can't remember when your fear of spiders or snakes or heights began, it might be because it has always been there. Both 'built-in' and learnt phobias (like Jan's fear of clowns) often ease over time if we begin to face the fear again (climb back on the horse, as it were). Phobias that are persistent tend to be linked with avoidance (no surprise there), usually because of that overestimation of risk and underestimation of coping ability we mentioned earlier. Jan overestimated the risk to herself — she believed that

75

she would 'fall to pieces and be a laughing stock' if she faced a clown – so no wonder she avoided them. Later she learnt that she could face clowns and remain quite calm – that was the end of her avoidance and the end of her phobia. Avoidance had stopped her from testing out the reality of the fear and also prevented her from developing the coping skills that would give her some confidence.

Earlier we talked about the skewed thinking that is common when we are anxious, and a particular one – scanning – is very common in those with phobias. If you are afraid of something it is understandable that you'd be on the lookout, but do this too much and it becomes a preoccupation that can make you more anxious, and you can even make mistakes and get scared over something that isn't what you fear – mistaking a bit of fluff for a spider, mistaking a harmless electrical buzzing for a wasp, for example.

You can see these patterns in Figure 6.

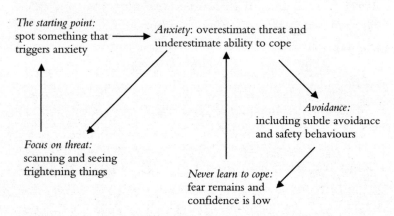

Figure 6: The way phobias are maintained

Even though we have not yet discussed coping strategies – these are covered in Part Three – you can probably see from the diagram that there would be ways of breaking the pattern. For example, facing the fear and building confidence would help, and not scanning would minimize the triggers for feeling afraid. Part Three will introduce you to the skills you need to do this.

Phobias can take many different forms, but two common categories are:

- specific phobia: fear of specific objects or circumstances
- agoraphobia: fear of being away from a safe base

Below are several descriptions of people's experience of different phobias. When you read them, see if they capture your difficulties. By now you are probably quite skilled at identifying maintaining patterns, so see if you can also work out just what keeps your own phobia going.

Specific phobias

Cat phobia

It might seem silly, and my family certainly thinks it is, but I go to pieces when I see a cat – even if it's only a picture of one. It sets my stomach churning and my heart racing and I think, 'I have just got to get away, I can't handle this!' And then I run.

I have been like this since I was three or four years old and I saw two cats fighting. They were all bloody and then one turned and looked at me. I was terrified. I am very careful not to go into areas where I might see a cat. I don't visit anyone

77

without first checking whether they or their neighbours own a cat. I don't browse in card shops – do you realize how many greeting cards have cats on them? I'm glad that I'm a man and I get sent ships and trains at birthdays! Although I'm joking a bit now, it's no joke. If I see a cat, or if I think I've seen a cat, it really affects my day-to-day life and I am restricted in what I can do and where I can go. It's getting worse, rather than better, as time goes on.

Vomit phobia

My husband is getting so tired of us having to take taxis home from local parties and clubs because I can't face walking down our main street. There are so many places where people can get drunk and might vomit, that I can't risk it. If my husband is really firm and insists that we walk home, I make him walk through backstreets so as not to encounter someone being sick. Also, I won't visit anyone who is ill and I don't go into work if there is a stomach bug going around. If I discover that someone I know is sick, I worry about it for days.

I've never been comfortable around sickness, but I've only been scared of it since coming around from an anaesthetic in hospital a few years ago and I heard the woman in the next hospital bed vomiting all through the night. It was awful. I started to feel nauseous and I began to retch so hard that I was convinced that I was going to die. It was one of the worst nights of my life and I made the hospital staff find me a side room for the rest of my stay. The thought of that time still makes me feel panicky and I can feel the nausea come over me. I'd rather not even think about it and I certainly never want to go into hospital again.

Specific phobias are fears of specific objects or situations and are probably the easiest to describe and to understand: fear of wasps, fear of heights, fear of mice, etc. Sometimes they are called 'simple phobias' but this does not mean that they are not distressing – so-called 'simple phobias' can be very disabling – just look at the examples above. They are called 'simple' because they are restricted to a definable object or situation. Historically, they have been classified by the name of the object of fear, and this has given us some interesting labels, for example:

- apiphobia (fear of bees)
- arachnophobia (fear of spiders)
- brontophobia (fear of thunder)
- emetophobia (fear of vomit)
- haematophobia (fear of blood)
- hydrophobia (fear of water)
- ophidophobia (fear of snakes)
- ornithophobia (fear of birds)
- zoophobia (fear of animals)

Don't be too concerned about finding just the right name for your phobia – the labels are far less important than you being able to understand *your fear* in the way that Frank and Jan did.

Some specific phobias are very common – most people are nervous around wasps or snakes and recoil from vomit, so you can understand some avoidance. This is, of course, exaggerated in phobia. Some fears are rarer – there are people with a fear of buttons or false teeth or baked beans and it is harder to identify with these, but there will be an explanation for them, just as there is an explanation for Jan's fear of clowns. Whatever the source of the fear, the reality is that a powerful anxiety response is triggered and this is what you need to understand, and, in particular, you need to discover what maintains the fear.

It is worth mentioning that not all fears cause a rush of adrenalin to prepare us for fight or flight – blood and injection phobias tend to make people feel weak and faint. This is because our bodies react differently when we see blood (or anticipate seeing blood). In this situation our blood pressure drops (rather than increases) and causes light-headedness. We can only speculate why this happens, but one popular theory is that it makes sense in evolutionary terms – if our ancestors saw blood it probably meant that they or their tribesmen had been injured. Anyone with lower blood pressure would lose less blood if they were injured and, therefore, a drop in blood pressure would be beneficial.

Agoraphobia

I have not been out of the house for six months – not since I had that funny turn in the supermarket and I thought that I was going to die. I did go to see my doctor at first, but I got into such a state getting there that I nearly collapsed, and now I get him to visit me at home. I feel safe here and I don't get the awful feelings, but I'm not even completely relaxed at home if I know a stranger is visiting. I often have a drink to calm me if the paperboy is coming to collect the paper money or the gas-man is coming to read the meter. Sometimes, though, I just refuse to answer the door.

I was always a bit nervous about going out and about, and gradually I went to fewer and fewer places on my own and I began to rely more and more on a glass or two of wine to give me Dutch courage. A year ago I was able to use the corner shop and to get round the block to see my sister but I can't do that now – even with the wine. Just talking about it makes me feel wobbly and breathless. I try not to think about the awful feelings I get – thinking about them makes me feel almost as bad as going out does. Sometimes I wonder if I'm going mad. My sister is very helpful, though – she does my shopping and visits me nearly every day.

Many people think: 'Agoraphobia – a fear of open spaces'. In fact, it is more subtle than that: agoraphobia is a fear of leaving a place of safety, a safe base. This can be the home or a car or the doctor's surgery, or a combination of safe places. The fear usually reflects an expectation that something terrible will happen to one personally – 'I could collapse!'; 'I could get lost!'; 'I could get ill and there will be no one to help me!'; 'I could lose control!'; 'People will look at me and think I'm stupid'. This last statement reflects something of a social anxiety (which will be covered later) and is a reminder that although professionals have devised diagnostic categories, there is often an overlap in symptoms and this is normal. Sometimes, but less commonly, agoraphobia centres around a fear that something will happen to loved ones – 'My baby could get ill and I wouldn't be able to get to a phone!' – or to the safe base – 'I could be burgled or the house could catch fire while I'm out!' Sometimes the fear is quite vague – 'I just have a sense that something bad will happen and that I won't be able to cope.'

Why don't these fears just disappear? Clinging to a 'safe place' is a form of avoidance and this means the person with agoraphobia simply doesn't learn how to cope. So in both examples above, you see the problem getting worse over time. You also see alcohol being used as a subtle form of avoidance in both examples – 'Dutch courage'.

Very commonly, agoraphobia is associated with other anxiety-related problems such as:

- social anxiety: this applied to Jan in the first example. She tried to stay at home or in a 'safe base' to avoid people noticing her because she was so shy
- trauma: following trauma some people have very painful or frightening memories. A trauma survivor might limit themselves to 'safe places' to avoid these memories being triggered
- panic attacks: the agoraphobia might have been triggered by a panic attack in the first place. This is a common scenario, and it might be maintained by the fear of having a panic attack when in public. This is the anxiety disorder most commonly linked with agoraphobia so let's have a look at panic attacks and panic disorder next.

If I have a phobia what should I do?
How can I break the cycle?

By using the guidelines in this book, you can aim to break the cycles by devising your own 'treatment plan', tailored to suit your needs. Once you are familiar with the various strategies, your plan might look something like this (though everyone will have a slightly different plan):

1. Identify your unhelpful thoughts and images about the thing you fear – this will help you appreciate why your fear is understandable (Chapter 7)

2. Take stock of your resources, particularly people who could support you

3. Learn how to manage the physical symptoms of anxiety, if these hold you back. This will begin building your confidence that you can take on something challenging (Chapters 8 and 9)

4. Learn to switch off alarming thoughts as this, again, can give you confidence that you can cope (Chapter 10)

5. Learn to re-think and question your frightening thoughts and images, to gauge just how realistic they are. When you can review, or even dismiss, alarming thoughts that truly are exaggerations you will be in a good position to face your fear (Chapter 11)

6. Learn how to stop scanning and looking out for the thing you fear, as this will only heighten your anxiety

7. When you've developed some confidence in mentally countering your fears, make a *graded* plan to face your fear. Facing your fears is key, but pace it carefully by stretching yourself without over-stressing yourself (Chapter 12)

8. Dare to drop unhelpful safety behaviours – again, carefully. Safety behaviours might help you in the short term but in the long term they will hold you back and keep your phobias alive

9. Keep facing your fears until your confidence has returned. Repetition will build your confidence and resilience.

10. Finally, make plans for keeping up your progress (Chapter 16)

Panic disorder

You might have heard the term 'panic attack' – it describes a very intense experience and one which most people find really unpleasant, if not terrifying. Typically someone having an attack notices both emotional and physical symptoms:

*   emotional: feelings of fear, apprehension or impending disaster
*   physical: difficulty breathing, chest pains, difficulty seeing clearly, dizziness

I will never forget the first time I had a panic attack – I thought I was dying! I was working on a stressful project and had drunk a lot of black coffee and very little else that day. By the evening, I was running late and knew that I'd have to rush to get to my friend Anna's on time. Of course, the traffic was bad and in the back of the taxi I found myself getting more stressed and then I became hot and dizzy and I could hardly breathe. Somehow I paid the driver, but in Anna's apartment I seemed to lose all control. I was sweating, gasping for breath, I had pains in my chest and my vision was getting dim. I couldn't hear what Anna was saying because of a ringing in my ears, but she had called a doctor because we both thought that I was having a heart attack. The doctor said that I had had a panic attack and that it was probably caused by the day's stress. This should have reassured me – and it did for a day or two – but then I had another attack and, again, I couldn't get 'in control' of the situation. Although I tell myself: 'Fran, get a grip, girl! These are not heart attacks and they cannot harm you!', I am now so frightened of the experience that I'm always worried I'm going to have another one and I avoid places where I've had them in the past.

As you can imagine, panic can be very alarming and the onset is rapid, which is why it's called an 'attack'. In this state, we often breathe very quickly, or hyperventilate – you might remember that one of the ways the body prepares itself for fight or flight is by breathing rapidly so that we have a good oxygen supply. Unfortunately, overdo it and it produces even more distressing physical symptoms, such as:

- dizziness
- tingling beneath the skin
- muscle pain(s)
- ringing in the ears
- a sense of things not being real (de-realization)

The onset of a panic attack can be so sudden that many people describe them as 'coming out of the blue' – actually, there will be a trigger but it can be hard to detect. In fact, there can be a wide range of triggers for a panic attack, but the most common are probably:

- facing a challenge and not feeling able to cope (for example, going outside alone or seeing a clown's mask)
- experiencing discomfort or pain and assuming this is serious, perhaps a heart attack or a stroke

If someone experiences repeated panic attacks, then we say that they have 'panic disorder'. This can occur on its own or with other anxiety problems such as agoraphobia (see above).

Why doesn't the panic simply go away? Well, our old adversary *avoidance* plays its part – in the example above you can see that Fran no longer visits places where she thinks she might have an attack, so she never builds up her skills in panic management or her confidence that she can cope. Therefore, her anxiety levels stay high – which then raises her risk of having a panic attack. Panic is also often fuelled by a particular sort of skewed thinking, namely a tendency to 'catastrophize' or jump to frightening conclusions: 'I can't cope!'; 'I am dying!'

This raises anxieties higher, panic can take hold and all those physical symptoms just feed the panic attack if we misinterpret them as dangerous. A very vicious cycle is then set up – and avoidance will only make things worse, as you can also see in Figure 7.

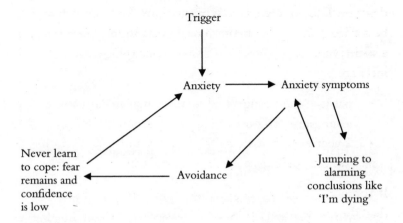

Figure 7: The way panic is maintained

If you want to know more about managing panic, there is an excellent book in this series called *Overcoming Panic and Agoraphobia*, which will help you learn even more about this particular problem and how to tackle it.

If I have panic disorder what should I do?
How can I break the cycle?

By using the guidelines in this book, you can aim to break the cycles by devising your own 'treatment plan', tailored to suit your needs. Once you are familiar with the various strategies, your plan might look something like this (though everyone will have a slightly different plan):

1. Identify what goes through you mind when you panic – the thoughts or pictures that make sense of your panic (Chapter 7)

2. Take stock of your resources, particularly people who could support you

3. Learn how to manage the physical symptoms of panic, particularly how to breathe during an attack. If you simply learn to combat hyperventilation you might begin to gain confidence and if you can also offset the other physical tensions of panic you will feel much more in control (Chapters 8 & 9)

4. Learn techniques to 'switch off' or distract you from alarming thoughts and images – this will help to stop the panic from escalating, particularly if you can stop the   catastrophizing thoughts and images (Chapter 10)

5. Also learn to review and question your problem thoughts and images, to see if they are true. This way you will develop more calming perspectives to bring to mind when you feel a panic attack coming on, or even during a panic attack. You will be able to reassure yourself (Chapter 11)

6. Try to not to scan your body for signs of panic and try to drop any other unhelpful safety behaviours as soon as you can (you can do this in a graded way). These will just hold you back in the long term

7. When you have more confidence, do things or put yourself into situations that you fear might bring on a panic attack so that you can consolidate your confidence – but do this carefully (Chapter 12)

8. Keep managing your panicky feelings and putting yourself in challenging situations until your confidence has returned. Repetition will build your confidence and resilience.

9. Finally, make plans for keeping up your progress (Chapter 16)

Social anxiety (Social phobia)

In its mildest form, social anxiety is simply shyness, but when it gets more disabling it becomes what we call social phobia. It can be 'generalized', which means that we get extremely anxious in many situations where there might be people around, or it can be 'specific' when it only applies to a certain situation – public speaking or eating out, for example.

The larger the gathering, the worse it is. Ever since I forgot my lines in a school play and everyone laughed, I have been terrified of public speaking. I know it seems ridiculous – I was an eight-year-old schoolgirl then and I am a teacher now – but I still feel just as frightened as I did as a child. I get clammy hands and I feel my throat tighten and my mind often goes blank or is beset by worries. I worry that I am making a fool of myself or that the audience will think that I'm stupid. I cope by teaching small groups rather than a big class when I can; and I know I shouldn't but I have very occasionally taken a tranquillizer to get me through parents' evenings. Sadly, it is just impossible for me to present academic papers and my career is suffering, which makes me very nervous. I'm OK at parties because I just merge with the crowd – but I won't play party games because I feel so vulnerable and scared if I'm being watched.

I was once quite outgoing and thought that I was confident. That all changed with my first pregnancy. I put on a lot of weight – much more than I should have – but I didn't mind because I was pleased about the baby and I thought that the weight would disappear after the birth. Partly because I was so huge, we didn't socialize much in the late stages of the pregnancy – I just didn't have the energy or the inclination to go out. We did go to a family wedding and I remember finding it quite hard work to mix and chat – but I decided that this was because I was tired.

After my daughter was born, I was overweight, a bit depressed and very tired. I no longer felt confident in myself and I had the most unpleasant time at the baby's baptism. I was already feeling self-conscious and then I overheard someone say: 'What has happened to Stella, she used to be so lively and attractive?' That just crushed any confidence that I had left and I wouldn't go out for weeks. I was so miserable that I couldn't get rid of the weight and that made me feel worse about meeting others. Now my little girl is five, I am still overweight and I still can't face going anywhere where there are people unless I have some false courage in the form of a drink or if my best friend comes with me. I do make myself attend my daughter's school events but I dread them and I sit at the back and keep myself to myself once I'm there. When I can, I persuade my husband to go instead of me.

If you have social phobia you might well be a 'fortune-teller' and a 'mind-reader', always predicting the worst and assuming that others think badly of you (this is me mind-reading, now, of course!). Stella had this problem; she was pretty sure that, if people noticed her, they would think that she was odd and probably that she was stupid and they would laugh at her behind her back. This made her feel really insecure and scared.

If you have social phobia, you might also notice that you become very self-conscious, perhaps finding it difficult not to focus on yourself. You might be hyper-aware of how you are feeling and how you are behaving: it is in this state that people often 'feel' as though they are blushing or shaking, which of course makes matters worse. Assuming that something is true because you feel it is very common in social anxiety – Stella *felt* that people were looking at her so she believed that they were and this made her even more self-conscious; she *felt* as though she was blushing so she believed that she was turning deep red, which again made things worse. Another common trait is being self-critical: Stella would find herself saying things like, 'Don't be so stupid!' or, 'You are such an idiot!' and this made her more self-conscious and nervous.

Why doesn't the social anxiety simply go away? By now you know that one of the main reasons is bound to be avoidance. Just like Stella, socially anxious people try to look after themselves by not going into situations where they would feel scrutinized. This saps their self-confidence and makes it increasingly difficult to face social challenges. Then there's the self-criticism, mind-reading and jumping to conclusions that are always negative, and the assumption that something is true just because we feel it. Finally, the acute self-consciousness, the self-focus that social anxiety causes, means that it is really difficult to 'stand back' and get a calmer perspective. All these psychological responses would make any anxious person more nervous and socially insecure.

If you are beginning to recognize that you have social anxiety and you are struggling to break the vicious cycles that it is so easy to get caught up in, then you might find that reading *Overcoming Social Anxiety and Shyness* helps. Again, details of this can be found under Further Reading at the end of this book.

If I have social phobia what should I do?
How can I break the cycle?

By using the guidelines in this book, you can aim to break the cycles by devising your own 'treatment plan', tailored to suit your needs. Once you are familiar with the various strategies, your plan might look something like this (though everyone will have a slightly different plan):

1. Understand your social fears by catching what goes through you mind when you are socially anxious. Sometimes this will be in anticipation and sometimes this will be during a social activity. Try to catch both thoughts and pictures (Chapter 7)

2. Take stock of your resources, particularly people who could support you

3. Being painfully *self*-conscious is a classic feature of social anxiety and it only makes things worse, so try to refocus your attention away from yourself in order to be less aware of yourself and how uncomfortable you feel (Chapter 10)

4. Learn to calm yourself physically, which will help you feel more in control of the physical symptoms that might worry and embarrass you (Chapter 8 and 9)

5. Review your frightening thoughts and images and see if you can develop less alarming perspectives. See if you can come up with reassuring alternatives to your socially anxious thinking (Chapter 11)

6. Be compassionate towards yourself and don't assume just because you feel or think something it must be true; you might be pretty sure that you are blushing or shaking and that people can see this – but more often than not these reactions are not obvious

7. Learn to be assertive, as this will increase your social confidence (Chapter 14)

8. Once you can calm your mind and body you will be feeling more confident and it's time to take on increasingly difficult social tasks, pacing yourself realistically (Chapter 12)

9. Keep putting yourself in challenging social situations until your confidence has returned. Repetition will build your confidence and resilience.

10. Finally, make plans for keeping up your progress (Chapter 16)

Hypochondriasis

Health anxiety, or hypochondriasis, as it is formally known, specifically describes anxiety about having or developing an illness and it is often associated with extra sensitivity to normal bodily sensations and a tendency to catastrophize. While it is a good thing to be concerned about our health, health anxiety represents over-concern.

I have always been aware of my health, but I was never really worried until a year ago when I heard an awful story about a young mother who suddenly died of leukaemia, leaving three small children. I've got three children so the story really resonated and that day I began checking for swellings and bruises. I was soon carrying out a full body check three times a day and calling in to see my doctor every few days. He kept telling me that there was nothing to worry about and that I had probably caused small bruises by prodding my body so much. I'd feel OK for a while but my doubts always returned and my fears became stronger.

Now, I also get my husband to check my body morning and evening so that I can feel confident that I haven't missed anything. He's getting fed up with this and we row a lot and this just makes me worse. Recently, my doctor told me that he doesn't want to have to see me nearly every day at the surgery and I am finding it so hard not to go – sometimes I pretend that one of the children is sick and use that as an excuse to get an appointment. The strange thing is, the more checking I do, the more worried I get, but, as I see it, you can never be sure, can you?

Why doesn't the health anxiety simply go away? Health fears are maintained in several ways:

- They can be so strong that they resist reassurance. As we saw in an earlier section, if reassurance doesn't ease

95

our worries in the long term we go looking for it again: this is typical of people with health anxiety; they repeatedly turn to their doctors, their friends and family, and the internet. So they never learn how to reassure themselves and to become confident about managing their concerns about their health.

- Sometimes a superstitious belief keeps the problems going; for example, 'If I think about the illness I won't catch it.' This can be comforting in the short term and so the preoccupation persists.

- Health anxiety is also maintained by repeatedly looking for signs of illness by 'scanning' and checking. We all have bodily discomforts from time to time and occasional swellings and skin discolorations that are not at all dangerous. Therefore, if we go looking and feeling for pains and lumps or changes in skin texture, we are bound to find them and it's most likely that they are absolutely normal. But if you suffer from health anxiety the discovery will scare you. If you go on to prod and rub swellings or spots, they get worse and become even more frightening.

- Avoidance of situations that trigger health fears (reading health columns in magazines or saying the word 'Cancer', for example) also maintains the problem for the now familiar reason that avoidance stops us from learning to cope and becoming confident – avoidance is anxiety's greatest ally.

**If I have health anxiety what should I do?
How can I break the cycle?**

By using the guidelines in this book, you can aim to break the cycles by devising your own 'treatment plan', tailored to suit your needs. Once you are familiar with the various strategies, your plan might look something like this (though everyone will have a slightly different plan):

1. Identify what goes through you mind when you become over concerned about your health – the thoughts or pictures that make your fears understandable. In particular, look out for catastrophic and superstitious thinking (Chapter 7)

2. Take stock of your resources, particularly people who could support you, but – and this is *really* important – learn to reassure yourself rather than turning to others

3. Learn to reassure yourself and to develop a less alarming outlook by taking stock and reviewing your anxious thoughts and the unhelpful pictures that run through your mind (Chapter 11)

4. Learn to live with the uncertainty of health worries – this will be easier if you can calm yourself physically (Chapters 8 and 9) and if you can put your worries to one side (Chapter 10)

5. Try to minimize scanning and checking as you will nearly always find something to concern you if you keep checking for signs of ill health. Again, Chapters 8, 9 and 10 will help

6. Now you are in a position to face difficult situations and build up your confidence. Such situations might include resisting reassurance seeking or might include reading a health-related article that you've been avoiding. It is absolutely essential that you face your fears but you must pace this so that you do not over-stretch yourself (Chapter 12)

7. Keep putting yourself in challenging situations until you have consolidated your confidence. Repetition will build your confidence and resilience.

8. Finally, make plans for keeping up your progress (Chapter 16)

Generalized anxiety disorder

If you have generalized anxiety disorder (GAD) you will be 'a worrier'. There is more to GAD than worrying, but worry is a very common feature and it is often exhausting. GAD is the label used to describe persistent feelings of anxiety, constant concerns and frequent 'What if . . . ?' thoughts. It is not unusual to hear sufferers saying: 'I never seem to be free of worry' or 'I can never relax, something is always troubling me. I am constantly on edge.' This is both physically and emotionally draining.

I always worry and I never relax nowadays. There is hardly a moment when I am free of aches and tension and my mind is almost always focused on worries. I can worry about anything, anywhere – and that means that I never know when I'm going to have an attack of anxiety, it's as if there's no escape. It makes me so tired and irritable and I have not been able to sleep or work properly and have not felt well in months. I'm not eating properly – and that worries me, too.

It seems to have crept up on me over the last year or two. Others have always said that I was 'highly strung' and 'a worrier' but this was never a problem – I just seemed to have more 'nervous energy' than most and I used this to my advantage or I've felt able to keep my worries in perspective. If anything, I should be more relaxed now that the children have left home, our finances are improving and my husband and I have more time to spend together. Instead, I'm even more edgy than usual – perhaps I haven't got enough to occupy my mind, I don't know.

I saw my doctor who said that I should join a yoga class and learn to unwind – I tried but I found it impossible to concentrate and I ended up getting more and more irritated! Now I try to cope by keeping busy in the shop, but this isn't easy because I am so tired that I can't seem to concentrate so I make silly mistakes and that stresses me and winds me up even more. I feel so hopeless that I just can't imagine when this is going to end.

If you have GAD you probably worry about the same things as everyone does – health, money, work and so on – you will just worry more and your worry will be really easily triggered. If you have not already looked at it, it is worth going back to the earlier section on Worry (pages 3–23), which will help you understand why it is such an unhelpful thinking style and also why it can take such a strong hold. Sometimes its most powerful hold is the worry that people have about worrying.

It is generally thought that behind GAD is the misinterpretation or the overestimation of a wide range of situations as being threatening. The example above shows how one 'can worry about anything'. It also shows how GAD can creep up on people and affect many aspects of their lives: sleep, appetite, social activity, and so on.

If you are going to address your GAD you need to start by doing two things:

1. try to tease out your individual anxieties. In the example, this GAD sufferer had particular anxieties about her health and her performance at work. But until she teased them out she didn't realize that she had such specific concerns. Her anxieties had seemed vague and that made them harder to deal with.

2. if your fears come to mind in the form of 'What if . . . ?' questions, then you need to be brave and try to answer the question – name the fear. Then you'll know what you are working with

Once you've done this you will have clarified your fears, and that is the necessary first step to managing them.

Why doesn't the GAD simply go away? A great deal of research has gone into understanding GAD and what drives it, and there are a number of different theories. If you think that you have GAD, see if you can identify with any of these ideas.

- **It's safer not to name the fear.** One view is that worrying 'What if . . . ?' is slightly less distressing than actually naming the fear. For example, worrying 'What if I'm ill?' might be less upsetting than 'I could have cancer and if it's advanced I could die'. So there is a tendency to cling to worrying, but unless you name a fear you can't begin to tackle it and the worries will continue.

- **Worry makes me worry.** The meaning of the worrying can drive it – if, for example, I think that worrying will drive me mad then I have more to worry about; if, on the other hand, I think that worrying is helpful and will prevent me from being taken by surprise, I will continue to worry. Either way, the worry will make you worry.

- **I can't stand uncertainty.** Another view is that people with GAD find uncertainty unbearable, it really makes them edgy. So they keep worrying about things, hoping that they will come up with some solution or knowledge that will make the difference. This is a stark contrast to being able to say 'Maybe it will happen, maybe it won't. No point in worrying', and then letting go of the concern.

- **I can't sort out my problems because of the worry.** Research has shown that the actual process of worrying gets in the way of problem-solving. Worrying sends us round in circles so it stops us from taking stock and tackling our difficulties. It almost goes without saying, if we don't solve our problems they remain there for us to worry about.

If I have GAD what should I do?
How can I break the cycle?

By using the guidelines in this book, you can aim to break the cycles by devising your own 'treatment plan', tailored to suit your needs. Once you are familiar with the various strategies, your plan might look something like this (though everyone will have a slightly different plan):

1. Try to identify what is at the root of your worries: name your fears, the thoughts or pictures that make your worries understandable. In particular, see if you have unhelpful beliefs about your worrying that might keep the worry alive (Chapter 7)

2. Take stock of your resources, particularly people who could support you

3. Some of your worries will be amenable to reviewing and re-evaluating and you might be able to take the 'sting' out of them that way (Chapter 11)

4. Some worries might not respond so well to self-talk and so distraction can help you to drop your worries and move on (Chapter 10)

5. It is often helpful to be able to calm yourself physically as this tends to calm the mind too. It also makes it easier to manage the physical discomforts that go hand-in-hand with GAD – and relaxation in particular has been shown to be a really helpful strategy for GAD sufferers (Chapters 8 and 9)

6. Learn how to problem-solve so that you can use this to work your way through problems rather than getting caught up in vicious cycles of worry (Chapter 13)

7. Once you have these coping skills in your 'tool-kit' you can start to face your fears more directly so that you effectively build your confidence. This might involve facing a difficult inter-personal challenge (use Chapter 14 on Assertiveness to help) or facing your fears about travelling, or about making decisions. With GAD the list is almost endless but whatever fears you decide to tackle, do this in a planned and graded way (Chapter 12)

8. Keep putting yourself in challenging situations until you have consolidated your confidence. Repetition will build your confidence and resilience

9. Finally, make plans for keeping up your progress (Chapter 16)

Obsessive-compulsive disorder

People who have obsessive-compulsive disorder (OCD) feel a strong compulsion to do certain things or to dwell on particular mental pictures or thoughts in an attempt to feel at ease, to feel safe and very often to ease a sense of responsibility (a common OCD belief is 'If something bad happens it's my fault'). In textbooks, these behaviours are called 'neutralizing' behaviours because they neutralize the fear – at least for a while. OCD affects different people differently – for example, Daniel felt compelled to wash his hands repeatedly (in case he carried germs) and to check over and over again that switches were turned off (in case of fire). Hester, on the other hand, struggled with a compulsion to bring to mind a mental image of her family being safe and well and to repeat specific and reassuring phrases because she feared that they might other-wise come to harm. These neutralizing behaviours are their best efforts to cope but they are ultimately a form of avoid-ance because neutralizing means never really facing the fear. This, as you now know, will stop Daniel and Hester from learning that things will be OK and that the rituals are really not necessary.

There is something of a typical pattern in OCD. Usually it starts with a person believing that a situation is threatening (the *overestimation of threat* that we looked at earlier), and this triggers a worrying thought or image. Next is a compulsion to do something to feel safe. Daniel feels compelled to check and Hester feels compelled to think 'good' thoughts. In the short term they will feel more at ease, but the worries will return because neither Daniel nor Hester has actually learnt to deal with the fears.

As with all anxiety-driven reactions, responding to a worrying thought or image (rather than ignoring it) can be a helpful response as long as it is in proportion to reality. If you were leaving your house and you thought: 'Did I switch off the gas fire? It would be dangerous to leave it on all day. . .' you might go back and check. This is a normal and helpful reaction. If a woman read an article about cervical cancer that triggered the worrying thought, 'I could be at risk, too. . .' she might be prompted to get a health check. If a father (who narrowly missed driving into a cyclist who did not have lights) had an unpleasant image of his own children being injured, he might be prompted to check that their bike lights worked. Each of these reactions is useful and would only present a problem if there was a compulsion to return several times to check the fire, or to make repeated appointments with the doctor, or if the frightening images didn't go away and then led to overprotection of children.

OCD and health worries: Nancy

I suppose that I have two compulsive problems: I worry that I could be contaminated by germs, so I wash a lot to avoid this. I also worry about my family's health and so I've stopped reading papers or watching TV programmes that could set off my worries. If I start to worry, my mind gets filled with the most awful images of death and I just have to think about everyone I love (always in the same order) while saying: 'You're OK. You're OK.' If I don't do this, or if I do it in the wrong sequence, I can't get rid of the worries and then the images stay in my mind and I feel so distressed that I just can't bear it. I know that this must sound really weird, and I would think it was weird if I didn't know how easy it is to get caught up in these worries, which will only go away if I wash or go through my 'You're OK' ritual. I can't actually remember a time when I didn't think like this, although there have been periods in my life where it's hardly been a problem, and times when it's dominated my days. The only way I know how to cope is to try to avoid situations that make me feel contaminated or worried about death. That's why I don't watch TV programmes about health issues, nor do I read that sort of article in the newspaper. If someone starts to talk about illness, I often make an excuse to walk away, and if I can't do this, then I have to wash or to go through my ritual as soon as I can. Sometimes I can't get away to do this and I feel absolutely terrified for hours.

OCD and safety worries: Judd

I never worried much until I was in the professional sports team. Winning and doing everything right was so important because so much rested on it. I think that we all became a bit superstitious about things. We would take 'lucky' items into matches and we had a 'lucky ritual' before every game. I suppose that we had such little control over what the other team did that we used these simple things to try to feel more in control. I can remember that I did get rather obsessional about checking – something that I could have control over – and I would double- and triple-check my equipment. Then I began checking more at home – lights, doors, and so on. Once I left the team, I gradually gave up a lot of my obsessive checking and, although my wife has always commented on my attention to safety, I've never had a problem with it. That is until six months ago.

It was around that time that I set a retirement date and was planning all sorts of changes in my life. Knowing that I only had another year with the firm, my boss suddenly promoted me to a position with a lot more responsibility – particularly financial.

He said that he wanted to send me off with a good bonus and a recognition of my abilities. Nice gesture but one that stressed me. I found myself worrying more and more about the safety of the office. I would travel home wondering if I had locked my office, locked the safe, set the burglar alarm, and so on. Very soon I could picture the safe being broken into because of my negligence and then I saw myself shamed in front of the man who had trusted me with this extra responsibility. By now I was so worried that I would return to the office time after time to check the safe, to check my office and to check the alarm. I could do this as many as twenty times and I began getting home later and later and more and more upset. My wife says that she can't stand much more of this.

The most common fears tend to concern contamination of oneself or others (as in Nancy's case) and safety (which was Judd's worry). However, some people with OCD are concerned about exhibiting inappropriate behaviour that could embarrass them – swearing in a public place or being rude to someone in authority, for example. In order to minimize the chances of this happening they carry out rituals or special behaviours – it's a way of trying to protect themselves. OCD is always about trying to protect oneself or others.

Another common OCD fear is about not being organized properly, with things arranged in the right way. The fear is that this will bring bad luck:

I know it's irrational but if I don't have everything lined up in order of size I feel very uncomfortable. I just sense that something bad will happen. I don't know why and I can't explain what I fear, I just feel safer if I've organized things properly.

Of course sometimes, purely by chance, this 'superstitious' behaviour is linked with good fortune or with a bad thing not happening. When that happens, it strengthens the superstition. Jon scored his best goal when he was wearing a certain kit and thereafter he wore his 'lucky pants' for each match. From then on he attributed goal scoring to his pants, not his skill, and got increasingly worried if he couldn't wear them. Sofia always lined up the cushions and shoes before she collected her two girls from school – she said that this would ensure that she found the children safe and sound. Her friend pointed out that there was no need to do this as the children were always safe at school. Sofia said that the fact that they were safe just confirmed her superstition and she really didn't dare stop.

People with OCD tend to feel uncomfortable about their behaviours because it is common to believe that they are not really necessary – 'I know it's irrational but . . .' – and yet the compulsion is strong. OCD is also often linked with feelings of embarrassment – and yet a sense of fear and responsibility still drives the compulsion to check, clean and ritualize. These conflicts often make OCD even more painful for the sufferer and, unfortunately, the embarrassment can make it really hard to ask for help. There are various self-help books on OCD that will give you a better understanding of the disorder and ways of managing it. You can find some recommendations under Further Reading in the back of this book.

Fears and anxieties: the labels

Why doesn't the OCD simply go away? As we saw in the examples, avoidance plays its part. Trying to cope by avoiding only saps confidence and tends to make things worse.

- Reassurance seeking is also a common reason for the problem becoming entrenched – we looked at reassurance seeking earlier, and you might remember that, like avoidance, it gives some short-term relief but stops us from gaining confidence enough to deal with the worries for ourselves.
- Another common way of coping is by *trying hard* not to think about an alarming thought or image. The problem here is that, if we try not to think about something, it will come to mind. See for yourself – try not to think about red balloons, absolutely clear your mind of red balloons, keep red balloons out of your mind. The chances are that you had images of red balloons. If so, you can appreciate that the strategy of trying not to think about something backfires.

If I recognize I have OCD what should I do? How can I break the cycle?

By using the guidelines in this book, you can aim to break the cycles by devising your own 'treatment plan', tailored to suit your needs. Once you are familiar with the various strategies, your plan might look something like this (though everyone will have a slightly different plan):

109

1. Identify what goes through you mind when you become over concerned about things. This might be very scary but you need to know what thoughts or pictures make your fears and behaviours understandable. In particular, look out for catastrophic and superstitious thinking and for vivid and alarming images and for thoughts about responsibility. Log your urges and your behaviours, too (Chapter 7)

2. Take stock of your resources, particularly people who could support you, but – and this is *really* important – learn to reassure yourself rather than turning to others

3. Look at your thoughts – try to learn to reassure yourself by being able to weigh up just how realistic your fears are. Are you overestimating threat and underestimating your ability to cope? This is common in OCD (Chapter 11)

4. In addition to using self-talk to help relieve your fears, distraction can help you accept uncertainty and to let go of your obsessive thoughts and worries. It can help you walk away (Chapter 10)

5. Absolutely crucial to overcoming OCD is facing your fears rather than succumbing to avoidance. Your biggest challenge will always be trying not to give into urges – but you really need to make sure that you actually test out whether or not your fears are founded: this has been proven over and over again to be the most effective way of breaking OCD cycles. You need to plan this carefully (Chapter 12)

6. In order to help you resist checking or cleaning or thinking in a magical way or reassurance seeking, you might need to call on the skills of realistic self-talk and distraction, but you will also find it easier to withstand the physical discomfort that can come with urges if you can calm yourself physically, too (Chapters 8 and 9)

7. Keep challenging yourself – both by resisting urges but also by doing things or visiting places that are likely to set off your urges – until you have built up your confidence. Repetition will keep building both your confidence and your resilience.

8. Finally, make plans for keeping up your progress (Chapter 16)

Post-traumatic stress disorder

Post-traumatic stress disorder, more commonly known as PTSD, is a stress reaction that sometimes follows a traumatic event such as a road traffic accident, an assault or witnessing a major disaster. It is quite normal to have a period of difficulty after a trauma and it's quite usual to be plagued by memories and distress for a while. There is probably a good reason for this replaying of frightening experiences, and one popular theory is that it gives us a chance to learn from our mistakes or close shaves. The car crash that I mentioned earlier kept replaying in my mind for a while, and each time it did, it gave me a chance to consider what I might have done to avoid it and what I did well that kept my child and me safe. This meant that I could keep learning from the experience without having to go through it again. In most cases these vivid recollections ease over time (sometimes days but often weeks or even months), but in PTSD it doesn't get easier. Then the distress of the memories affects behaviour and PTSD sufferers avoid whatever might trigger the memories: places, people, reading newspapers, and so on. You can see that life becomes restricted and fear sets in.

The first studies of PTSD involved soldiers who all showed similar patterns of extreme stress reactions after combat. The main features were classic symptoms of anxiety but with recurrent, vivid memories or dreams of the trauma, too. These especially vivid memories are very typical in PTSD and the particularly vivid ones are known as 'flashbacks', as they seem to transport the sufferer back to the moment of trauma. And the memory isn't always just visual – some people have flashbacks of smells or physical sensations or sounds. What they have in common is that flashbacks refresh the fear each time they occur and this keeps the problem alive. Sufferers often fear the flashbacks because they think that they are going mad or that each flashback is a reminder that they'll never get better. But most people do recover from PTSD and learn to manage flashbacks and bad memories.

Getting back to the soldiers – in some instances they were much more 'emotional' than before; for example, becoming fearful or tearful more easily. Sometimes the post-traumatic reaction was the opposite and they experienced emotional numbing – that is, feeling very little or having blunted or deadened emotions. Probably the most common emotion felt in PTSD is fear, but sometimes the main feeling is grief or disgust or anger – all very powerful in fuelling distress and avoidance. The message is that there is quite a range of emotional reactions linked with PTSD – not just fear – and sometimes the emotional consequence is a numbing rather than feeling more emotional.

Since the early studies it has become clear that PTSD can happen to anyone, not just to soldiers.

After the car crash, I started to have dreams about it. I expected these to go away within a few days, but they were persistent and so vivid that I would wake up really believing that I had just been in the accident. I know, from talking to others, that this is a common reaction, but my terrifying dreams kept on for weeks and weeks and they were affecting my sleep and my ability to work the next day. Eventually, the doctor gave me some sleeping tablets to help me cope with this.

Although I was then less bothered by the dreams, I still could not bring myself to go back to the junction where the accident had happened, nor could I bring myself to drive the car again. I thought that I'd soon get over my fear of driving and of that junction, but I found that it got worse rather than better and I became very dependent on my wife to do the driving and to plan routes that didn't take in that junction. If we did get close to the scene of the accident, I would start to have really vivid memories – like a flashback of the original scene. This upset me so much that my wife soon learnt lots of alternative routes and we now stick to them. She's been so understanding about this and she has really put herself out to help. Although it's now been six months since the crash, I still don't feel confident that I will be able to drive again and being so restricted in my freedom to travel is affecting my work.

Why doesn't the PTSD simply go away?

- The traumatic memories play a big part in this. Our brain generally deals with traumatic memories by 'replaying' them for a while, but gradually the intensity fades and recollections feel more like a bad memory rather than a vivid re-run of the trauma. However, the flashbacks can be so powerful and 'real' that they can re-start the distress all over again.
- It's understandable to be fearful of the memories (or what the flashbacks might mean in terms of going crazy, for example) – but being in a state of heightened anxiety and fear can actually make us more prone to having scary memories.
- Avoiding doing things or going to places that bring back memories (as we saw in the example above) is also understandable, but, as you well know, avoidance stops us from regaining confidence.
- Many trauma survivors restrict their lives because they grow less confident, and limiting social and physical activities only makes us increasingly withdrawn and fearful.

If I have PTSD what should I do?
How can I break the cycle?

By using the guidelines in this book, you can aim to break the cycles by devising your own 'treatment plan', tailored to suit your needs. Once you are familiar with the various strategies, your plan might look something like this (though everyone will have a slightly different plan):

1. Try to understand what goes through your mind and, therefore, what explains your PTSD. This is likely to be a combination of vivid memories, and worrying thoughts about your vulnerability and likely danger (Chapter 7)

2. Take stock of your resources, particularly people who could support you.

3. Remind yourself that powerful memories are normal after a trauma: the brain is set up to replay traumatic memories. Just understanding this can ease the stress and make the recollections less intense

4. When you are familiar with the sort of thoughts and images that trigger your fears, use constructive, soothing self-talk to remind you that you are safe and that the danger is over now. Also try to develop soothing images of you coping and being safe (Chapter 11)

5. Use distraction to build your confidence in order to get rid of unwanted, intrusive thoughts and images if necessary (Chapter 10)

6. And use relaxation and controlled breathing to give you the confidence that you can calm and soothe yourself when you begin to get stressed (Chapters 8 and 9)

7. Now, you can gradually 're-claim' your life, taking up hobbies and activities again, but pace yourself so that you don't feel overwhelmed (Chapter 12)

8. Also aim to *gradually* face the situations you have been finding difficult because they trigger memories and fears, and use soothing self-talk and soothing images to reduce your mental tension. Plan this carefully and pace yourself realistically (Chapter 12)

9. Keep putting yourself in challenging situations until you have consolidated your confidence. Repetition will build your confidence and resilience

10. Finally, make plans for keeping up your progress (Chapter 16)

A word about 'Burn-out'

Burn-out is a rather vague term that has been around for years and it is used to describe a different form of anxiety or stress problem from the ones that we've talked about so far. Burn-out is the reaction to constant stress that tends to go unnoticed until we realize – or someone close to us realizes – that we are not coping. It creeps up on us. The cause can be what you might think of as 'active' stresses, such as overwork, pressured deadlines or impossible targets, or 'passive', such as job boredom, lack of autonomy or frustration. The stress can even be 'positive' in that it reflects something enjoyable – spending too many hours at the job you love; taking on too many chores and favours for the people you like to help, for example. Whatever the origin, the symptoms are similar to those in other stress-related problems, but they can be more severe because we ignore or dismiss the stress until it has reached levels that interfere with our work, our home life or our sense of well-being.

Looking back, all the signs were there but I never took any notice. I had always wanted to be a nurse and I was ambitious for myself and concerned about my patients. So I never stopped to look at how hard I was working. Actually, it is difficult to slow down in my job – the culture of an emergency ward is one of self-sacrifice and hard work. And I loved being a part of that. Then I began to get digestive problems, but I simply took antacids, and when I was diagnosed as having irritable bowel syndrome, I thought it was a nuisance but I did not realize that it was a warning sign. I began to get more and more run-down and told myself that this is what happens in the winter and that we still have to run the service. I was losing weight, feeling exhausted and getting so irritable that some of my staff were obviously giving me a wide berth.

The most frightening part of my experience was that I began to make mistakes – often really stupid ones that I wouldn't expect of a student. Fortunately, I had not made many before my line manager insisted that I was signed off work to recover from stress. At the time I was shocked and it took a while to sink in, but now I recognize that I was lucky that my boss saw what was happening and gave me a much-needed break. Thank goodness the decision hadn't been left to me – I don't think that I would have realized that I was suffering from burn-out until I had made far too many mistakes and perhaps made myself quite ill and those around me miserable.

Why doesn't the burn-out simply go away?

- A common reason is that we don't even notice it – it creeps up on us and the gradual changes don't set alarm bells ringing
- Another common reason is that we are quite driven to stretch ourselves – perhaps because we enjoy what we are doing, perhaps because we have a sense of obligation, perhaps because we can't say no
- Burn-out tends to make us less efficient and we don't achieve as much as we hope or we make more mistakes. This can fuel a drive to work harder to compensate for our mistakes or lack of production, and this will only make us more tired and less efficient: a vicious cycle.

If I recognize I have burn-out what should I do? How can I break the cycle?

1. Catch the thoughts that drive you so hard – and then try to counterbalance them with more moderate ones (Chapter 11)

2. Learn to say no so that you are not forced to overstretch yourself or to settle for boring or frustrating work just because it's hard to be assertive (Chapter 14)

3. Learn to time-manage so you have realistic goals and you can make time for rest and relaxation – and schedule in enjoyable activities (pages 350–69)

4. Listen to the people around you when they suggest you slow down or take it easy or when they point out that you might not be fulfilled in what you do – sometimes it takes an outsider to spot problems

5. Learn what your warning signs are – in the example above it was digestive problems, but someone else's warning sign might be headaches, back pain, drinking more, comfort eating, and so on. Discover what tells you that it's time to take stock

Summary

- Worries, fears and anxieties are sometimes grouped into specific categories or 'diagnoses'

- the most common diagnoses are: phobias, panic disorder, social anxiety, health anxiety, generalized anxiety disorder (GAD), obsessive compulsive disorder (OCD) and post-traumatic stress disorder (PTSD)

- Burn-out is also a recognized form of stress that CBT can tackle

- There are tried-and-tested CBT treatments for most of the anxiety diagnoses

- Recognizing your own problem in one of the diagnostic groups can give you some ideas for coping

Part Two

Managing Problems using CBT

5

Managing problems using CBT

I have suffered with my nerves for years and I have always managed by taking the odd tranquillizer. I always take one before I go to a social event or if I have to visit the doctor or dentist. Although this has worked for me, I do worry that I might be dependent on the tablets. I did get into a terrible state on holiday when I went without them but ended up panicking, which ruined the holiday for everyone. After that, my husband said that I should try to cope without them but I haven't the courage. There must be another way . . .

Our view on managing anxiety-related difficulties has changed quite dramatically over the past thirty years. There have always been two options for managing worries, fears and anxieties: psychological methods and/or medication. Using medication was very popular in the 1970s and early 1980s, and then more and more research showed that psychological methods were effective – in particular, a therapy known as CBT (cognitive behavioural therapy).

Medication – usually in the form of tranquillizers or anti-depressants – is not necessarily a bad thing as long as it is used cautiously and *always* under the advice of a doctor. In fact, medication might be invaluable for helping you through a crisis; but its long-term use is generally considered to be unhelpful for several reasons:

- resorting to medication stops us from learning to manage our own anxiety. Then we don't develop the self-confidence that we need in order to overcome anxiety-related problems
- there is some evidence that tranquillizers lead to physical (not just psychological) dependency
- there is good evidence that medication is no more effective than psychological management in many instances
- there is the possibility that medication will simply mask symptoms of worry, fear and anxiety but will not address the root of the problem, which may then remain a source of vulnerability to stress
- medication can cause unpleasant side-effects that might even worsen the anxieties of someone who is very sensitive to bodily changes

Fortunately, there is really convincing evidence that CBT can help with anxiety problems and, better still, that a large number of people can use CBT in the form of self-help, such as this book. Part Three of this book will take you through a self-help CBT programme that is based on years of running anxiety-management sessions in an NHS clinic. Therefore you can be confident that the techniques are tried and tested and that this recovery programme is realistic. The programme itself is presented in a systematic way and covers coping strategies for managing physical, psychological and behavioural symptoms. The requirement from you is that you read the text thoroughly and be prepared to take time to tailor this approach to meet your needs. This means:

- keeping diaries of *your* anxieties and worries
- trying out different techniques and discovering what works for *you*
- finding time to practise the techniques
- pacing yourself realistically

Mediation

If you are currently taking medication and are planning to reduce your use, this is an ideal opportunity to learn strategies to replace it. Introducing CBT techniques will make it easier for you to ease off the medication (see the note on coming off medication at the end of this chapter). It is very important to make sure that you come off any medication under the guidance of your doctor.

CBT: what it is and why it works

I began to think that I was never going to be able to live my life normally again. Since I began to get anxious about what others might think of me, I went out less and generally did less. I was becoming house-bound and socially isolated. Then a friend recommended a book on CBT because it had helped her when she struggled with anxiety in the past. I have to say she was a good advertisement for CBT as I would never have realized that she had ever had a problem. I read the book at once and it first helped me to understand that anxiety is basically normal (this immediately made me feel better) and that it can get out of hand and that there were reasons for this. I began to see that my anxieties had got out of hand because I had simply just had to deal with a lot of stress at one point in my life. This reassured me that I was not weak or silly – just unlucky. Next, the book helped me to appreciate that I had become caught up in what it called 'vicious cycles' of worry and anxiety. These held me back and took away my confidence – but the book also showed me how I could break these cycles and regain my confidence. The book outlined lots of techniques to help me to manage the horrible physical sensations and my worrying thoughts, and it encouraged me to take on increasingly difficult challenges until I managed to get back my old life. In fact, I think I did better than that. Armed with a better understanding of anxiety and lots of ideas of how to cope, I don't think I will be as vulnerable to falling into the anxiety trap again.

CBT is a talking therapy, which was developed by Professor Aaron T. Beck in the 1960s, and it was first used as a therapy for depression. It was so successful that in the 1980s it was used with other problems like anxiety and eating disorders. Over time, it has been shown to be an excellent talking therapy for a wide range of psychological problems, and the books in this series reflect this. There has been a considerable amount of research on the ways in which CBT can help with anxiety.

What we have seen over and over again is that it helps many people by giving them the understanding and the 'tools' they need to manage their own difficulties.

The simple notion on which CBT is based is: what goes through our mind (thought processes or cognitions) affects the way we feel and ultimately what we do (our behaviour). For example, Josh is in an aeroplane and it begins to shake a little. His thought is: 'Oh no – there is something seriously wrong here – we could have engine failure and crash!' Understandably, he feels frightened and this makes his thinking even more extreme (our old enemy the vicious cycle). His panic affects his behaviour – he is no longer sitting calmly, he is rigid with fear and he clutches his lucky St Christopher's charm, keeping his anxieties to himself.

Marty, who is sitting across the aisle, has a different thought: 'Could be a bit of turbulence – this is quite normal on a flight.' He feels relatively calm and simply turns to his partner and shares his idea – she agrees with him and they both settle back in their seats.

One situation – two different views, each view leading to different feelings and actions (see Figure 8). If only Josh had been more open to the idea that he might be safe, he might not have felt so afraid.

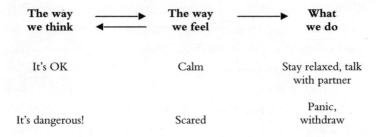

Figure 8: The way we think affects the way we feel and what we do

In turn, what we do can change the way we feel and the way we think. Josh remained tense and clung to his 'lucky charm'. This kept his anxiety going – he tensed up and it made him feel more anxious. A few minutes later when the turbulence ended, he felt relief but it was an uneasy relief because he had not been properly calmed and assured and he was worried that it might happen again and that next time his lucky charm might not work. He remained anxious. Marty, on the other hand, had checked out his 'minor turbulence theory' with his wife and they had assured each other and both felt safe. Like Josh, he was aware that it might happen again during the flight, but he felt relaxed about this because he could remind himself that this was normal and it would soon pass safely. This interaction between the way we think (cognitions) and what we do (behaviours), and how it affects the way we feel, is shown in Figure 9.

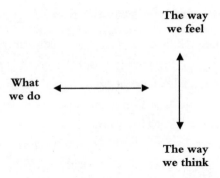

Figure 9: What we do affects the way we think and feel

If you have problem anxieties, worries and fears, CBT will help you to change the way you feel by teaching you to address the way you think and what you do. You will learn to recognize your own patterns and this will help you to catch your anxious thoughts, feelings and behaviours before they get out of hand. By learning some of the most widely used CBT techniques, you will be able to take charge of the *cognitions* (thoughts and images) and the *behaviours* that could make your difficulties worse – in short, you will learn to follow the path of Marty rather than Josh.

One of the best things about CBT is that it is a coping style for life – once you get the skills under your belt they are with you for good. Yes, there will be the odd time when the going gets tough because life throws difficulties in our path, but you will still have the skills and knowledge to get you through – even though it might be more of a struggle at those times. We know from research that CBT not only helps people to get over their anxieties, it protects them from slipping back or *relapsing*.

A note about coming off medication

Learning self-help skills to replace the medication is the surest way of being able to stop taking it, but it is possible that the process will be difficult because of 'withdrawal symptoms'. These are simply the reactions of a mind and body in recovery but they can be uncomfortable. Many people do not experience withdrawal symptoms, so don't *anticipate* suffering as you cut down on your medication because you might actually be someone who can do this with ease. However, you should always seek the advice of your doctor before changing any drug regime and you should tell your doctor if you are experiencing discomfort.

Common, *and temporary*, withdrawal symptoms to be aware of are:

- feelings of anxiety
- loss of concentration, poor memory
- agitation, restlessness
- stomach upsets
- oversensitivity
- feelings of unreality
- physical tension and pains
- appetite changes
- difficulty sleeping

If you do experience these symptoms, reassure yourself that they are temporary and that your body and mind will eventually adjust to not using medication. When you do reduce your medication, try not to substitute alcohol, drugs, food or smoking for comfort, as these can cause you further worries. Instead, use the self-help strategies in Part Three of this book.

Part Three

Managing Worries, Fears
and Anxieties

6

What can I do?

I had given up thinking that things could be different. My old doctor had always given me tablets to help me deal with difficult situations. When a new doctor told me that I could manage without them, I thought that she did not realize what she was asking. She explained that, over time, I could develop ways of managing my distress for myself and then I could cut down on my pills. It didn't happen overnight but I did manage to learn how to deal with stress by myself. That boosted my self-confidence and then it became even easier to cope. I felt so much better in myself for not having to turn to drugs and much more able to take on new challenges.

Strategies for coping

In Part One of this book, you saw that worry, fear and anxiety are not just common but they are crucial to survival. However, you also saw that they can develop into problems when they are excessive and cycles of distress get set up. Now it's time to think about breaking those cycles by developing practical ways of dealing with the feelings, thoughts and behaviours that bother you.

You will be relieved to learn that there is a wide range of

coping strategies to help you do just this, and Part Three of this book will guide you through them.

In summary, you will discover:

- ways of recognizing your anxieties and stress
- ways of taking charge of bodily sensations
- ways of managing problem thoughts and images
- ways of changing unhelpful behaviours
- ways of coping for life

These approaches will help you bring your problems under control – but they are skills that need to be practised and learnt. Because of this you might find that some don't come naturally at first – that's only to be expected. You wouldn't expect to be fluent in French after a few evening classes. Think of the process of acquiring these skills as being like mastering a new language: you will need time to practise. You will then develop your own 'tool box' of effective ways of coping, which you can use whenever you are under stress or anxious.

Some of the strategies that you are about to read might seem familiar – perhaps they are similar to coping techniques that you have tried already. Don't assume that they will be redundant or unhelpful until you've given them another chance. Even familiar and previously tried strategies might have some life left in them. Perhaps they didn't work in the past because you didn't use them properly or at the right time for you or because they needed more practice. Give them another chance and they might prove to be very useful after all.

Other coping techniques in this section will be quite new to you. Don't be put off by novelty – you might find some good ideas here – but do recognize that the unfamiliar strategies are likely to need extra attention and practice.

When you have taken yourself through the *entire* programme, you'll discover which techniques, or combinations of techniques, suit you best; these will form your personal 'toolkit' for coping. Everyone's 'kit' will be different and it is important that you tailor yours to meet *your* needs because personalizing your approach can make all the difference. You are much more likely to keep up a way of life that helps you combat anxieties if it feels comfortable and right for you. Whatever your choices of coping strategies, the golden rule is that you will be most successful if you tackle your stress when it is at a low level. Although it is not always possible to catch anxieties early, do try to nip things in the bud. Once you are aware of your own patterns of stress and worry and once you have created your own 'kit', you can relax, knowing that you are carrying around with you effective ways of dealing with these challenges – then you can simply get on with your life.

Top tips when choosing your strategies for coping

Your best starting point is to really understand your own personal experience of worry, fear and anxiety. For this reason, you will be encouraged to keep diaries (see page 144) to help you get a handle on your anxieties. This is very important groundwork, so don't skimp on this part of the programme even though you might be tempted to do so. You will also need to spend some time considering:

- what is feasible for you
- your preferences
- your resources

You need to build a realistic coping plan, one that will work for *you*. You can't plan to overcome your fear of flying by taking flying lessons unless you have the finances and freedom to do so; you can't anticipate relaxing at an expensive gym if you hate gyms, you have three small children at home and no money; but you *can* make plans that involve the support of others if you have helpful family and friends, and you *can* make plans that impinge on your daily work if you have sympathetic employers.

Hilary wanted to overcome her fear of snakes and her husband suggested a day at the zoo, with him, visiting the reptile house and then on to a nice restaurant at the end of the day to give her something pleasant to look forward to. In this case this was sound advice – they lived fairly near a zoo, they could afford the entrance fee (and the meal later), Hilary's husband could take the day off to be with her and she felt confident in his company. For Frances the same plan would have been less good because it would be difficult for her to take the time off work during the week and at weekends she had no reliable childcare, she also had a long-standing dislike of zoos (all the smells and noises put her on edge) and her husband was her worst critic so she would have felt stressed and unsupported – far better for her to start to face her fears by looking at pictures of snakes in the evening with her best friend encouraging her.

You will discover more about keeping diaries to identify

your personal needs and resources in the next section. Once you've kept records for a while, you will be in a good position to judge what will work best for you.

Another tip is to look for coping strategies that 'match' the problems you have. For example, if you suffer from the physical discomfort of stress, make sure that controlled breathing and relaxation (see pages 160–88) are on your skills list. If, on the other hand, you are more bothered by constant worries and nagging fears, invest extra time in learning distraction techniques (see pages 189–204) and how to counter worrying thoughts (see pages 205–41). The best way to match strategies to your needs will be covered in more detail in the next chapter. You can work though this after you have had an opportunity to keep some records of your difficulties.

Coping strategy or safety behaviour?

As you saw in Chapter 2, it is crucial to distinguish between a coping strategy and a safety behaviour. Coping strategies build our skills and confidence while safety behaviours undermine our sense of being able to take command of challenging situations. It would be great if I could now list the safety behaviours that you should avoid, but it is not that simple. The difference is not absolute, it is in our interpretation – it depends on how we view the behaviour.

- **Coping strategies:** in both the long and short term, we view these as ways of helping us to help ourselves, and when we have used them we feel more confident that we 'can do'

- **Safety behaviours:** these often seem helpful in the short term, but in the long term they erode our confidence. We tend to view them almost superstitiously as a means of just getting by and we grow dependent on them

Sam and Bill were both nervous about having an injection at the dentist's surgery. Both got through the difficult situation by using distraction in the form of a soothing image. Sam's confidence grew: 'This is great – I realize that I've got strategies that I can use to give me the edge in difficult situations. There are things I can do, which means that I can manage my stress. I needn't be so worried in the future.' On the other hand, Bill felt lucky that he'd got through the situation but he felt no more confident: 'Phew – managed it this time but only because I used my image. . . Suppose I can't remember it next time? What will I do then? I couldn't have coped without it.' Bill certainly had not got the idea that he was learning to control his problem, he was becoming dependent on carrying out a particular distraction ritual.

Same situation, same strategy, different interpretation – but can you see the difference that Sam and Bill's attitudes make?

When you have come through a difficult situation, you need to review your conclusions and make sure that you are giving yourself credit where it's due. Ask yourself:

- What have I just achieved?
- What have I learnt about my strengths and abilities?
- Knowing this, what will I do next time?

Had Bill done this, he might have appreciated that he could take credit for deciding to use a very appropriate coping strategy that helped him realize his coping potential and challenge his old prediction (the prediction that he could not cope). He might have concluded that in similar situations he could make similar choices and this would mean that he could take charge of his problems.

A footballer doesn't score a goal because he is carrying a lucky mascot or wearing 'lucky pants'– he scores a goal because he has skill and ability. The only thing the 'lucky charm' does is undermine his confidence and prevent him from realizing just how good he is. Make sure that you don't make the same mistake.

Safety behaviours: friend or foe?

Having made the distinction between safety behaviours and coping behaviours, you might be surprised that I now want to say a few things in support of safety behaviours. They have had negative press over the years, they've been seen as the bad boys of anxiety disorders, and, to be fair, they don't help us if we over-rely on them. However, they can be helpful if we use them to get us started on the road to recovery. The advice simply to drop them completely is unhelpful if it means that we are left feeling bereft of ways of coping and hopeless about ever having the courage to start facing our fears. Faced with that scenario, some people just give up. So you need to consider how you can make safety behaviours work for you without becoming reliant on them.

Alicia had spent years managing her fear of collapsing in public by using safety behaviours: she carried smelling salts and glucose tablets to combat the light-headedness that she feared might lead to collapse; she always walked close to a wall so that she could steady herself if necessary; she wore flat shoes to give her stability and did as much supermarket shopping as possible so that she could lean on a trolley. Using all these 'crutches' ate away at her confidence and it got harder and harder for her to dare to go out. So she sought the help of a therapist who helped her realize that the safety behaviours were actually making her less confident, and then the therapist advised Alicia to drop them all. Poor Alicia was paralysed. Without any of her 'crutches' she was simply too afraid to venture out. So the therapy plan was revised and it was agreed that Alicia would drop one safety behaviour at a time, starting with the one that she felt she used least – the smelling salts. Armed with her remaining 'crutches', she did continue to go out and she grew confident to manage without the smelling salts – then she was able to leave the glucose tablets at home and later she dared to experiment with shoes with higher heels. And so it went on until she built up the confidence to venture out under her own steam without fear of collapse. She said that the therapist's first suggestion had left her feeling hopeless and scared, like someone who had been confined to a wheelchair being told that now they should simply walk. The second approach was not so off-putting because (to continue her metaphor) she had been given crutches, then walking sticks so that she could make progress at her own rate, stretching herself but never terrifying herself.

The lesson to learn here is one of balance – using 'crutches' enough to give you the confidence to move forward but not so much that you lose faith in your ability.

Coping alone or with the help of others?

Although this is a self-help guide, you can enlist the support of others if you think that it will make things easier for you. Partners, family and friends can be helpful allies in coping, as can professionals such as counsellors and medical practitioners. It is worth spending some time reflecting on what would be most helpful to you: perhaps it would be a partner's company when you are learning to relax or a friend's support as you try to go out and face your fears, or your doctor's help in reducing your medication. Involving others can also be a really helpful way of educating them – helping them learn what your fears and anxieties are about and what helps you. You could even ask someone close to read this book if you think that would help them understand your difficulties and your needs. Most of us are fortunate enough to have people in our lives and some of those people would be happy to help – so give it some thought because, with extra help, you could beat your fears and anxieties sooner.

What to expect from the self-help programme

You will be reassured to know that many anxious people have already benefited from the plan in this book. In fact, the whole programme is based on a successful group treatment that I began in the 1980s – so it has really stood the test of time.

Over the years, colleagues and I also used this approach with individuals and we learnt things from our patients – things that might now help you.

> *'You are not alone if you are scared or worried or stressed – there will be a reason for it and it's nothing to be ashamed of.'*

> *'To overcome fear you have to face it – it's that simple – but you can make it easier for yourself by careful and sensible planning.'*

> *'Make no bones about it – this is hard work but it's so worth it. I would advise anyone to keep at it as the practice pays off.'*

> *'Ask for help – this is an important step you are taking, and don't blow your chances by being too independent.'*

Some of you will find that this self-help guide is all you need; some of you will get some relief but you might not feel that you have *taken control* of your problem and you might need a bit more support. This support could come from friends, family or professionals. For example, you might well learn to relax, and you will get physical relief from this, but you still might not be able to resist the impulses to check without some support from your family; you might learn to sleep better and get benefit from this, but you still might not be able to dismiss your daytime worries without the guidance of a therapist; you might learn to catch worries and put them on hold but you might need help in actually learning to let go of them. Even if you need some extra support you will still have gained from following the programme – give yourself credit for that. You will have taken an excellent first step in trying out self-help and everything you learn from this book will be fundamental to further work. So, if you are one of those people who requires more support, don't be dismayed; simply get in touch with a professional such as your family doctor, who can advise you where to go for help.

Summary

- You can learn to recognize your anxieties and stress

- You can take charge of bodily sensations, problem thoughts and images and unhelpful behaviours

- You can discover ways of coping for life

- Enlisting the support of others can really help you in achieving all this

7

Getting to know your fears and anxieties

For a long time, I thought that my panic came out of the blue. This made me even more frightened because I felt out of control. Then I started to keep a diary of my panicky feelings and, to my surprise, I saw a pattern. This made me feel less helpless and I started to reorganize my life to try to stop the panics. For example, I got the feelings if I hadn't eaten for hours (and I get so absorbed in my work that I do forget to eat), so I began to carry snacks in my briefcase; I felt panicky when I had to see my boss, so I attended an assertiveness-training class to help me feel more confident around her. I took control again.

Keeping diaries and records

The actual experience of worry, fear and anxiety is different for each of us – bodily sensations, worrying thoughts, problem behaviours – and the triggers for anxieties vary enormously from person to person. Before you can begin to learn how to manage *your* problem you must really understand *your* problem. This is your starting point. You can do this quite easily by keeping records when you are particularly worried, fearful or anxious. Simply note:

- your physical feelings
- your thoughts (or mental images)
- what you do in response to this distress

Diary 1 is a typical record for doing this, and you can use it to help you structure your own record keeping. You will see that, as well as having columns for noting the onset and the experience of stress and anxieties, there is an opportunity to rate the level of your discomfort from 'Wholly calm' (1) to 'Worst feelings possible' (10). There is a final column for recording how you tried to cope and how you felt afterwards.

This detailed information will help you see how your stress and anxiety levels vary from situation to situation. This will help you appreciate when you are particularly vulnerable or less so. The extra information will also give you an insight into what works and what doesn't work for you as a coping response, because, under 'What did I do?', you will be noting how you reacted to feeling anxious and then what happened to your distress levels.

This might seem like an awful lot of information to keep, but knowledge really is power in overcoming anxiety. The more you understand your difficulties, the better you can manage them. You don't need to keep detailed records for ever, but it would be a good idea to keep detailed accounts for a week or two (you'll find extra diary sheets at the end of the book). Then look back over your entries and you should find that you can answer the following questions:

- what things or situations trigger *my* distress?
- what situations are easier or harder for me?
- what are my bodily feelings and my problem thoughts?
- what do I do when I'm distressed?
- what helps me best cope with my distress and what makes it worse?

'What helps me best cope with my distress?' is a particularly important question as you must distinguish between the coping strategies that help and are good for you in the long run, and those that might make you feel better in the short term, but are not helpful over time. We have seen how reassurance seeking, avoidance and escape can give short-term relief, but we've also seen that they are confidence-destroying in the longer term. You need to be on the lookout for other ways of coping that might feel good at first but that ultimately work against you.

To help you see how this sort of diary might be used, three examples are given in diaries 1(a)–(c). These are records made by a person with a dog phobia (1(a)); a person with social anxiety (1(b)) and someone with OCD (1(c)). Of course, your experience will be unique to you and quite different from the examples, but the idea is that you can see how the diaries can be used. As time goes on, you can use simpler versions that will help you to monitor your progress.

Getting to know your fears and anxieties

Diary 1

Where and when?	How did I feel?	What was it like?	What did I do?
When did I feel anxious? Where was I and what was I doing?	What emotion(s) did I feel? How strong were they? 1 (calm) – 10 (worst possible)	How did it feel in my body? What thoughts or pictures did I have in my mind?	How did I try to cope? How did I feel when I'd done this? 1 (calm) – 10 (worst feelings possible)

Diary 1(a) Dog phobia

Where and when?	How did I feel?	What was it like?	What did I do?
When did I feel anxious? Where was I and what was I doing?	What emotion(s) did I feel? How strong were they? 1 (calm) – 10 (worst possible)	How did it feel in my body? What thoughts or pictures did I have in my mind?	How did I try to cope? How did I feel when I'd done this? 1 (calm) – 10 (worst feelings possible)
Saturday: Walking in town and I saw a dog from the corner of my eye	Anxiety (Emotions: 8)	I was a bit shaky and felt a bit sick. What if it comes over here and starts to attack us? He could harm the children. I couldn't cope with seeing that.	I walked the children into a café and we stayed there for half an hour. (Immediate emotions: 3.) Later I felt disappointed with myself, and I was very anxious when we had to leave the café.
Saturday: Leaving the café	Anxiety (Emotions: 7)	Shaky, butterflies in my stomach. What if the dog is still there? We could be in danger.	I marched the children very quickly to the car park and didn't look in any shops on the way – just thought about getting to the car. (Emotions: 7)
Wednesday: Jade suggested that we go to the park at the weekend	Fear (6)	Shaky and tense. The park is full of dogs – they are running free! It is a dangerous place and I won't be able to cope with my fear. Just thinking about it is frightening.	Talked with Jade about my fears. She said that she understood and we could take a walk somewhere else. (Emotions: 3)

Getting to know your fears and anxieties

Diary 1(b) Social anxiety

Where and when?	How did I feel?	What was it like?	What did I do?
When did I feel anxious? Where was I and what was I doing?	What emotion(s) did I feel? How strong were they? 1 (calm) – 10 (worst possible)	How did it feel in my body? What thoughts or pictures did I have in my mind?	How did I try to cope? How did I feel when I'd done this? 1 (calm) – 10 (worst feelings possible)
At work on Wednesday: had to contribute to a meeting	Fear (Emotions: 8)	Felt paralysed, dry throat, hot. I can't do this – I'll say something stupid and everyone will see that I'm stupid. They are all looking at me. I'll be humiliated.	I said what I had to say without looking anyone in the eye and immediately afterwards I left without speaking to anyone. (Emotions: 5 – I was still tense)
Wednesday evening at home	Anxiety (Emotions: 7)	Nervous, agitated. Thoughts going round: I made a hash of my presentation. I had an embarrassing picture of this in my mind.	I had a couple of drinks. (Emotions: 2)
Sunday evening: dinner at Anthony and Kat's place	Anxiety (Emotions: 8)	Tense, shy, dry throat, blushing. I don't know that couple – I don't know what to say to them. They must think I'm a fool. I must look like a fool – I'm blushing.	I drank to calm my nerves but it just made me less able to talk sensibly and I still felt self-conscious. (Emotions: 6)

149

Diary 1(c) OCD

Where and when?	How did I feel?	What was it like?	What did I do?
When did I feel anxious? Where was I and what was I doing?	**What emotion(s) did I feel? How strong were they?** 1 (calm) – 10 (worst possible)	**How did it feel in my body? What thoughts or pictures did I have in my mind?**	**How did I try to cope? How did I feel when I'd done this?** 1 (calm) – 10 (worst feelings possible)
At home, trying to leave the house	Fear (Emotions: 9)	Tense and breathing fast. If I don't make sure that all the electrics are switched off the house could go up in flames. I can't afford the shame or the expense. I'm so worried I can see a picture of the burning house in my mind's eye.	Went back nine times (and was late for work). Still felt worried (Emotions: 8) so I called a friend and asked him to drive to the house to check it. (Emotions: 4)
At the shop doing the accounts for Sima who is on holiday	Worry and anxiety (Emotions: 8)	Tense, agitated. I must get this just right. I must keep checking. What if I get this muddled? I'll cause problems for the shop owners and they'll know that it was my fault.	Double-checked the figures (twice) and then told myself that Sima's bosses agreed to me doing this so they have to carry some of the responsibility if I make a mistake. (Emotions: 4)

A step further: getting to know your coping skills

I thought that I knew how to deal with my stress at work – I grabbed a chocolate bar and instantly felt a bit better. But keeping the diaries helped me to see that this never worked for long. Very soon I was writing another entry that said that I was still stressed and now worried about eating so much – I was getting anxious and miserable! This trick for coping just wasn't working for me.

Hard as it was, I made up my mind to visit the dentist. It was dreadful at the time and I was a nervous wreck sitting in the waiting room. When she called me in for my check-up I almost ran away – but I made myself go in and have the examination. I felt great afterwards! At first I didn't want to write up my diary in case it brought me down, but writing it made me see what an achievement this had been and how – although it felt bad at the time – it was well worth the effort and the right thing to do.

These two examples show how the last column of your diary can help you see what really works for you. The obviously unhelpful strategies can be dismissed straight away, leaving you to consider your 'short term only' and 'long-term' coping methods.

- **'Short term only' strategies** give immediate relief but are counterproductive if you keep relying on them – for example, turning to tranquillizers or alcohol, avoiding difficult situations or scolding yourself. 'Short-term' strategies can be useful if they buy you time to put into action a 'long-term' strategy, or if the 'short-term' strategy is a planned last resort.

- **'Long-term' strategies** build up your confidence and they are the real foundation to overcoming anxiety; they are beneficial both in the short term and in the long term. However, their impact might not be as immediate as some of the 'short term only' strategies, and therefore we often need more self-discipline to put them into action. In the example below, Harry's 'long-term' strategies are physical activity and talking through his problems. Other 'long-term' coping skills might include yoga exercises, planning and problem-solving, or talking to yourself in a soothing, constructive way.

Once you are familiar with your short- and long-term strategies, don't feel that you have to abandon all your 'short-term' solutions: this can be too alarming a prospect. Instead, think how you might begin to mix and match them so that you build your confidence while using short-term strategies less and less. The story of Harry, a very tense shop owner, illustrates how you can successfully combine short- and long-term coping.

Harry often gets home from work far too stressed to settle. If possible, he relaxes by running and, if this is not possible, he does physical work around the house (both good long-term strategies). If he can't run or busy himself, he would rely on talking through his stress with his wife; if she wasn't available, he would telephone a friend (again, good long-term methods). On one occasion, he gets ready to run but finds that he is too stressed and physically tense to do this – he feels too agitated and anyway it has begun to rain. Unfortunately, his wife is not at home and he cannot get his friend on the phone. He then falls back on his 'last resort' strategy and heads for the kitchen where he has a stash of good-quality chocolate. He takes some and settles in front of the TV. Harry regards this as a 'last resort' because, when he gets home, he wants to be able to unwind and then do things with his family – helping with homework, taking his daughter to her music lesson and so on – he doesn't want to 'chill out' so completely that he has no energy for his family (he usually saves this complete unwinding with chocolate and the TV until later, before he goes to bed). Clearly, comfort eating would have been an unhelpful strategy if Harry had simply spent the evening over-eating or if he routinely turned to eating in response to stress. However, on this occasion he has soon unwound enough to find the energy and focus to go running after all – his 'last resort' gave him the tension release he needed in order to do what he had wanted to do in the first place.

This is quite a different picture from Richard, who didn't get the balance right, and his short-term strategy worked against him:

Richard also came home feeling too tense to get into his usual routine of running, and he poured himself a very large glass of wine to unwind. He hoped that this would ease his tension and then he could get on with other things that needed to be done that evening. He did manage to unwind, but so much so that he became sleepy and a bit drunk. His children asked for help with their homework and he couldn't really support them and he certainly couldn't sort out the accounts that needed to be submitted the next day. Overdoing the short-term coping left Richard unable to be productive. So the 'last resort' strategy didn't work quite so well for Richard, his children didn't get their dad's help, he didn't get his work done, and he ended up feeling very stressed in the morning.

When you complete your diaries you need to study them to work out what works best for you so that you don't fall into the trap that Richard did. Eventually, you will be able to see clear patterns, and once you've reached that stage it can be useful to make a list of your 'short term only' and your 'long-term' strategies for reference when you are feeling stressed. You can use Table 1 opposite.

Table 1: Coping skills

My ways of coping		
Long term	Short term only	Absolutely last resort

A final note about coping with stress concerns the use of stimulants. When you are trying to cope, it is especially important to try not to turn to substances such as alcohol and nicotine, or caffeine-containing food and drink such as chocolate, chocolate drinks, coffee, energy drinks, cola or tea. In the short term these can provide a pleasant distraction from your problem, but as soon as the caffeine or nicotine enters your system, it can increase the unpleasant bodily symptoms and this can then make managing your stress more difficult. Alcohol is deceptive in that it *is* relaxing in the short term, but the breakdown products (metabolites) of alcohol are stimulants, and so you can find yourself more tense than ever, once the alcohol has been processed (metabolized) by your body. Also, if you drink heavily, you can find yourself with a hangover that will almost certainly get in the way of coping. Instead, try to acquire a taste for decaffeinated or non-caffeinated drinks and foods, and try to cut back on smoking and drinking alcohol when you are stressed.

Using your diaries to catch maintaining cycles

I hope I've persuaded you just how useful your diaries can be. They will show you what bothers you most when you are anxious and *what keeps your problems going*. The latter – what keeps your problems going – is particularly important. You really need to study these patterns, these vicious cycles. You might recall that the key to managing anxieties is to break the patterns that maintain them, so search your diaries for explanations: are your cycles of distress driven by bodily sensations, or by worrying thoughts and images, or by avoidance, or by a lack of social confidence, or by a lack of planning skills? Maintaining cycles will point you in the right direction for taking the next step – creating a personal management programme. If you need a reminder about the way in which problems are maintained, look back over Chapter 2 in Part One.

When you have pinpointed your maintaining cycles, you will be ready to link the self-help skills in Part Three of this book to your particular needs. For example, is physical discomfort behind your problems? If so, focus particularly on the techniques for getting bodily sensations under control – especially if you find that you hyperventilate when stressed. If worrying thoughts or images are your main source of stress, make sure that you learn well the techniques of distraction and thought testing. Should you find that your main difficulty is rooted in avoidance and a lack of confidence, make plans to prepare yourself for a programme of graded practice. If you discover that your fear is about communicating with people, consider assertiveness training as part of your personal programme. I'm sure that you get the gist, but Table 2 on page 158 summarizes the options for you.

Table 2: Creating your personal programme

Coping strategy	When should I give this special attention?
Self-monitoring diary-keeping	Throughout your programme. This will help you to build up an accurate picture of your needs and will also provide a record of your progress.
Techniques for managing bodily sensations	
Controlled breathing	If you experience panic attacks, difficulty in breathing, dizziness. It is also a good idea to learn this as part of your relaxation training.
Applied relaxation	If you have much physical tension or bodily discomfort when you are stressed. This is also very helpful with sleep problems.
Techniques for managing psychological symptoms	
Distraction	If you have difficulty dismissing worries and upsetting mental images. This is also very useful in panic management.
Thought management	If distraction is not sufficient to manage your worrying thoughts. If you need a powerful and enduring means of self-reassurance.
Techniques for dealing with problem behaviours	
Graded exposure to fears	If you avoid what you fear, you *must* emphasize this, as exposure is the only sure way of overcoming a phobia or OCD.
Problem-solving strategies	If you have difficulty organizing your thoughts and making plans when you are under stress.
Assertiveness training	If interpersonal problems stress you.
Time management	If your stress management is undermined by poor organization/delegation.
Techniques for coping in the long term	
Blueprinting	This is an essential part of the programme for everyone.
Coping with set-backs	This is essential and should be given attention throughout the programme.

The coping strategies in this book are laid out systematically, so it should be easy for you to find the techniques you will need. However, it's a good idea to try all of the strategies, as you will most probably need to use several of them in combination. Having said that, it is also important to remember that each of us has different needs and different capabilities, so always aim to tailor your self-help programme to meet *your* needs and to reflect your realistic goals.

Summary

- Keeping logs, diaries or records will help you discover: the characteristics of your difficulties; what drives your problem; your own ways of coping and how effective they are

- This is the foundation for taking charge of your problems

- Your records must be detailed enough to give you the information that you need

---

8

Managing bodily sensations I: controlled breathing

I was in agony, my chest hurt and my limbs ached. Now I realize that stress is very physical and I learnt how to keep the physical discomfort to a minimum simply by learning how to breathe properly. I had been breathing far too quickly and this just made matters worse for me. Now I take things easy, breathe slowly and am more relaxed in stressful situations. I still get some discomfort, but nothing that I can't tolerate.

Breathing comes naturally – we can all do it so we tend not to think about it. But it is like standing or walking – if you don't pay attention to your posture you can end up with problems; if you do pay attention you can avoid all sorts of discomforts. In Part One of this book we looked at the way our breathing changes when we are stressed – it becomes rapid and shallow and we inhale a good deal of oxygen. You'll find yourself doing this after you have just run to catch a bus or raced to get to an appointment on time – it's a perfectly normal response to exertion and also to stress and it's called *hyperventilation*.

We all hyperventilate when we are tense or exercising. Breathing faster at these times gets oxygen to our muscles so our body is prepared for action – running away, for example.

Rapid breathing isn't a problem in the short term – in fact, your body will need the extra oxygen if you have just run to catch a bus – but if you keep over-breathing, you will force too much oxygen into the bloodstream and this will disrupt the delicate oxygen–carbon dioxide balance. Your body will let you know that things have gone out of sync by triggering unpleasant physical sensations, like:

- tingling face, hands or limbs
- muscle tremors and cramps
- dizziness and visual problems
- difficulty in breathing
- exhaustion and feelings of fatigue
- chest and stomach pains

You won't necessarily get all these symptoms, but even one or two of these sensations can be very alarming. For this reason, they often trigger more anxiety and therefore more hyperventilation: a vicious cycle. Sometimes – *but not always* – this cycle of stress can lead to a panic attack. Figure 10 shows how this simple but powerful cycle of reactions can escalate.

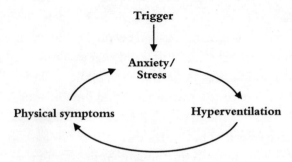

Figure 10: The hyperventilation cycle

So far this probably sounds quite dramatic – and if you are stuck in a panic cycle then it will feel dramatic – however, the good news is that you can easily learn to correct over-breathing and control the symptoms for yourself by developing the skill of regular breathing. This means learning to breathe gently and evenly, through your nose, filling your lungs completely and then exhaling slowly and fully. Below is an outline of a breathing exercise that will help you to take control of the symptoms of hyperventilation, and you'll see that it really is quite simple. The key to using it is in being so practised in the technique that you can switch to it whenever you need to, even when you are stressed.

Breathing regularly: how to do it

First a few guidelines before you start:

- Use your lungs fully and avoid breathing from your upper chest alone
- Breathe smoothly, without any gulping or gasping
- When you first practise, do this exercise lying down, so that you can better feel the difference between shallow and deep breathing. As you become more practised, you can try the exercise sitting and later standing. Eventually you will be able to do this even while walking
- Place one hand on your chest and one on your stomach
- As you breathe in through your nose, allow your stomach to swell. This means that you are using your lungs fully. Try to keep the movement in your upper chest to a minimum and keep the movement gentle

- Slowly and evenly, breathe out through your nose
- Repeat this, trying to get a rhythm going. You are aiming to take eight to twelve breaths a minute: breathing in and breathing out counts as one breath. This might be difficult to gauge at first, so practise counting five to seven seconds for a complete breathing cycle (i.e. one inhalation and one exhalation)
- *Do not deep breathe rapidly*

Controlled breathing in action: managing a panic attack

After my very first panic attack, I was really sensitive to every sensation in my body – especially in my chest. When I had the first panic, I was sure that the ache in my chest meant that I was having a heart attack. That fear stayed with me even though my doctor had told me that I had a healthy heart and that we all suffer aches and pains from time to time. His words reassured me in the surgery, but as soon as I had the chest pains again, I began to panic. I went back to see him and he tried something else. He explained how we all breathe quickly when we are frightened and this can bring on chest pains. He suggested that, in my case, this made me more frightened and so I breathed even faster, and so on. I wasn't convinced. Then he did a sort of test in the surgery and this made me realize two things:

1. *that the way I breathed really did affect the way I felt, and*
2. *that I could control my symptoms.*

First he showed me how to breathe slowly and evenly, then he asked me to start panting (hyperventilating) while we stood together. Well, it was a real eye-opener. Within seconds of beginning to pant, I started to get the chest pain and the dizziness just like when I have the 'heart attacks'. Next, he began to talk me through controlled breathing, and my dizziness went away and the chest pains eased. He asked me to do the exercise again, and again I seemed to be able to switch on and switch off the symptoms.

After that, I was more confident and I found that, whenever I got anxious and uncomfortable, I could simply choose to change the pace of my breathing and this would make me more comfortable and take the edge off my fear. I took control. The doctor told me to practise this regular breathing during the day so that it would become a habit. So, every time I go to the bathroom, where it's nice and peaceful, I spend two minutes doing my breathing exercises. I find it really relaxing and I get to practise half a dozen times a day. As time goes on, I am getting better and better at switching off the sensations and they bother me less and less.

Difficulties when using controlled breathing

It is usual to have a few 'glitches' when trying out any of the coping strategies in this book. This will probably be the case when you try to control your breathing, so I've listed a few common difficulties and their solutions below.

Difficulty in breathing naturally and comfortably

At first the smooth, regular breathing might not come naturally and you might feel that it's awkward and uncomfortable. You may feel that you are not getting enough air or that the air is not really filling your lungs. All of this is quite common. With practice, however, you will find this slower rate of breathing gets easier and is actually quite comfortable. Often, all you need to do is give yourself time to develop the skill. If you do continue to feel that you can't breathe in fully, begin the exercise by exhaling as much as you can. In this way, you will empty your lungs and the first in-breath should be deep and comfortable.

Feeling strange during the practice

You are probably quite sensitive to physical sensations and now you are trying out something new which affects the way you feel physically. You are bound to be very aware of even slight physical changes and there will be some new sensations associated with controlled breathing. These won't be harmful; they'll just be new to you. Try to be curious about them – just observe them and see what happens if you accept them and continue with your practice.

Forgetting to practise

This is possibly the most common problem, but I can't stress enough how important it is to practise the exercise whenever you can – you are trying to develop a new habit, which will only come through repeated rehearsal. To help you to practise, try using reminders: a regular alarm on your mobile phone, a coloured mark on your calendar, whatever you know will grab your attention from time to time. Most of us look at our watches regularly throughout the day, so you might find it useful to put a little eye-catching mark on your watch (I used a small blob of nail varnish).

Be assured that, as your skill improves, you will find it easier and easier to switch to controlled breathing whenever you need to, and it will even become a habit to correct your breathing as it begins to get too rapid.

Summary

- Stress and anxiety can make us hyperventilate, but that's not unusual

- However, hyperventilation can make stress and anxiety worse if we are alarmed by its effects

- Simply learning to breathe in a regular, controlled way can combat hyperventilation, but it takes practice

9

Managing bodily sensations II: applied relaxation

My tense and panicky feelings eased as soon as I began to do my relaxation exercises regularly. At first, I hadn't done them often enough and I didn't get much benefit. Then I decided to make a real effort and it paid off. Much to my surprise, I found that I got mental relief as well as physical relaxation and this gave me hope that I could learn to manage my anxiety. Now I can feel relaxed very quickly and I can 'switch off' the tension in all sorts of situations that used to bother me.

Under stress, the muscles in our bodies tense: that's normal. However, if it is exaggerated or if it goes on too long, muscular tension can cause an incredible variety of uncomfortable feelings. You'll appreciate that we have muscles throughout our bodies, so we can find tension-related aches and pains virtually anywhere in our bodies. Not everyone experiences these feelings, but commonly they include:

- stiff neck
- painful shoulders
- tight chest
- difficulty in breathing

- trembling
- churning stomach
- difficulty in swallowing
- blurred vision
- back pain

Of course, when these sensations get distressing, they can trigger more tension and so our old enemy the vicious cycle is set up.

The most effective way of controlling bodily tension is learning how to relax in response to it: to 'apply' relaxation as and when we need it. Easily said but often a challenge to do. This 'applied' relaxation isn't just a matter of sitting in front of the television or having a hobby (although these recreations are important, too); learning applied relaxation means developing a skill that enables you to reduce physical tension whenever you need to. In time you will become confident about reducing your anxiety and tensions in a variety of situations – in effect, you will have a portable skill to use when you need it. Even better, when your body is free of tension, you will find that your mind will tend to relax, too. So all in all, it's worth taking the time to learn how to relax.

It does take time, though – the ability to relax at will is only achieved through practice, practice and a bit more practice. One of the most effective ways of mastering the skill is by working your way through a series of structured exercises, such as the four below. These are designed to help you learn to relax step by step. The first two routines are quite long and you may find that recorded instructions are helpful.

You can make your own recording following the relaxation scripts (see pages 370–80). Be sure to use slow, gentle speech so that you give yourself the best chance of relaxing – you won't find it very soothing if you bark efficient instructions at yourself!

General guidelines for relaxing

You won't be able to relax and read the instructions at the same time, so first familiarize yourself with all the exercises – you'll see that they get shorter and shorter, so that might spur you on! Once you are familiar with the routines, you can start to work through them one at a time. When you can relax using the first exercise, move on to exercise two; when you have mastered this, begin exercise three. By the time you get to exercise four you will be ready to learn a very brief, rapid relaxation routine that will easily fit into your day-to-day life. This whole process of learning a series of exercises should be done gradually, possibly over several weeks. Of course, the length of time needed will vary from person to person, so don't worry that you are not progressing fast enough – this will only make you more tense – and don't try to rush things. Only move to the next exercise when you feel fully relaxed at the end of a routine.

Some 'top tips' before you begin:

- Plan your practice. Try to get a routine going and keep to the same time each day. That way you'll stand a bet-ter chance of keeping up the practice

- Practise frequently. Aim to practise at least twice a day: the more you practise the easier it will be to relax at will, and that's your goal

- Choose the right place: practise somewhere quiet where you won't be disturbed. Make sure that it is not too hot or too chilly. Give yourself the best chance of relaxing

- Choose the right time: avoid relaxing when you are feeling very tired or if you are either hungry or full. It's hard to relax under these circumstances

- Get comfortable: when you first try to relax, make sure that you have found a comfortable position and wear comfortable clothes. You'll probably begin by lying down, but later you will be able to practise sitting or even standing

- Get into the right state of mind: try to adopt a 'passive attitude'. This means not worrying about your performance but just having a go. Be curious and see how it goes; don't judge yourself

- Breathe! It is so important not to hold your breath or to hyperventilate during your relaxation practice; if you do, you could feel worse rather than better. Remember to breathe through your nose, filling your lungs completely so that you feel your stomach stretch a little. Keep the rhythm slow and regular. It is best to get the hang of controlled breathing (see Chapter 8) before you start your relaxation training and then you can be sure that you are breathing in a way that will help, not hinder

- Record your progress. Use a sheet like Diary 2 (see page 172) to keep track of your progress. You can expect a certain amount of day-to-day variation (as we all have ups and downs in our tension levels), but by keeping a log over time you will be able to see patterns and then you'll be able to work out what makes it easier or harder for you to relax. The more you understand about your physical tensions, the more control you'll have over them

- Practise! I've emphasised this so much that you probably predicted this final 'top tip'. But there's no getting round the fact that practice will improve your skill

The relaxation exercises

And finally – the exercises themselves. There are four:

- Lengthy relaxation
- Shortened relaxation
- Simple relaxation
- Applied relaxation

You will see that the first exercise demands quite a lot of time and effort – but it is worth the investment. The skills you learn are the foundation for the brief, applied relaxation that will allow you to counteract tension as and when you need to do so.

Lengthy relaxation (LR)

This lengthy relaxation is based on a very well-established relaxation routine devised by Edmund Jacobsen in the 1930s – so you can feel confident that this is a tried and tested

Diary 2: Relaxation Diary

Where and when?	How I felt before the exercise	What exercise I did	How I felt after the exercise	Notes
Note the time and place	How relaxed were you? 1 (not at all) – 10 (deeply relaxed)		How relaxed were you? 1 (not at all) – 10 (deeply relaxed)	What did you notice about the exercise and its effects?

routine. His aim was to develop a systematic programme to help his patients achieve a deep level of relaxation. His solution was a series of 'tense–then–relax' exercises focusing on the body's major muscle groups. An additional advantage of this approach is that it helps us learn to distinguish between tense and relaxed muscles. Sometimes we can become so used to being tense that we don't even realize that we are. These exercises help us recognize when we are tense – and when we do that, we can relax in response.

The basic movement that you use at every stage of the exercise is as follows:

- tense your muscles, but do not strain: concentrate on the sensation of tension
- hold this for about five seconds, then let go of the tension for ten to fifteen seconds
- concentrate on how your muscles feel when you relax them: notice the difference between tense and relaxed muscles

LR asks you do this for many different sets of muscle groups throughout the body, so it really is a very thorough exercise. It is important to breathe slowly and regularly between each stage in the procedure and during the exercise. When you have decided where and when you will carry out your exercises, get comfortable and start to focus on parts of your body, as follows:

Feet   Pull your toes back, tense the muscles in your feet. Relax and repeat.

173

Legs	Straighten your legs, point your toes towards your face. Relax, let your legs go limp, and repeat.
Abdomen	Tense your stomach muscles by pulling them in and up – as if preparing to receive a punch. Relax and repeat.
Back	Arch your back. Relax and repeat.
Shoulders/neck	Shrug your shoulders, bringing them up and in. Press your head back. Relax and repeat.
Arms	Stretch out your arms and hands. Relax. Let your arms hang limp. Repeat.
Face	Tense your forehead and jaw. Lower your eyebrows and bite. Relax and repeat.
Whole body	Tense your entire body: feet, legs, abdomen, back, shoulders and neck, arms and face. Hold the tension for a few seconds. Relax and repeat.

Some of us still feel tense at the end of the routine – if this is so for you, simply go through it again. If only parts of your body feel tense, just repeat the exercise in those areas. If tensing and focusing on certain muscle groups is really uncomfortable or distressing, then skip that group for now and plan to go back to it later when you have more confidence and skill in relaxing. The important thing is not to stress about your performance.

When you have finished the exercise and feel relaxed, spend a few moments relaxing your mind. Think about something restful: whatever scene or image works best for you. Breathe

ter exercise that you can practise as you
enced at achieving the relaxed state. It is
developed in the 1970s by a cardiologist
on. He simply wanted to help his heart
tress levels, but the exercise has become
rsally helpful relaxation technique. For
need to find a restful 'mental device' to
. This means finding a sound or word
nd relaxing. You might use the word
f the sea; or the image of a soothing
ure or an ornament that you like, or
ing, such as a quiet country spot or a
n't have to be complicated: sometimes

ked out what is most effective for you,
s:

ible position with your eyes closed.
y growing heavier and more relaxed.
our nose and become aware of your
hale. As you breathe out, think about
, while breathing easily and naturally.
her or not you are good at the e
of your tensions and rel
ng thoughts will p
worry about
n to think
attern.

178

slowly through your nose, filling your lungs as completely as you can. Continue for a minute or two, then open your eyes. Don't stand up straight away; only when you are ready, move *slowly* and stretch *gently*. Feel good.

Lengthy relaxation should be practised about twice a day until you always feel fully relaxed at the end of the exercise. Then you can move on to the shortened and adapted LR. Remember, it takes time to learn how to relax. Give yourself a chance and don't expect to succeed too soon. As we said earlier, some people find it easier to follow this exercise if they have recorded instructions to guide them. Remember, you can make your own audio recording by reading the relaxation script at the end of the book. Be sure to speak slowly and gently; you are aiming to calm yourself.

LR in action: Managing sleep problems

I've never been a 'good' sleeper and it usually takes me a while to drift off, but I became a terrible sleeper after my illness and one of the thoughts that used to keep me awake was: 'I'll never be able to get to sleep while I'm this uncomfortable', and pretty soon I would also begin thinking: 'Perhaps I am getting ill again!' These thoughts and the physical discomfort would keep me awake for hours. Needless to say, the next day I would feel tired and the aches and pains would seem worse.

My doctor explained that the aches and worries were probably feeding on each other and contributing to my sleeplessness. She went on to say that I could break out of this vicious cycle if I learnt to relax at bedtime. She described a relaxation exercise that involved systematically un-tensing my muscles and she gave

175

me a recording of instructions to follow at home. I then practised relaxing once or twice a day. This was no hardship because it gave me relief from my aches and pains during the day, too. I soon knew the exercise well enough to be able to use it when I went to bed. Instead of dwelling on the discomfort in my body, I focused on relaxing my body and I rarely stayed awake long enough to complete the exercise! I would then wake up better able to cope with the strains of the next day, and if I did get aches during the day, I would simply do the relaxation exercise in a chair. It's made a real difference to me.

LR in action: Managing physical pain

After the crash I was badly hurt: my ankle and shoulder were fractured, my back had been injured and I had whiplash. I also had terrible headaches for weeks – really bad ones. I had several operations on my ankle – even so, it still gives me pain and I can't walk well and I'm angry and embarrassed about that. Months later, I still found that I suffered from pain throughout my body and the headaches kept coming back. I went to see my doctor and she told me that I was getting very tense, perhaps because of my memories of the crash and because I was angry, and this was giving me aches and pains throughout my body. I didn't like the idea that she was telling me that it was all in my mind and I told her that my pain was very real and very physical. She reassured me that she was not suggesting that I was imagining it and she explained that anyone with very tense muscles can experience real pain. She thought that the solution was to help me learn how to relax my muscles. It would be challenging for me because I really did have cause for pain (my

---

ankle) but
She gave
me how t
learnt to
became g
disappea
do: I co
so much
part an
often u
eases a
to be
painfi
ankle
relax

Short

Once
routi
go th
the
do t
ada
For
lyir

Managi

Simple relaxation

This is an even shor
become more experi
based on the exercise
named Herbert Bens
patients reduce their
established as a unive
the exercise, you will
use during the routin
or picture that you f
'calm' or the sound
object, perhaps a pict
a scene you find calm
deserted beach. It does
simple is best.

When you have wo
follow these instruction

- Sit in a comforta
  Imagine your bo
- Breathe through
  breathing as you i
  your mental imag
- Don't worry whe
  cise; simply let go
  own pace. Distract
  your mind. Don't
  them; simply retu
  or your breathing

- You can keep this going for as long as it takes for you to feel relaxed. This might be two minutes or twenty minutes: the criterion for finishing the exercise is you feeling relaxed. When you do finish, sit quietly with your eyes closed for a few moments, and then sit with your eyes open. Don't stand up or begin to move around too quickly.

As this is a brief exercise, you can practise it more frequently than the earlier ones. You could do it for a minute or two every hour; or at coffee, lunch and tea breaks; or between appointments; or at every service station if you are driving on a long journey and feeling stressed. The options are endless and the most useful thing you can do is to discover a regular routine that fits in with *your* lifestyle.

Simple relaxation in action: Managing worries and discomfort

My family has always said that my problem is that I never unwind and that's why I feel so tense and physically unwell all the time. The truth was that I didn't know how to unwind. I'd tried sitting with a book or watching TV, but my mind always wandered back to some worry or other and I'd soon become tense and uncomfortable again. Then I learnt a simple relaxation routine. This gave me something constructive to focus on as well as easing the aches and pains that used to concern me so much.

I had to find a few minutes each day, at regular intervals, to sit and concentrate on breathing calmly and then imagining a sooth-ing scene. My first choice didn't work too well – it was a tropical beach and I thought of myself lying in the sun, listening to the sea. I'm such an active person that this actually began to irritate me! My next choice did work. I remembered a formal garden that we had visited earlier in the year – I'd loved it. So, in my mind, I went for a stroll around this garden, noticing all the different trees, shrubs and flowers and imagining the scent of the roses and the feel of the sun on my shoulders. I managed to find a postcard of the garden that helped make my mental picture more vivid.

I did this exercise three or four times a day – whenever I got to the end of one chore and before I began the next. It was wonderful: my mind wasn't so tense and I had no physical pains to worry me. I even found that I had more energy if I relaxed during the day. Every now and then I get a worry or a twinge or an ache and I am alarmed, but I use this as my cue to relax and, so far, the physical discomfort has always gone away and the worries have become manageable.

Cued relaxation

By now, you will be familiar with three relaxation exercises, and if you've been practising you will be getting more and more skilled at relaxing. Once you have mastered the first three exercises, you can begin to use your relaxation skills throughout the day and not just at your designated 'relaxation time'. In this way, you will get better and better at being able to relax at will. You'll need to start by learning how to relax 'on cue' and all you need for cued relaxation is something that will catch your eye regularly and remind you to:

- drop your shoulders
- untense the muscles in your body

- check your breathing
- relax

As a cue, or reminder, you could use something that you look at regularly during the day – your watch, an office clock, your diary, for example. Every time you see the cue, you will be reminded to relax and so you will be practising your relaxation skills several times a day. There are all sorts of cues that you might use; just work out what catches your eye frequently and use this as a reminder.

Applied relaxation – the grand finale

The final stage of relaxation training is learning to put it into practice whenever you need it, using stress as your cue to act. To do this, you need to start trying it out during your day-to-day activities. If possible, begin with situations that are not too stressful then work up to more challenging situations as your skill and confidence improve. With time and regular practice, relaxation will become a way of life and you will find that you can relax just when you need to. Of course, you are bound to continue to experience some tension from time to time – this is normal – but now you'll have a better awareness of it and you will have the skills to bring it under control.

Applied relaxation in action: Keeping calm in public

I've always been shy and nervous around people. That's just me. In public I get tense and then I can't think straight and I don't usually manage to enjoy or achieve what I want to do. Recently I learnt how to relax and I could get into quite a nice

181

'chilled' state where my body and mind felt calm. I knew that I had to start using this ability in real life, but to be honest I was quite daunted by the prospect. My mum was really helpful – she said that I didn't have to 'jump in at the deep end'. She told me to write out my list of difficult situations and then choose the ones that didn't scare me too much. She said I should start there. So I began by meeting up with friends for lunch. Sure enough, when I sat in the café waiting for them, I felt myself getting tense but I imagined myself relaxing into the chair, my shoulders dropping. I checked that I was breathing nice and evenly and I simply said to myself: 'It's fine, you know how to unwind.' I felt calmer and was OK when my friends turned up. Next I put myself into a more challenging situation and I volunteered to show a visitor around our department – again I was able to combat my tension. Next I plan to try my applied relaxation skills when taking something back to a shop.

Throughout this chapter you have been given the message that relaxation is a *skill* and therefore it takes time to develop it – don't skimp on the effort you put into learning how to do it properly. A useful analogy for relaxation training is learning to play the piano. You would start with the laborious, but necessary, scales (lengthy relaxation) and graduate to arpeggios (shortened relaxation). With this as a foundation, you would be able to play simple tunes (simple relaxation) and gradually more sophisticated music (cued relaxation). Only after a lot of practice would you be able to sit at a piano and play spontaneously (applied relaxation). You wouldn't be able to play spontaneously if you had not worked through the earlier stages;

and you might find that you can't relax when you need to if you have not done the groundwork.

Applied relaxation in action: Managing worries

It was helpful when the psychologist gave me a label for my problem – GAD – but I was still plagued with the worrying and the tension. She explained that it would take time to get my problem under control and that she would first teach me how to relax my body and mind. I remember thinking that I had tried everything to relax and that she wasn't going to teach me anything new. I told her that I'd hired gentle, entertaining DVDs, I'd gone out to dinner with friends, I'd even joined a Pilates class. Then she explained that she was going to teach me an additional way to relax so that I could add this to my list of relaxing things to try. Her method was different from my other activities because I did the exercise alone and focused on myself and the way I felt. It was quite difficult to get into at first, especially as the early exercises took fifteen to twenty minutes, and I have to be honest here – they were a bit boring. If she hadn't stressed how important it was to practise, I think that I would have moved on too soon. However, as the exercises got shorter, I began to enjoy them more and I was more motivated to practise. Nonetheless, I didn't think that it was going to take so long – I spent weeks learning to relax!

Eventually, I reached the stage of being able to tune into when I was tense and then I was able to drop my shoulders, check my breathing and empty my mind of worries. This is no mean feat, believe me. It was hard work and I nearly gave up several times, but now I'm glad I kept going because it has really changed the way I feel. I am no longer dogged by that sense of doom and gloom because I can shake it off by relaxing whenever and wherever I need to.

Difficulties in relaxing

If you find that you have some difficulties when you are working through your relaxation training, you are not alone. Below are some common obstacles:

Peculiar feelings when doing the exercises

It's usual to feel strange if you are doing something physical that you are not used to. Don't worry about this (as your tension will only rise if you do). I remember feeling tense and annoyed the first time my tutor took us through a relaxation exercise, but now I find being able to relax is effective and invaluable. Try to accept that it will take a few practice sessions before you begin to feel comfortable with the exercises, and you will find that the unusual or annoying sensations will soon disappear. Also, make sure that you are not hyperventilating (over-breathing) during the exercise, or standing up and moving around too soon, or practising when you are too hungry or full, as any of these things can cause unpleasant feelings.

Cramp

This can be painful but never dangerous. There are a few things you can try to make it less likely that you will get cramp: avoid tensing your muscles too vigorously; in particular, avoid pointing your toes too enthusiastically. Try not to exercise when your muscles are cold, and use a warm room for your practice. If you do get cramp, ease the pain by gently rubbing the affected muscle and take a break from the exercise – you can always return to it later.

Falling asleep

Sometimes this isn't a problem – it's what you hope for – but if you don't intend to fall asleep, you can try sitting rather than lying down, you could time your exercise so that you are not tired when you start, you could hold something (unbreakable) so that you would drop it and wake if you dozed off.

Intruding and worrying thoughts

The human brain has evolved to allow us to think creatively and have lots of ideas. This is great but it does mean that we all get lots of thoughts intruding on our consciousness. So when your relaxation is interrupted by other concerns, don't worry as it's quite normal and not a serious obstacle to your practice. The best way of making sure that unwanted thoughts go away is by not dwelling on them. Accept that they will drift into your mind from time to time and then simply refocus on your relaxation exercise. If you try *not* to think of them they will not go away. If I tell you *not* to think about a pink car, the chances are that you'll immediately get an image of a pink car in your mind; and if I stress: 'No really, clear your mind of pink cars', then the image will probably become even more fixed. Just tell yourself that it's normal to get intrusions. Don't pay them much attention and simply turn your thoughts back to relaxing.

Not feeling relaxed

This can be a problem when you first begin relaxation training. When you are new to the exercise, you may not feel much benefit, because the benefits come with practice. The most important thing is not to try too hard as this will create tension. Just let the sensations of relaxation happen when they happen. It is also worth asking yourself whether you are in the right state of mind (or body) to relax and if your environment is suitable. If not, do the exercise later or somewhere else – give yourself the best chance of succeeding.

A word about exercise

A very effective way of unwinding physically is to take exercise. If you can't get on with the relaxation exercises, for whatever reason, you could try to do something physically demanding as this will *always* reduce muscle tension. It is also a good way of distracting us from worries, particularly if we have to concentrate on rules or techniques (playing squash or taking a dance class, for example). Another great thing about exercise is that you also gain a sense of mastery and increased self-confidence.

If you are worried about the physical symptoms of anxiety, doing exercise means that you can bring on feelings of breathlessness, a racing heart and other physical sensations in a controlled way and you can grow confident that these responses will come and go without harming you. It puts you in control.

In recent years research has shown us the particular benefits of exercise for stress and anxiety management. Most importantly, regular exercise seems to raise the 'fight–flight threshold', and that means that it takes more to get us stressed, which in turn means that we are more at ease. Physical activity also appears to combat the effects of stress on the brain itself (by bathing it in a cocktail of 'good' neurochemicals) and it lowers blood pressure: this is very reassuring if you are worried that long-term stress might be taking a toll on your health. The 'cocktail of good neurochemicals' also improves our mood and again this helps in stress management because the better our mood the more hopeful and capable we are. And the benefits of exercise don't end there, as taking regular exercise speeds up our ability to learn, and an improved memory usually means that we are that bit more confident and a bit less anxious. So what these findings also suggest is that you would get more out of this programme if you took regular exercise while working your way through it.

In short, there is now a lot of research supporting the link between exercise and reduced anxiety and stress, so it really is worth thinking about getting more active. And it's really worth thinking about enjoying yourself while you do this: cycle or run in a beautiful area, go to the gym with your best friend, join a fun exercise class – make exercise something that you want to fit into your life.

Summary

- Physical tension can fuel stress and anxiety

- You can combat this by learning to relax and you can learn to relax in a series of exercises that get shorter and easier to apply

- You need to practise to get skilled in applied relaxation, but it is possible to learn to relax at will

- Taking exercise can also combat physical tensions and improve your stress management

10

Managing psychological symptoms I: distraction

What I like about distraction is its simplicity. Instead of dwelling on my worries and feeling worse and worse, I have learnt to switch off from them. With practice, I can now do this in almost any situation. Furthermore, I've discovered that nothing terrible happens if I don't worry, and that I've been wasting such a lot of time, in the past, fretting about things.

In this chapter and the next you will learn strategies for keeping the psychological aspects of worry, fear and anxiety under control. This means managing the alarming thoughts and images that run through our minds.

As you already know, cycles of worrying thoughts (or mental pictures) and increasing anxiety can develop and these keep tensions high. For example, at a party, a woman who easily blushes and has difficulty speaking fluently could easily get worried about her social appearance (she might even have a mental image of herself being flustered and embarrassed) and this anxiety would make it even more likely that she blushed and found it hard to speak: a cycle of social anxiety could develop. If a man had a slight chest pain and thought: 'This could be a heart attack!', his stress levels would rise and he would get tense. Then, increased muscular tension would worsen the pain, and his thoughts might become even more alarming: 'This *is* a heart attack!' The anxiety would get worse and set up a cycle of increasing tension and worrying thoughts. It's clear that modifying the thoughts could break the cycle.

What triggers psychological symptoms?

Sometimes you will find it easy to catch what is going through your mind, but sometimes you might simply be aware of feeling fear or anxiety. It will have seemed to come out of the blue, as if there is no trigger. The link between thoughts and feelings is *so* efficient that an emotional reaction often seems to happen automatically without any obvious thoughts or images. This is normal and it happens all the time. You could walk by a bonfire or smell old paint and feel content or afraid without realizing why. If you really reflected on it you might realize that this was because the smells reminded you of happy childhood experiences of firework displays or helping your grandpa in the shed or of upsetting memories of being burnt or getting told off for playing with paint. It works for pleasant and unpleasant feelings. Even when this automatic response is a stress reaction, it is often no bad thing: when a car comes round the corner too quickly, you jump out of the way *without seeming to think about it*; if a child looks as though he is about to stumble into a fire, you grab him *without seeming to think about it*. There is actually a chain of reasoning behind such actions; but it becomes so well established that it is almost as if we 'short-circuit' the conscious thinking process and thus save precious time in dangerous situations.

This 'short-circuiting' can underpin problem anxiety, too. Imagine a woman who is happily walking round a church filled with flowers. She suddenly has a surge of anxiety and feels that she has to get out of the church. It is only later that she realizes her feelings were triggered because she smelled chrysanthemums and this took her back to her childhood when she was terrified of her piano teacher who always had a vase of them on the piano. She 'short-circuited' the reasoning process and suffered powerful feelings of distress that she did not understand at the time.

Whether or not you can actually put your finger on the mental component of these cycles of anxiety, they do drive our distress so it is good to have some strategies for tackling worrying thoughts and images. In essence, there are two ways of breaking the cycles of worrying thoughts:

- *distraction*, which refocuses our attention away from the cycle
- *testing*, which helps us identify and review exaggerated worries

Distraction

You are probably so used to multi-tasking that it will be a surprise to learn that we can only fully concentrate on one thing at once, but it's true and we can use this to our advantage because it means that when we turn our attention to something neutral or pleasant, we can *distract* ourselves from worrying thoughts and images. By using specific techniques of distraction, you can break the cycle of worrying thoughts and prevent your anxiety increasing.

There are three basic distraction techniques, and with a bit of effort you can tailor these to suit your needs.

- physical activity
- refocusing
- mental exercise

As we run through each of these distraction techniques, you need to think how you can make them work for you – try to link them with your preferences and interests. You also need to bear in mind that the key to successful distraction lies in finding something that needs a great deal of attention, is very specific, and holds some interest for you. If a distraction task is too superficial, too vague or too boring, it tends not to be effective.

Physical activity

Physical activity is possibly the easiest of the three exercises and it is particularly useful when you are so stressed that you just 'can't think straight'. Using physical distraction simply means keeping active when you are stressed. If you are physically occupied, you are less likely to be able to dwell on worrying thoughts. There are so many possibilities:

- taking exercise such as walking, jogging, playing squash, taking the dog for a walk, and so on. These sorts of activities are particularly beneficial as they help use up the adrenalin that can otherwise make you feel tense, and, as we have already seen, exercise is a powerful way of managing stress

- taking on minor social chores: for example, if you felt self-conscious at a party you might offer to take drinks around to people to keep yourself and your mind busy

- domestic chores: clearing cupboards, mowing lawns, reorganizing the garage . . . The list is endless and the advantage of keeping yourself active in this way is that you'll probably feel good for having done something that needed doing anyway. The chores don't have to be on a grand scale – tidying a handbag or reorganizing a messy personal organizer would work, too

- fiddling: a really easy and much underrated strategy. It doesn't require much mental energy and it can be quite discreet. For example, if you are sitting in a waiting room feeling edgy and tense, you could wind and unwind a paperclip, or fold a sweet wrapper into an interesting shape, pull apart and put together a ball-point pen. None of these requires skill, but each task can absorb your attention enough to break the cycle of anxious thinking and feeling stressed

In different situations you will need different activities, so make sure that you have several up your sleeve. You might play squash in the evening in order to take your mind off the day's stress; take a brief walk up and down the corridor when you are very tense at the office; reorganize your desk when you are not able to leave the office but are alone; unwind and rewind paperclips to take the edge off your anxiety in meetings or in a waiting room. If your physical task requires a degree of mental effort, so much the better, because the distraction effect will be more powerful.

Refocusing

This means distracting yourself by paying great attention to things around you. If you were in a crowded street you could try counting the number of men and women with blond hair, or look for certain objects in a shop window; in a café, you could listen to others' conversations (discreetly!) or study the details of someone's dress (again discreetly!) or note the details of a poster on the wall. The task does not have to be complicated or sophisticated; you just need to find a range of objects to absorb your attention. For example, if someone was anxious about using the supermarket, he or she could read car number plates as their friend drove them to the store, attend closely to their shopping list while moving round the supermarket and, at the checkout, read the details on food packages, count the number of items in their own or another person's basket or browse through a newspaper or magazine.

Refocusing is particularly useful if you are self-conscious or worried about physical symptoms. When we are socially anxious or worried about our physical health we tend to focus on ourselves – how fast we breathe, how hot we are, how much we shake, what pains we have – and this can make us more uncomfortable and even more anxious. Refocusing takes our attention away from us and this can break the cycle of self-focusing and increasing anxiety.

The great thing about refocusing is that everything you need is around you – you don't have to stress yourself by wondering what you are going to think about – the possibilities are all within view. But it is not just the things that you can see that can distract you – what can you hear? What can you smell? How does the gravel feel and sound as you walk over it? How does the seat beneath you feel? And the sun on your shoulders? You can use all your senses to absorb your thoughts.

Mental exercise

Mental exercise requires you to be creative and to use more mental effort by coming up with a distracting phrase, picture or mental task for yourself. A distracting phrase might be a line or two of soothing poetry, a distracting picture could be the recollection of a beach where you'd felt good, your mental task could be reciting an entire poem, recalling in detail a favourite holiday trip, practising mental arithmetic or studying someone nearby and trying to guess what they do, what interests they might have, where they are going and so on. You could try dwelling on an imaginary scene to take your mind away from worrying thoughts; by making your scene come alive with colour and sounds and texture, you can distract yourself even more successfully. Some people enjoy imagining a dream home and then walking through every room, studying the detail of the furniture and fittings; some people like 'listening' to a well-loved tune; others are soothed by recalling cycling over a familiar and much-loved track, paying attention to the scenery; some people find that they can become absorbed in imagining all the stages involved in making a complex flower display (and perhaps imagining the scent of the blooms) or redesigning their home. The more detailed the mental tasks, the more distracting they are, but it is important that you work out something that suits you, something that reflects your interests and preferences.

General rules for distraction

- Before you use a distraction technique you must select one which is suited to you and the situation in which you need to be distracted. There is no point in dwelling on a picture of a sun-soaked beach if you hate the sea and you sunburn easily, or if your real love is skiing. Similarly, relying on physical activity to distract you will not be helpful if your anxiety attacks happen during interviews. Work out your preferences and needs and then tailor distraction to suit you. Try to make use of your own interests: if you are a keen gardener, you might use pruning and weeding as your physical activity; looking through the bus window at gardens and identifying plants as a refocusing exercise; and holding an image of a beautiful formal garden as a mental task.
- When you have established what you need, be inventive in developing your own selection of distraction techniques, but always be specific in your choice of task and choose exercises that demand a lot of attention.

- When you have a repertoire of distraction techniques for different occasions, practise them whenever you have the chance. In this way, when you are stressed, you can switch your thoughts to your distraction quite easily.

Now consider when and where you could use distraction techniques by recalling the situations you find difficult and then planning which of your techniques you might use. An example is shown in Figure 11. Try compiling a list for yourself using the blank Figure 12 or on a separate piece of paper. This list should be as long as you need it to be – aim to have more than one or two entries and remember that a single anxiety-provoking situation can have more than one distracting solution.

My anxious situations	Examples of distraction in action
Sitting in stationary traffic	*Listen to soothing music*
Waiting in doctor's clinic	*Read book/magazine*
Standing in line at passport control	*Read the posters and read them backwards, too*
Tense at home	*Go for a walk to the shops and back*

Figure 11: My anxious situations and examples of distraction in action

My anxious situations	Examples of distraction in action

Figure 12: List of distraction techniques for anxiety-provoking situations

So far, this has been a very theoretical exercise and you've simply been considering what is likely to help you – now you need to give your distraction techniques a try. Put your distraction strategies into action when you are feeling anxious and see what happens. You will find that some of your ideas will be successful right from the start, which is great, but others will need refining. Look back on the experiences that are less successful and try to understand why a strategy might not have worked for you: maybe the image you chose didn't really reflect your preferences so it wasn't that engaging; perhaps the mental arithmetic you set yourself was a bit too difficult; maybe the setting wasn't right for the physical distraction you chose and a mental distraction would have been better. There can be many reasons for a strategy not working well, and everyone will discover different obstacles; the key is to work out why something did not work for *you* at *that time*. In short, see if your ideas work in real life – if they don't quite do the trick then tinker with them and get them just right for you.

Worry and distraction

You might remember that, in the introductory sections of this book, we noted that some of you might be 'worriers'. If you are, then distraction will be a really helpful part of your coping toolkit. If you can identify your worry (if you can answer the 'What if . . . ?' question) then you can first consider if there is something you can actually do about the worry. If there is, then do it and use problem-solving (see pages 267–84) to help you, but if there is nothing else to be done and you still find yourself going round in increasing circles of anxiety, thinking about the future with lots of 'What if . . . ?'s, then distraction can break the pattern. Use distractions to let go of the worries. This will give you relief, but it will also help you learn that you can stop worrying and things will be OK. You can take charge of your worrying.

The same can be said for the cycles of anxiety that are set up when we look back with 'If only . . .' thoughts (we called this rumination rather than worry). Repeated 'What if . . . ?' and 'If only . . .' thoughts only increase our distress and, again, distraction helps us disengage and escape the vicious cycles. We can then use our minds for something more pleasurable or useful.

Distraction in action: Managing claustrophobia

I just can't bear enclosed spaces – I'm all right in the street where I feel that I can breathe, and I can manage at home because I feel relaxed there. But theatres, churches, lifts, crowded shops: no! Ages ago I accepted that I wouldn't be able to get about as much as most people and at first it wasn't too much of a problem: we hired videos, I went shopping in the week when things are quite quiet and I never felt inclined to go to church, anyhow. However, things changed: it seemed that my children and my nieces and nephews were all getting married and having babies and baptisms. Suddenly, I was expected to go to church and go into hospitals. I was so torn. I wanted to see my children married and my grandchildren baptized but I was also terrified and I wanted to stay away. Fortunately, I discovered a way of getting through the ceremonies – although I have to admit that I always sat near the back of the church so that I could escape, if necessary. I taught myself ways of distracting my mind from my panicky thoughts. There were three things that really helped me. First, I always carried a good book so that I could get lost in that if we had to sit around for any length of time. I know that it might seem rude to sit in a pew reading until the bride arrives, but it was often that or not going to the wedding. Second, I took my worry beads with me everywhere I went so that I could fiddle with them to take my mind off my worries – these were more acceptable in church but alarmed a few visitors at the hospital! Finally, I taught myself a sort of meditation: I would be able to stand or sit, just like everyone else, but I imagined that I was somewhere else, somewhere safe. In my imagination I was back on the farm where I grew up and I could imagine walking through our fields with my father. I recalled the smells and sounds of the farm, and as I filled this lovely image with more and more details, I could feel myself relaxing.

I've used these strategies and they have given me the confidence to be present at some of the most important occasions of my life. I had only intended them to be a means to an end – a way of being physically present, but do you know what? Little by little, I began to feel more confident about being in enclosed spaces because I was learning that nothing bad happened – I could cope just like everyone else. I find now that I don't need to use my distraction techniques so much and I'm so much less anxious when I think about the next challenge. I no longer have to sit close to an exit because I know that there are things I can do to manage my anxiety.

Distraction in action: Managing worry

The best advice my dad ever gave me was: 'If you can't do anything about it, don't worry.' Good advice – but I used to find it so difficult to let go of the worry. I would ask myself: 'Can I do anything about this worry?' and if I could, I'd do it; but if I couldn't, the worry would just rattle round in my head and I'd get more and more wound up. Now I have learnt to distract myself, and if I can't do anything more to ease my worries, I simply switch off from them by using distraction. It happened the other day at the post office. I was in a long queue and I was getting tense. I realized that I was worried about not getting back to the car before my parking ticket ran out. I asked myself if there was anything I could do and there was – I could text my daughter and ask her to wait for me

201

by the car so that she could tell the traffic warden I was on my way. Maybe it would help – who knows, but at least I'd done something constructive. I was still worried and so I asked myself if there was anything else I could do – there wasn't, so I took my mind off my worries by studying the shelves in the shop. In my head I counted the number of brown envelopes, and then white envelopes, that it is possible to buy in a post office. Then I turned my attention to the rest of the stationery – there was plenty to keep me busy. I felt myself calm down and then I was able to do something more interesting and I began to plan my daughter's birthday party. The more plans I made, the more distracted I became. Before I knew it, it was my turn at the kiosk.

Difficulties in using distraction

I just can't seem to do it

It could be that you are simply not practised enough. This is common and easily remedied as long as you are able to find time to rehearse your skills, especially when you are not anxious. The challenge here is to find ways of building regular practice into your day-to-day life.

It didn't work for me when I tried it

It is possible that the technique was not suited to the situation. Again, this is a common problem and easily overcome if you have a range of strategies in your toolkit. Make sure that you have considered plenty of different ways of taking your mind off worries – if necessary, go back to your list and ask friends to help you increase your ideas. Think about the anxiety-provoking situation in advance and try to choose the best strategy from your toolkit – but have a back-up idea, too.

Perhaps you were already too stressed to cope. There comes a point when we are too stressed to cope very well – so always try to catch your anxiety as early as you can. Make sure you are familiar with your 'early warning signs' next time. Any coping technique will work better if you are less stressed, but a useful tip is to use the physical activities more when you are very stressed as they are often easier to put into action than the mental activities.

A final and very important note: Like many people you will find distraction invaluable in dealing with worries, fears and anxieties, and it can give you an opportunity to think and plan more productively. However, it can be counterproductive if it is used as a way of *avoiding* difficult situations, if it is always used as a safety behaviour. For example, if you were anxious about speaking with guests at social gatherings and you *always* distracted yourself by handing round the drinks, then you would never face your real fear and it would not go away.

If you are using distraction as a safety behaviour, or you find that the worries keep returning, then you will need to learn another strategy for thought management: namely, *testing and reviewing* problem thoughts and images.

Summary

- Frightening thoughts, images and worries drive anxiety and stress

- We can only properly attend to one thing at once, and if this is neutral or pleasant it can distract us from the alarming thoughts and images

- Both physical and mental activities can be used as effective distractions, but they need to be chosen carefully to match your needs and preferences

- Then they need to be practised

11

Managing psychological symptoms II: reviewing anxious thoughts and images

I had always known just what thoughts set off my worrying and feeling miserable, but it had never occurred to me to ask myself if these thoughts were realistic. When I started to stand back and look at them properly, I discovered that many of them were unfounded and that there was another way of viewing the situation. Once I'd done this I was even able to shake off my worries or reassure myself. There was the odd occasion when my worry was well founded, but, more often than not, I quickly realized that I'd no need to be so alarmed and that I could re-think my troublesome thoughts – and that took the sting out of them. Sometimes, I asked my partner to help me re-examine my worries and between us we've managed to make life a lot more bearable for both of us.

You already know that anxiety makes us think differently and that we can get caught up in a cycle of worry and increasing anxiety. Questioning our anxious thoughts – testing and reviewing them – is another way of breaking the cycle of increasing tension and anxiety. This time we do it by taking the 'sting' out of a worrying thought that isn't worth worrying about. The technique of testing and reviewing negative thoughts and images involves several steps, and I have to be honest and say that it requires a fair bit of practice, but it is worth it because once you've mastered this approach you will be in a very strong position to deal with all your anxieties.

- **Step one** is a familiar one – catching just what is going through your mind (and keeping a thought diary will help you to do this).

- **Step two** is a new one and it involves you asking yourself: 'Is this a realistic worry?' Of course, the answer to this question could be 'No' or it could be 'Yes' and we'll consider how to respond to both. In this chapter we'll look at ways of managing concerns that are exaggerated, that are out of proportion to the real situation: you'll learn to review this sort of troublesome thought or image and come up with more realistic or constructive statements that won't upset you so much. Of course, some worries and concerns are realistic, and Chapter 13 on Problem-solving will guide you through dealing with these. So you'll have all bases covered.

Back to this chapter: sometimes it is really easy to put your finger on the thought or mental picture that has triggered anxiety and sometimes you'll be able to see a less upsetting possibility quite quickly:

I had this sudden feeling of tension – a real knot in my stomach. I realized it was because Sue had just said that I might be expected to present a retirement gift to our boss. I used to be nervous about these things but then I thought: 'You know, there's nothing to be worried about – I've done it so often now that I know I'll be OK.' Once I'd got that perspective I felt fine.

However, there will be other times when you'll find it hard to catch the worrying thought and perhaps even harder to set your mind at rest. That's not unusual and you can be reassured that the steps described in this chapter will guide you through the process of catching, testing and reviewing your alarming thoughts and images. The approach is based on a very helpful and structured procedure developed back in the 1970s by the father of CBT, Dr Beck. The strategy he suggests involves three basic steps:

- identifying anxious thoughts and images
- standing back and reviewing anxious thoughts and images – deciding if your anxiety is realistic
- finding a balanced, alternative way of thinking if it isn't realistic

Step 1: Identifying anxious thoughts and images

When you are feeling calm, it is not always easy to recall the thoughts or images that triggered your anxiety – these are often called the 'hot thoughts' because they cause the strongest emotions. Your best cues for catching them are the actual sensations of anxiety and tension. When you are aware of your tension rising, ask yourself: 'What is going through my mind?' Your worries may be in words, such as 'I am going to make a fool of myself', or 'I think that I am having a heart attack!' They may be in pictures, such as a scene where you are losing control or an image of something terrible happening. It is not always easy to recognize what is going through your mind, but with practice you will become better at it, so don't give up too soon.

Keeping a written record of what's in your mind near the time of the anxious episode can be the best way of discovering the words, images or phrases that cause your tensions. You can use a thought diary like the one opposite (Diary 3), writing down whatever is in your mind when you are anxious. Some people find the paper diary very helpful, but others find it a bit cumbersome and prefer to note their thoughts and images on their mobile phones, for example, as it's easier than getting out a piece of paper to write on. That's fine – always aim to make the strategies in this book work for you. The diary is a means to an end – a way of capturing important thoughts and images – so try out different approaches until you discover what suits you best. It's very important to have an efficient means of catching what's going through your mind, as some 'hot thoughts' are very fleeting and if you don't catch them as they occur, you can lose them.

Diary 3: Catching what goes through our minds

Where and when?	How did I feel?	What went through my mind?
When and where was I and what was I doing?	What emotion(s) did I feel? How strong was it? 1 (none at all) – 10 (the strongest possible)	What thoughts or pictures did I have in my mind? How much did I believe them? 1 (did not believe at all) – 10 (absolutely sure they were true)

Try not to shy away from examining what you feel and think. In the short term it might be uncomfortable to do this and you may feel upset by looking closely at your thoughts, but if you do identify your worries you'll be in a much better position to take control of them. Consider Leanne, a student who always used bacterial wipes for opening doors and cleaning seats when she was at college. When asked why, she said: 'I don't like germs and I don't want to talk about it.' Clearly, she is afraid of something and she's avoiding thinking about it. But while she is reluctant to spell out her fears it is difficult to understand them and even harder to help her cope with them. Perhaps she is afraid of catching a nasty disease that could also harm her family and friends; perhaps she is afraid of picking up a bug that will make her vomit in public; perhaps she fears she could contract a life-threatening illness – we could speculate at length, but only when she describes the fear will she be able to address it using the strategies in this section of the book.

Once you have put your finger on what's causing your worry or fear it can be helpful to try to rate just how much you believe your alarming thought and how it makes you feel. This rating is optional – if it's one task too many, just don't do it – but it can give you a more precise idea and understanding of your fears. For example, one day I might identify my worrying thought as: 'If I don't go back and check the house door is locked we'll be burgled.' I might believe this 90 per cent and have a fear level of 85 per cent. On another day I might believe it only 40 per cent and have a fear level of 50 per cent. It's normal for ratings to vary from time to time and you can learn from this. In this example I might realize that

I have lower anxiety when I'm only going a short distance, or if I've a friend with me or if I'm just less stressed in general. All of this information gives me a better 'handle' on my fears. You can also re-rate your beliefs and anxieties when you've worked through all the steps and then you can see how this strategy works for you.

Step 2: Standing back and reviewing anxious thoughts and images

When you have recorded your stressful thoughts or images, you can stand back and take a look at them. Sometimes this process alone will make all the difference:

A really useful thing I learnt was to write down my fears. Just putting them on paper helped me. I'd jot them down, stand back and look at them. It was as if I could suddenly get a different perspective and things didn't seem so bad or I could see a way through.

At other times you'll need to do a bit more than this in order to feel OK. First you can study your automatic thoughts and see if there are biases in your thinking. Have a look again at pages 30–44 for a detailed reminder, but the general categories are:

- extreme thinking
- selective attention
- relying on intuition
- self-reproach
- worrying

Looking for thinking biases will help you judge how realistic your fears are – maybe they are well founded, maybe not – but you need to be able to make that judgement. At this stage you are simply trying to get a feel for whether or not you need to be quite so worried or concerned by examining your thoughts for biases.

If you do spot thinking biases, don't be critical of yourself, just 'step back' and note them. Sometimes we can change our perspective just by appreciating that our thinking is skewed – standing back and appreciating that we've been exaggerating things can often give us a more balanced outlook straight away. Use Diary 4 to help you do this.

If you find that your thinking is rather 'skewed' but that you still feel distressed even though you can see the biases, don't worry about this either because later you can move onto the next step of counterbalancing your fears by systematically reviewing alternative, less alarming, ways of seeing things (Step 3).

A very common stumbling block is not being able to spot biased thinking when we are actually feeling anxious or worried. This is totally understandable as our rational perspective is not at its best when we are tense and scared. If you find that this happens to you, then don't try to scrutinize your diary when you are upset – instead look at it later when you are feeling calm and more able to view the situation clearly. If you still have difficulty standing back and getting a more detached perspective, ask a friend to look through your diary and to comment on the accuracy of your perceptions and predictions.

Diary 4: Catching thinking biases

Where and when?	How did I feel?	What went through my mind?	Can I spot any thinking biases?	Is there another way of looking at things?
When and where was I and what was I doing?	What emotion(s) did I feel? How strong was it? 1 (none at all) – 10 (the strongest possible)	What thoughts or pictures did I have in my mind? How much did I believe them? 1 (did not believe at all) – 10 (absolutely sure they were true)	• Extreme thinking • Selective attention • Relying on intuition • Self-reproach • Worrying	Is there a less alarming way to view things? Can I think of a more balanced possibility? How much do I believe the new possibility? 1 (not believe at all) – 10 (absolutely sure it is true)

Always remember that you can use other people to support you – you don't necessarily have to do this alone. Some people find that just naming the thinking biases helps them detach from their worries and then they can get a new perspective, while for others it's just the starting point. In either case it is a valuable step in managing anxieties, worries and fears.

Ivana: When I looked at my diary a few hours later I could see that it was full of 'all-or-nothing' thinking. No wonder I felt so bad – I was jumping to all sorts of extreme conclusions. We'd miss the plane! I'd lose the tickets! Our luggage would go missing! I was a bit surprised to see this because at the time I didn't know that my thinking was so skewed. My fears felt realistic at the time. I showed my husband and he laughed and said, 'I could have told you that you think like that!' I guess I needed to discover my biased thinking for myself. I wasn't upset by his laughing – I know that he wasn't being cruel. In fact, I joined in with it. Now when I get into a state and start making extreme predictions, he just smiles and says: 'OK, what's happened to your thinking?' That stops me in my tracks; I realize what's going on. I call it my 'A to Z thinking' because I jump to an extreme conclusion without considering that there might be options lying between A and Z. I find that as soon as I notice this I can get a better perspective on things. Sometimes things just fall into place then and I feel calmer.

Artie: I kept a record of the things that went through my mind when I got nervous and stressed at work. When I looked back over what I'd written, I noticed some subtle biases in the way

I always viewed things. First, I noticed that I had quite a harsh attitude towards myself – I kind of assumed that things were difficult because I'd done something stupid or because I was weak. That just made me despise myself and then I felt so unconfident. Second, when I actually managed to detail what was going through my mind I discovered that I ran a sort of video through my head and in it I was always struggling – I always jumped to the conclusion that I would not cope, I always assumed the worst. I hadn't appreciated this before, but now it was clear why I got so nervous. Now that I know how I tend to think, I try very hard to be kinder to myself (and just doing that helps so much), but I also know that I need to start working on my predictions. I need to learn how to take stock and think about things differently. I know that this might not be easy, but I feel more hopeful now.

Step 3: Finding a balanced, alternative way of thinking

By this point you will probably be familiar with the thoughts and images that make you anxious and also with the particular thinking biases to which you are prone. So now you can take the third step and begin to find constructive alternatives to your exaggerated thinking. When you are about to do this you will feel less afraid and more confident about coping with challenges. We'll deal with tackling realistic anxieties and concerns later in this book.

If your thoughts are skewed and not realistic, there are six questions to work through:

1. Why is it understandable that I have this worrying thought (or image)?
2. Are there reasons for *not* worrying or being afraid?
3. What's the worst thing that could happen?
4. If the worst thing happened, how would I deal with it?
5. What's a more balanced way of looking at my original fear?
6. How can I check out this new possibility?

Diary 5 (see pages 218–19) will help you to work through these questions.

Question 1: Why is it understandable that I have this worrying thought (or image)?

You will see that this first step reviews why you might hold a worrying thought or jump to an alarming conclusion. This might seem odd – by now you have decided that your worries might not be realistic and your aim is to get a more tolerable perspective. So why are you being asked to justify your concerns? Well, this first step will help you be more understanding towards yourself – it's the step that encourages you to say: 'It's no wonder that I got so scared or concerned . . .' By doing this you are less likely to be critical of yourself and more likely to begin this exercise with a compassionate attitude. You will also be able to identify the grain of truth in your fears (if there is one) and to better recognize your 'Achilles heels' or the things that regularly set off your worries. So I hope that you can see that it is worth spending time on this first step even though it might, at first glance, seem an odd question.

Question 2: Are there reasons for *not* worrying or being afraid?

Now you can move on to considering what might counterbalance your worries. There are a number of useful questions you can ask yourself at this point, questions like:

- what do I know which just doesn't support my fears or concerns?
- what experiences have I had which don't fit with my worries?
- when I'm feeling confident, how would I see things?
- what would I say to a friend who was scared or worried?
- what would a friend say to me if they were trying to calm or reassure me?

By asking yourself these sorts of questions, you can begin to get a different take on your fears. This is a key strategy in cognitive therapy – discovering other possibilities and widening your viewpoint – and the more you do this, the more skilled you become and the easier it gets to come up with alternative, more helpful, perspectives.

Question 3: What's the worst thing that could happen?

This question is often a really hard one to face, but if you can answer it then you have named the worst fear and you'll know just what you need to get to grips with. This is particularly important if your scary thoughts are in the form of questions such as: 'What if . . . ?'; 'What will they think of me?'; 'How will I cope?' None of us can tackle such questions, so you

Diary 5 : Catching and testing what goes through our minds

When and where	How did I feel?	What went through my mind?	Why is it understandable that I have this worrying thought / image?
When did I feel anxious? Where was I and what was I doing?	What emotion(s) did I feel? How strong was it? 1 (none at all) – 10 (the strongest possible)	What thoughts or pictures did I have in my mind? How much did I believe them? 1 (not believe at all) – 10 (absolutely sure they were true)	What have I experienced that makes sense of my fears or worries?

Are there reasons not to worry or be afraid?	What's the worst thing that could happen? How would I cope?	Is there another way of looking at things?	How can I check this out?
What have I experienced that doesn't fit with my fears or worries? What do I know that might reassure me?	What skills and support do I have to help me deal with my fear?	Can I think of a more balanced possibility? How much do I believe the new possibility? 1 (not believe at all) − 10 (absolutely sure it is true)	How can I put my new idea into action? What do I need to do to see if I'm right?

need to turn it into a statement such as: 'I'm scared that I have a serious illness' or 'I think that people will laugh at me' or 'I'm worried that I will faint in public'. Once you have identified the worst thing for you, your frightening prediction, then you can try to answer the next question.

Question 4: If the worst thing happened, how would I deal with it?

Naming your personal worst-case scenario and being able to come up with a solution might end your worries straight away because you'll have the sense that 'I can deal with this if I have to'. Even if that's not quite enough to reassure you, you will have begun to change your outlook just by coming up with ideas about coping. It's a helpful step and worth rising to the challenge of facing just what lies at the heart of your fears. This is an opportunity to reflect on your personal strengths and supports, to think about ways you've coped in the past and to begin to see your way through your difficulties. Some people find that it is really helpful to imagine a picture of themselves coping, dealing with the situation in a way that makes them feel strong and able. More and more research shows us that using imagery is a powerful way of changing our feelings, so why not try it?

Question 5: What's a more balanced way of looking at my original fear?

Now you can pull together your new ideas and summarize them as a new possibility that is not so scary. When you look back over questions 1–4 you will see that you have lots of new ways of viewing your original fears – see if you can now sum up your new perspective in a way that is balanced and less alarming. Because coping imagery can build our confidence, you could also create a mental picture of your new, balanced way of looking at things. You could imagine coping in a different, effective way. If you can, picture yourself facing your fear, 'see' this in your mind's eye and imagine feeling more calm and assured. This isn't the time to give yourself a reassuring platitude that you don't really believe; it's time to take an honest look at the work you've done and to draw an honest conclusion. You will only be assured if you believe your new statement, so it's often useful to rate just how much you do believe it – if your rating is low, you can re-visit each question and see if you can come up with more compelling arguments. Sometimes, however, our belief rating is low because we are not easily convinced by words or images of ourselves coping (the cognitive argument) – we want more proof. This is where the behavioural side of CBT comes in – testing out just how realistic our new statement is. This is a healthy, sceptical attitude and one you should embrace – always look for proof. This then leads us onto question 6.

Question 6: How can I check out this new possibility?

Up until now you've been using your mind (your cognitive abilities) to come up with new ideas. You've been a 'philosopher'. Now it's time to become a 'scientist' and test out your ideas. The best way to check out whether or not a new possibility is realistic is to put it into action and then see what happens. Do be scientific about this – that means being curious and not judgemental – try it out and just see how it goes. Sometimes it will go smoothly and your confidence will improve and sometimes there will be a glitch and you'll need to go back into 'philosopher' mode in order to think about what you might do differently to get a better outcome next time. This is an important pattern in CBT – shifting to and from the thinking of the 'philosopher' and the doing of the 'scientist'.

- PHILOSOPHER (analysing results and coming up with new ideas)
- SCIENTIST (testing out new ideas and being curious about the outcome)

Sometimes the glitch occurs simply because we take on too much too soon. The new ideas might well be sound; some-times we need to test them out in a graded or step-by-step fashion.

Denise was nervous about saying what she wanted; she had difficulties in being assertive. She worked through questions 1–5 and came up with a new statement that she believed 98 per cent: 'It's understandable that I'm nervous, I've never really been encouraged by my parents, but I know I am just as capable and worthy as the next person and I have rights and I deserve to be heard.' She thought of a way to test this out: 'I can test this out by speaking up for myself. I need to tell people what I need and what I want.' However, she took on her boss and the matter of her salary straight away and this proved far too difficult: she failed to make any real impact on her boss and she felt pretty upset afterwards. Her notion that she deserved to be heard and that she would benefit from practising being assertive had been absolutely correct – the set-back hadn't occurred because her line of thinking was wrong – but she did need to devote more time to her planning. On reflection (philosopher mode), she realized that she could build her confidence better if she took on tasks that would stretch her but not risk overwhelming her. So next she returned a faulty pair of shoes and asked for a refund – an easier and ultimately successful task that left her feeling good about herself, more confident and ready to take on another challenge.

If you look back over Step 3 (Finding a balanced, alternative way of thinking) you will see that it involves a whole series of steps in itself, each one building on the next. Therefore it is quite demanding. When you first start to work your way through the six questions in Step 3 you can expect it to take time and you will probably find that you need to keep rather detailed notes. However, you can also expect it to get much easier. With time, most people find that they reach a stage of being able to review their unhelpful thoughts (or images) automatically, without having to use notes or having to consciously work through each step. If you have ever learnt a new language or if you are a driver, you will have had this experience of consolidating a skill. In the early days you will have had to refer to your notes on vocabulary and grammar in order to string together a coherent sentence, or to talk yourself through each of the steps involved in getting the car going and moving off down the street – but after a while (and much practice) you do these things automatically. It will be the same with reviewing unhelpful thoughts and images. I've put a few examples in the text so that you can see how to work your way through the questions in Step 3: I've chosen three people who could successfully follow Step 3 because I wanted to show you how its done and how it could work for you. If these examples make it look a bit easier than you first find it, don't get disheartened, just reckon that you'll need more practice. Sometimes you'll find a more helpful way of thinking does come about first time around, but quite often you'll need to review the process and give it another go. Ultimately, though, you can look forward to being able to do this increasingly quickly.

Finding a balanced way of thinking in action, 1: Anxieties about a friend

'Sara is late for our meeting. She might have had a car crash and have been injured.'

I believe this 5/10 and my fear is 8/10.

1. Why is it understandable that I have this worrying thought? Are there reasons for my thinking like this? Yes, there are: I read about people being killed in road accidents, and she is travelling on a main road where she could have an accident. I am not being completely ridiculous. Other people might have similar fears.

2. Are there reasons for *not* worrying or being afraid? Yes, when I think about it there are: plenty of people use that road day in and day out and never have an accident. The weather conditions today are very good for driving and so an accident is even less likely than usual. Even if Sara were in an accident, she need not be badly hurt – quite a few of my friends have had accidents and experienced very minor injuries, if any. There are roadworks on the road she uses – they could account for her being late. I feel a bit better already. As I think about this I realize that she might have got the date wrong and she's not even on her way here.

3. What is the worst thing that could happen? The worst thing is that she's had an accident and is injured.

4. If the worst happened, how would I deal with it? How would I cope with this? There is no doubt that this would be a difficult situation for me, but I could get my husband to support me. We could contact the accident services at the hospital to find out how badly she'd been hurt. I would want to visit and could take my husband with me. I would remind myself that she would be well looked after in the hospital.

5. What's a more balanced way of looking at my original fear? A more constructive way of viewing the situation is that it's unlikely that Sara has had an accident and she's probably late because of roadworks or because she's forgotten the meeting. Although I know this is probably true, I still feel jittery. I need to remind myself that if she has had an accident, then she is not necessarily badly injured; and if she were, I could reassure myself that the hospital staff are the best people to deal with this and use my husband to support me if I am distressed. I believe this 100 per cent and my fear has gone down to 2/10.

6. How can I check out this new possibility? Easy, really – I'll ring her mobile as she might be able to answer it and put my mind at rest. If she doesn't answer, it doesn't mean that something is wrong – maybe she's driving and can't answer. If she doesn't answer, I'll give it another fifteen minutes to see if she turns up. There's absolutely no point in worrying and worrying, so I'll distract myself by reading the notes I've prepared for the meeting. If she's still not here in a quarter of an hour, I'll give my husband a ring and ask him what he thinks I should do. Two heads are often better than one.

Finding a balanced way of thinking in action, 2: Dealing with physical symptoms

'I feel dizzy and light-headed. I am beginning to sweat and feel sick. I am sure that I am going to pass out in this shop and make a fool of myself.'

Belief rating: 8.5/10. Fear rating: 8.5/10.

1. Why is it understandable that I have this worrying thought? I suppose it's understandable because my friend works in a shop and he says that he has had two customers feel faint and pass out in his shop and people do pass out in public places. I once fainted in school, so I know that it is possible. It's not unreasonable to worry about this. When I look at what goes through my mind when I'm anxious, I realize that I have a second fear – I worry that I'll make a fool of myself, that people will judge me badly. It's understandable that I have that worry because I was teased at school and I know that people can be harsh and cruel.

2. Are there reasons for *not* worrying or being afraid? Let me see – are there reasons against my holding this thought? Yes, there are: I know from experience that I often feel like this when I am anxious. I'm probably simply experiencing symptoms of anxiety. I know that worrying and over-breathing makes the light-headedness worse and I'm so tense that I'm probably hyperventilating. My friend would tell me to remind myself that a quick relaxation exercise and some even breathing always calms me and then I can get back in control. He'd also remind me that the customers in his shop recovered and everyone was very nice to them. When I fainted in school it wasn't really unpleasant, I didn't hurt myself and the people around me were kind. I was also ill when that happened and I'm not ill now, so I'm not likely to faint. When I recall being teased, it was by other children; adults are probably more sensitive.

3. What is the worst thing that could happen? The worst thing is that I would faint here in the shop and I'd look foolish – but now I've started to think this through, I don't believe that I would look foolish, I don't think that I'd be ridiculed. It's funny how daring to think about fears actually helps to put them into perspective.

4. If the worst happened, how would I deal with it? If I actually fainted, how would I cope? I think there's a good chance that someone would come to my rescue: my friend says that in his shop the staff are always ready to deal with this kind of emergency. I suppose I'd come round like I did before and I'd probably ask someone to help me if I felt unsteady. But I really have begun to think that I probably won't faint.

227

5. What's a more balanced way of looking at my original fear? Now I'm thinking quite differently – I realize that it's very hot in here and that could have triggered these unpleasant feelings; my anxiety is probably making them worse and I know that I can control things by taking a minute to relax and check my breathing. Even if I fainted, I would recover and feel all right, as I did after I'd passed out in school. My friend says that people do feel faint in large shops, so a staff member won't be surprised if I ask for help. I never think that someone is foolish if they feel unwell, so people are unlikely to think that I am. I believe that I'm just anxious and I'm not going to faint 8/10, and I believe that people would be understanding and helpful and wouldn't think I'm foolish 9/10. When I look at things this way my anxiety goes down to 2/10 and I feel loads better.

6. How can I check out this new possibility? I can check out the possibility that I'm simply anxious by taking the time to relax myself and I'll do that straight away. Checking out that people wouldn't think me foolish – that's not so easy. I know – I'll just ask some of my friends. I'll see what they think if they see a person faint. The way I'm feeling now I expect that they'd feel sympathetic – but I'll actually ask them so that I can be sure.

Finding a balanced way of thinking in action, 3: Fear of spiders
'It's a cobweb. That means a spider – I'm not going to cope – I have to get out of the room.'

I believe there's a spider here and that I won't cope 100 per cent. My fear levels are 8/10.

1. Why is it understandable that I have this worrying thought? Cobwebs and spiders go together. It's that simple. I know from experience that I can go to pieces if I see a spider. I've been hysterical before.

2. Are there reasons for *not* worrying or being afraid? Sometimes I have mistaken cracks and bits of hair for cobwebs, so I suppose that it's possible that it is not a cobweb that I've seen. I also know in my mind that British spiders are not harmful and I have told this to my kids when they've been afraid – I believe it when I say it to them. I have recently had experiences of being able to deal with very small spiders, so I *might* not go to pieces like I did in the past.

3. What is the worst thing that could happen? It could be a cobweb, I could see a spider and I could become terrified and feel sick or freak out.

4. If the worst happened, how would I deal with it? How would I cope? In the recent past I had to get rid of one or two extremely small spiders that had made their home in my classroom. I managed to appear calm in front of the children (I breathed slowly and kept telling myself it would be OK) and I just took a glass and a piece of card and captured them one by one. I guess I could remind myself of this and that might calm me. Actually, if I run that picture through my mind I feel calmer already. I know I can do it – I can 'see' myself do it. If the spider were large I wouldn't be nearly so confident, but if the worst came to the worst, I could always just leave the room: I don't have to stay and become hysterical.

Managing Worries, Fears and Anxieties

5. What's a more balanced way of looking at my original fear? If I look back over what I've just written I can see things differently. There might or might not be a cobweb in the room (I don't have to jump to the conclusion that there is) and that might or might not mean that there's a spider here. Even if there is a spider, it could be small enough for me to tolerate or I might be able to stay reasonably calm. If I do feel overwhelmed then I could simply leave this room – although that would be my last resort. Now I only believe that I've seen a cobweb 7/10 and I don't assume that this means that I will see a spider. If I did see a spider I now only believe 2/10 that I would become hysterical. My fear level is down to 4/10.

6. How can I check out this new possibility? Well, I'll go and look at the so-called cobweb to see if it really is one. If it isn't a cobweb then that's the end of my worries, so it's worth being brave and checking out my fears. If it is a cobweb then I'll stay here and see how I get on by reminding myself that I can cope with some spiders and I'll keep my breathing slow and steady and I'll try to be as relaxed as I can. I'll keep my mental picture of coping in mind, as that helps. I'll find out if a spider does appear (and now I believe that it might not), and, if it does, I'll find out how strong I am. If I have to leave the room, I'm not going to give myself a hard time as I know I will have done my best to deal with my fears.

These examples raise some important points that you might need to bear in mind when you are re-evaluating your own anxieties:

230

- You can see that sometimes what seems like a single worry turns out to be two or more – it is important that you tease out the different strands to your alarming thoughts so that you can tackle all aspects of your fears. Leave no stone unturned! In the example above there were three parts to this woman's fear: the assumption that she's seen a cobweb; the prediction that there would be a spider nearby; the conclusion that she would not cope. In her final review, she addressed all three aspects and then she did something else which is also very good practice . . .

- . . . in this same example you saw her being prepared to give herself credit for trying to deal with her difficulties and she wasn't going to beat herself up if she didn't cope too well. A wise decision because it would help her build her confidence in herself and encourage her to keep trying.

- In all the examples, you saw people doing something to check out if their fear was well founded (they addressed Question 6). In the first example, the worried colleague checked out her concerns in the moment. She dealt with it there and then – and that was appropriate for that specific concern. In the second example of a man who was afraid that he might faint, you saw that he took his 'scientific' work beyond the moment and he planned to check out his fears further by asking his friends about their attitudes towards people who are unwell or faint in public. This would help him build up a 'data bank' to which he could refer when he next felt worried that he might be judged badly. So you can see that it's a particularly good way of tackling persistent and recurring anxieties. It's so useful that I want to spend a little more time on it now.

Re-evaluating your worries and fears: the scientist in you

Let's revisit the second example and we'll call this man Steve. Steve identified two fears: (i) a fear that his physical discomfort meant that he was about to faint; (ii) a fear that others would think badly of him if he fainted. These were recurring fears and they had become so strong that Steve was beginning to avoid going out to very public places. Through ongoing observing and testing he built up a body of evidence that helped him re-evaluate his long-standing worries. He used three strategies:

- testing a prediction by reviewing 'Theory A vs. Theory B'
- trying out a new behaviour and reviewing the outcome
- surveying others for their opinions

1. Testing a prediction by reviewing 'Theory A vs. Theory B'

The scientific approach Steve used to test his prediction that physical discomfort meant that he was going to faint is often called 'Theory A vs. Theory B' because you explore two competing theories – two possibilities. It's a strategy devised by Professor Paul Salkovskis, a cognitive therapist, who used it to help people with health anxieties. However, you'll see that it can be used to test all kinds of anxious beliefs. Put as simply as possible, you have two theories (A and B) that you test out: one theory is that your fear is well founded and is true, and the second theory is that it is simply your anxieties that are causing the problem. To begin with, the 'jury is out', so to speak. You are not trying to prove one theory over another, you are being open-minded. Then you simply collect evidence and see which theory gains most support. It's not a trick to con you into thinking in a certain way, but a genuine experiment to see what is really most likely. Steve's theories look like this:

- **Theory A**: My physical feelings mean that I am going to faint
- **Theory B**: My physical feelings are normal or a result of my anxieties – either way they are harmless

First he kept a simple record of times when he felt physically unwell and he documented the outcome. His 'body of evidence' looked something like this:

Situation	Physical feelings	Thoughts / Images	What happened	Theory A or B?
Wed: in pub with friends	Bit light-headed	I'm going to faint – I can feel it	I sat down and was fine within a minute or two. I probably drank the first pint a bit quick and it went to my head.	Theory B
Thurs: on the train to work	Light-headed, not easy to breathe	I'm going to faint. I'll fall here in the gangway	I remained standing, looked out of the window and described (to myself) what I saw. I didn't feel great but I didn't faint and I was actually OK by the time I reached town. The train was crowded and I was standing – no wonder I felt odd.	Theory B
Sat: shopping in High Street	Chest tight, 'fuzzy' in my head, feeling a bit sick	I hate shopping! I can't cope – I'm going to pass out	Jumped on the bus home. Felt better straight away.	I don't know because I ran away
Mon: in a meeting	Heart racing, jittery, light-headed	I'm nervous and it's causing these feelings and I'm going to faint	I stayed in the meeting and gave my presentation. As soon as it was done I relaxed and felt better. I didn't faint.	Theory B

Steve kept this diary for over a week and collected many more experiences. He then reviewed them, keeping as open a mind as possible. When he looked back over his entries he drew this conclusion:

> On balance, Theory B has proved itself: I did not faint even though I felt faint and dizzy at times. So I have learnt that when I do feel odd it's probably normal or my anxieties making me feel worse, and most importantly I now know that I can feel uncomfortable and not faint. I've also learnt that distraction can help me if I am in a genuinely unpleasant situation like being crushed in a crowded train.

2. Trying out a new behaviour and reviewing the outcome

As he gained confidence, Steve also took things a step further by putting himself in situations that would have been difficult for him in the past. For example, it was not easy for him, but he went to a shopping mall that was larger than his local one and discovered that he could cope – it wasn't plain sailing but he learnt that he could succeed and this added to his confidence. Buoyed up by his success, he arranged to go to a multiplex cinema. This was a major challenge so he arranged to go with a friend, and again it went reasonably well. What Steve discovered was that he needed to repeat these sorts of tasks in order to begin to feel OK. He found that his first attempt would be successful but he'd often feel uncomfortable, but with repeated attempts he felt increasingly at ease. A great asset for Steve was his curiosity – rather than viewing challenges with fear he began to wonder how things would turn out and that made him prepared to give something a go. An open and curious mind is always a bonus in overcoming anxieties.

3. Surveying others for their opinions

Steve tackled his second fear – that people would think badly of him – by carrying out a simple survey of his friends. He emailed seven people (whom he felt he could trust to be honest) with the following message:

Hi. Would you mind answering a quick question for me? It will only take a minute. I'd just like to know – if you saw someone faint in a public place, what would you think of them? Thanks – Steve

He got his responses quite quickly and they included statements like:

I'd feel sorry for them – I'd want to help if I could.

I'd think 'poor person' and feel concerned.

I've been there myself so I'd imagine that they felt vulnerable and shaken; so I'd check that they were OK.

I'd wonder if they were ill – I'd look round to see if someone was looking after them.

If it was outside a pub or bar I'd wonder if they were drunk and then I'd not be impressed!

I'd assume that they weren't feeling well – perhaps the shop was too hot, or the train was too crowded – and they just passed out. People do, it's not their fault.

I know what it's like so I'd feel sympathetic.

Steve reviewed all the responses and noticed just how many of his friends said that they would feel sympathetic; only one person was negative, and that was only if he thought that the fainting person was drunk. The conclusion that Steve drew was: Even if I fainted (and now I don't think that's likely), people would probably not think badly of me and would want to help me. I believe this 100 per cent. You can see that this is a really good way to check if your 'mind reading' is accurate.

Another way of testing out his fears had also crossed Steve's mind. He had seen a TV programme where a woman who was afraid of fainting had actually gone out to a supermarket with her therapist. The therapist had pretended to faint so that his patient could see what would happen (she saw that one or two people were really helpful, many people minded their own business and no one made an embarrassing fuss). This gave the woman the confidence to pretend to faint herself (in another shop, of course), and she again discovered that nothing bad happened and in fact people were considerate and caring. She quickly overcame her fears. However, Steve couldn't imagine being able to do this without the help of a therapist so he just stuck to his survey. Interestingly, though, his wife was in the early stages of pregnancy and she began to faint through low blood pressure. This meant that Steve was able to witness someone fainting in public and he became extremely confident that even if a person faints, it's OK: his wife always had time to steady herself or ask for help, and in every single instance she encountered kindness. Steve, the detective, used his observations to build up his confidence.

As you work through the questions in Step 3, you might find it helpful to summarize your thoughts in Diary 5 so, in addition to the example in the text, there are some blank templates at the end of the book (see pages 393–9). This should help you to capture your thoughts and review them more quickly, making it even easier to balance your thinking. Eventually you won't need the diary because you will have developed a new habit of standing back and reviewing alarming thoughts and images, but you might need a bit of help while you are building up this skill.

Difficulties in counterbalancing anxious thoughts and images

'I can't believe that it is as simple as that'

These examples might make it seem very easy to counterbalance worries and fears – and sometimes it is. But it's not always so simple: if it were, you would be doing it all the time and would not need to read this book. Like all skills, it comes with practice, and so you do have to put in the hours. Where possible, practise when you are not feeling too anxious – then you are more likely to be as objective as possible. You could review your anxious thoughts sometime after the distressing event, perhaps when you felt calmer or had a friend to help you. Use Diary 5 to help you structure a detailed response to your anxious thoughts. In time you will become skilled at doing this and you will be able to work through the six questions quickly, and counterbalancing your worrying thoughts will become more automatic. Eventually, you'll be able to do this on the spot and get more 'instant' results: it really can be as a simple as that.

'I can't hold on to my worrying thoughts'

You are not alone if you find that this is a problem – your best strategy is to record your thoughts as soon as you can, because thought management is more effective if you can clearly spell out your worries. Use your phone or a scrap of paper – whatever is to hand – to try to catch what is running through your mind at the time.

'I can't get to grips with reviewing my thoughts'

Anxious thoughts often come in the form of questions: 'What is going to happen, will I pass out?' or 'Are they thinking that I look foolish?' If this is the form your thoughts are taking then it's no wonder that you can't review them – you can't argue with a question and you can't test it out, so turn it into a statement: 'I am worried that I will pass out', or 'I am worried that they will think that I look foolish'. If you need help in getting the hang of reviewing your problem thoughts or images, ask for help. Friends and partners can be very supportive and can be particularly good at pointing out alternative possibilities and perspectives.

'The same types of thought keep coming up'

This is good because it will make managing your worrying images or thoughts easier. It is common for there to be a theme to our concerns – and this means that we can prepare a 'one-size-fits-all' counterstatement. If, for example, your worries are around being ill, then you could devise a statement to give yourself assurances in response to many different health worries: 'I know that I tend to get over-concerned about health issues but I also know that each time I've visited my GP she has found nothing for me to worry about. I'm probably being over-sensitive and I can afford to put my worries to one side.' Of course it is important that you believe what you are telling yourself; as we've said before, a simple platitude won't do the trick if you don't actually believe it.

'I can't hold on to my new, balanced thought'

No wonder – this is a new perspective and it can take a while to 'bed in'. You will probably find it helpful to write down your new, balanced statements in full. They will have more impact if you spell them out. In addition, you will better develop the skill of thought management if you get into the habit of examining your fears and anxieties really thoroughly – a vague review can result in a vague new possibility and this won't be as assuring as a clear statement.

'It's taking too long to take effect'

Eventually, the balanced response to a distressing thought or image can become as automatic as the anxiety response is now. However, you should expect to have 'good' days and 'bad' days: we all do. There are going to be times when you are not feeling well, or you are feeling tired or just too distressed to review your thinking in the stressful situation. Don't worry about this too! Try to use distraction as a way of coping with the anxiety and, when you are feeling calmer, then think about the balanced perspective. Also, if it has been particularly difficult to counterbalance your worries, try to understand why it was difficult for you on this occasion: there will be a reason and it is important that you appreciate your vulnerabilities.

Summary

- What goes through our minds affects the way we feel and the way we behave

- Anxieties are often driven by 'skewed thinking'

- We can review the way we think and decide if the worry, the anxiety, is realistic

- If it's not, we can find a balanced and rational alternative

- This involves being a 'philosopher' who can think about thinking, and a 'scientist' who can test out new behaviours and new possibilities

12

Facing your fears I: graded practice

> *My father always used to say that if you fell off a horse you should get on again as quickly as possible. He was right and that's what I've learnt to do, but I've also learnt that you don't have to get back on the horse in one leap. I've learnt to face my fear by taking it one step at a time and building up my confidence in the process. Sometimes this is a slow process, and sometimes it requires a lot of planning, but I always get there in the end.*

As you saw in Part One of this book, people have many different fears: fear of heights, public speaking, arguments, travelling, animals, illness, humiliation, busy places . . . the list is endless. Avoiding or putting off facing a fear will maintain it better than any other behaviour, so Chapters 12 and 13 are devoted to strategies to help you face your fears so that you can stop avoiding and procrastinating. You now have an understanding of why you might be afraid or worried and you have some strategies for countering the physical and mental stresses of fear and anxiety so you are in a good place to start facing your fears.

Where possible, it is best to do this *at your own pace*, which means not taking on too much too soon, and the approach called **graded practice** is designed to help you to do just that, to pace yourself. But before launching into the details of graded practice, it's only realistic to acknowledge that sometimes you might not have time to do this – sometimes we have to rise to an imminent challenge and on these occasions the strategy of **problem-solving** (Chapter 13) will help you to cope. I mention this now because I want you to know that there are ways of tackling impending problems as well as ways of tackling those which we can take our time over. There are also other chapters that you'll find make it easier to face your fears: Chapter 14 teaches you how to be assertive, which will help you to face difficult interpersonal situations, while 'Time management in a nutshell' (page 350) will help you to deal with tasks that you might otherwise put off.

Facing fear through graded practice

First you must understand your fear: you need to know exactly what frightens you because different people fear things differently.

- Two people with a spider phobia: one person can tolerate a medium-sized spider at the other side of the room, and only become frightened if that spider moves nearer; the other becomes panicky just looking at a picture of a small spider.
- Two people have social phobia: one person is afraid of becoming inarticulate when she speaks and she fears that others will think her stupid; the other person also fears looking stupid, but only if she shakes when she signs her name in public.
- Two people who fear travelling: one cannot go long distances because he is afraid of being ill when he is far away

from home or a hospital; the other cannot take even short journeys on public transport in case he faints in public.

You can see that even fears that at first seem similar can actually be quite different from each other. Therefore, you need to ask yourself:

1. *What exactly triggers my fear?* What goes through my mind? What size of spider makes me anxious? Just what do I fear will happen when I am out in public? What is it about travelling that upsets me so? It is also helpful to consider your strengths:

   _____

   _____

   _____

2. *What can I already achieve?* How near can I tolerate a spider? What things can I do in public? How far can I travel, and how? Then think about the details:

   _____

   _____

   _____

3. *What makes it easier for me?* Think about the time of the day, about different places, the company you are in, and ask yourself what eases your distress:

   _____

   _____

   _____

When you have answered these questions, you will be able to describe your fear in more detail. If you had a spider phobia, you might discover:

I think that I'll just go to pieces if I am anywhere near a spider. But my anxiety is only triggered by medium-sized and large ones; I can actually tolerate small ones. I can't bear a large spider in the same room as me, but I am reasonably comfortable if I know one is in another room. I am less afraid of spiders during the day or in good light (when I can see them) and I feel much less anxious when I have someone with me. I'm also better in a familiar room as I think I know where spiders might lurk.

If your fear focused on public speaking, by asking yourself specific questions, you might discover:

My problem is a fear of speaking in front of an audience of a dozen or so in a semi-formal setting. I worry that I will make a fool of myself. I am not scared of small, informal discussions or of large, very formal lectures when I read from a script. I know that it is more difficult for me if I am already stressed – when I'm abroad, for example, or very tired. I find it easier to have a colleague sharing the responsibility and if I've planned my presentation thoroughly beforehand.

If your fear was of travelling short distances on public transport, you might discover:

I'm scared of fainting in public and I feel most at risk on public transport where I'm hemmed in and often feel I can't get enough air. I can use taxis and there is a local minibus which is OK because I know the driver and he lets me sit near a door with a window and I know he would let me get off if I needed to. I'm better on minor roads where it is easy to pull over and I'm more confident when I take a beta-blocker, which my doctor has prescribed for me to help with my anxiety. Failing that, I can go a bit further if my daughter is with me.

You may have more than one fear; if so, do this exercise for each of them. The first step is to describe your fear accurately: page 247 has a space for you to write down your fears in detail. You'll see that there is an example of how this might look.

Once you are able to describe your problem(s) in detail, you will have the information that you need to devise a plan of *graded* practice – a plan that will build on your strengths and achievements. Although the notion of facing your fear might seem alarming, you can do it gradually, so that you never need feel *very* afraid. Your aim will be to *stretch yourself* not to *stress yourself*.

This planned, graded approach helps us overcome fears by providing an opportunity to build our confidence step by step, thus learning that certain situations (or objects) are not really dangerous and that we can cope. It will challenge you because it's not easy to face our fears, but you can make it easier by planning and preparing. It is best to attempt something relatively easy at first, and then move on to more challenging situations at your own pace. In this way, you will build on your success and increase your confidence.

Facing your fears I: graded practice

My fear	What it's really like for me
Spider phobia	*My anxiety is triggered by medium-sized and large spiders, I can tolerate small ones. I can't bear a large spider in the same room as me, but I am reasonably comfortable if I know one is in another room. I am less afraid of spiders during the day or in good light (when I can see them) and I feel much less anxious when I have someone with me. I'm also better in a familiar room as I think I know where spiders might lurk.*

There are three stages in graded practice:

1. Setting targets: clarifying your long-term objective.
2. Grading tasks: planning steps carefully to build on success.
3. Practising: putting plans into action – repeatedly.

1. Setting targets

Look at your description of what you fear. Then consider what you want to be able to do. Be realistic and be precise. Your description of what you want to be able to do is your **target**. If you have several fears, you will need to do this for each of them. Your targets might look something like this:

I want to sit in a room that is not well lit and feel comfortable. I want to be able to stay there if there is a medium or large spider crawling on the wall or the floor and I want to be able to do this even if I'm on my own and even if the spider gets close (less than a metre). I want to be confident enough to go into my garden shed by myself.

I want to be able to present a work project in front of an audience of a dozen or so in a semi-formal setting. I want to be able to do this without using a script and I want to be able to do this even when I am stressed and when I am performing alone.

I want to be able to use the local bus system to get around the county. In particular, I want to travel to Longtown to visit my daughter and grandchildren and I want to be able to do this

alone at any time of the day and sitting in any seat on the bus.
I also want to do it without using beta-blockers.

These targets are reasonably precise – although some state-ments would benefit from a bit more precision. For example, what exactly does 'not well lit' mean, and how many is 'a dozen or so'? You might be wondering why it's important to define your targets so very clearly. Clearly defined targets give us exact instruction (so we know just what we are aiming for) and they define the end point clearly (so we know when we have achieved our target). We can all too easily get deflected from vague targets and all too easily not give ourselves credit for attaining them, so precision is good.

If you do have more than one target, decide which to take on first – only take on one at a time. It's often a good idea to tackle the easiest first, but sometimes it's necessary to prioritize a target that is particularly urgent. Even if you select a target that is not the easiest, you can make it easier by breaking it down into achievable tasks.

2. Grading tasks

Now it's time to plan a series of small, specific steps of increas-ing difficulty, which culminate in achieving your target. The first task has to be manageable: remember *stretch not stress*. So ask yourself: 'Can I imagine myself doing this with a bit of effort?' If you answer 'No', then make the task easier. While you will need to stretch yourself, you don't need to take risks: the aim of graded practice is to build on a series of successes, so try to plan for success. In describing your fear, you asked yourself the question: 'What makes it easier for me?' Now you can use this information to tailor your plans to match your abilities – this will increase the likelihood that the earlier tasks will be manageable. As you progress, the tasks will become more challenging – but at a rate you can manage.

In grading a series of steps, first consider your starting point or baseline – what you can do now. And build on this by asking yourself: *If I can do this step, what can I imagine being able to take on next?* Again, being precise is important.

The series of tasks will vary from person to person because you need to really personalize your programme – make it work for *you*. However, a typical graded approach for the person with a spider phobia would look something like this:

Starting point: sitting in a well–lit, familiar room (our liv-ing room) with my partner: watching TV or reading in the evening.

Step 1:   sitting in well–lit, familiar room on my own: watching TV or reading.

Step 2:   dimming the lights (halfway) in a familiar room with my partner: watching TV or reading.

Step 3:   dimming the lights (halfway) in a familiar room on my own: watching TV or reading.

Step 4:   sitting in the room, dimmed lights, with a live spider in a jar near the window (about 3 yards away). With my partner.

Step 5:   sitting in the room, dimmed lights, with a live spider in a jar about 2 yards away. With my partner.

Step 6:   sitting in the room, dimmed lights, with a live spider in a jar about 1 yard away. With my partner.

Step 7:   sitting in the room, dimmed lights, with a live spider in a jar by my feet. With my partner.

Step 8:   Sitting in the room, dimmed lights, with a live spider in a jar by my feet. Alone.

Step 9:   sitting in the room, dimmed lights, with a live spider loose in the room. With my partner. I will aim to stay there for at least five minutes.

Step 10:   sitting in the room, dimmed lights, with a live spider loose in the room. Alone. I will aim to stay there for at least five minutes.

Step 11:   going into my garden shed with my partner.

Step 12:   going into my garden shed alone: I will have achieved my target!

This is only one way of tackling a spider phobia. A different person's graded tasks list could look quite different. The important thing is that *your* list is tailored to *your* needs. Another person might have felt it necessary to look at pictures of spiders before having a real one in the room, or to have a dead spider in the jar before using a live one. This particular plan relies on the help of another person, but not everyone has that option so things like this have to be taken into account. But even when you have really personalized your graded tasks, the steps are not set in stone – they can be modified if necessary. For example, whilst working your way up your hierarchy of tasks, you might discover that you'd underestimated your ability and that you can actually tackle two steps at once – or you might discover that you have overestimated your ability and you need to break a step down into two or more smaller steps. This ongoing adjustment is normal *and necessary* if you are going to create the best opportunity for yourself.

Going the extra mile: research has shown that it can really build your confidence if you stretch yourself beyond your target. So this is something that you might consider. The person in the example above decided to 'go the extra mile' by holding the jar with the live spider in it, letting the spider loose in the room, recapturing it using the jar and a piece of card, then letting it free in the garden. Achieving this stretched her beyond her goal and it really consolidated her confidence in coping.

To help you get a better idea of the possibilities for graded practice, here are possible steps for overcoming a fear of public speaking and of using public transport.

Fear of public speaking:

Starting point: speaking informally in front of four or five colleagues or reading a script in front of a large, impersonal audience. In familiar surroundings (i.e., my office) when I am reasonably relaxed and feel well prepared. Sharing responsibility for the presentation.

Step 1:   speaking informally in front of four or five colleagues or reading a script in front of a large, unfamiliar audience. In familiar surroundings when I am reasonably relaxed and feel well prepared. Being wholly responsible for the presentation.

Step 2: speaking informally in front of ten to twelve colleagues. In familiar surroundings when I am reasonably relaxed and feel well prepared. Sharing responsibility for the presentation.

Step 3: speaking informally in front of ten to twelve colleagues. In familiar surroundings when I am reasonably relaxed and feel well prepared. Being wholly responsible for the presentation.

Step 4: speaking informally in front of ten to twelve colleagues. In unfamiliar surroundings (e.g., in the Birmingham or London office) when I am reasonably relaxed and feel well prepared. Being wholly responsible for the presentation.

Step 5: speaking informally in front of ten to twelve colleagues. In unfamiliar surroundings when I am reasonably well prepared but a bit stressed (perhaps I will have travelled up to the office on that day, perhaps I will have left some of the presentation for me to be spontaneous, or perhaps the presentation will be abroad). Being wholly responsible for the presentation. I will have achieved my target!

'The extra mile': taking the opportunity to give a completely impromptu presentation.

In this example, you'll see that there is scope for choice and flexibility – for example, the size of the audience or the location. Your plan has to be realistic, and building in such options can make it more so.

Fear of using public transport:

Starting point: travelling several miles (up to 15 miles) in a taxi or in the local minibus (as long as I'm near the door with a window and I know that I can trust the driver to stop and let me out). Doing this on minor roads and with a beta-blocker <u>or</u> my daughter to help.

Step 1: travelling several miles (to Longtown, 12 miles away) in a taxi or in the local minibus, near the door with a window and a trusted driver. Doing this on minor roads and with my daughter but no beta-blockers.

Step 2: travelling several miles (to Longtown, 12 miles away) in a taxi or in the local minibus, near the door with a window and a trusted driver. Doing this on minor roads alone and using no beta-blockers.

Step 3: travelling several miles (to Longtown, 12 miles away) in the local minibus, but using a seat in the middle of the bus. Doing this on minor roads, alone.

Step 4: travelling several miles (to Longtown, 12 miles away) in the local regular bus, the one that uses major roads. I'll go at a quiet time (mid-day) and sit near the exit and a window. I'll ask my daughter to come with me.

Step 5:   travelling several miles (to Longtown, 12 miles away) in the local regular bus. I'll go at a quiet time (midday) and sit near the exit and a window. I'll go alone.

Step 6:   travelling several miles (to Longtown, 12 miles away) in the local regular bus. I'll go at a busier time (8.30 a.m.). I'll sit near the exit and a window, alone. I will have reached my target!

'The extra mile':   I'll make this journey and sit further and further away from the exit so that I can be confident that I'll always be able to make the trip even if I can't sit near the exit. I will also take a bus ride to a place that is further away – the local city is 25 miles away, so I could try that.

In this example, you'll see again that there is scope for choice and flexibility.

Although this might sound obvious, you need to make sure that your plans fit your budget and your lifestyle. It can be easy to be overambitious or overoptimistic about your resources. For example, someone on a limited income could not afford to take taxis on a regular basis, and a mum with little or no childcare help could not get out on her own very often. You need to plan carefully and realistically.

The box opposite can be used to help you set out your plan, but remember that this is not set in stone and you will probably need to adapt and update it as you progress towards your target.

Managing Worries, Fears and Anxieties

My starting point	
Steps	
My target	
My 'extra mile'	

3. Practising

By now you have your well-thought-through plan and it's time to combine this with what you know about stress and anxiety management. You might not feel confident at the outset – after all you are being asked to face the thing you fear – but you need to try out each step, using your coping skills, until you can manage the step without difficulty. Then you can move on to the next task, and so on. Don't be put off by some feelings of anxiety – these are only natural, because you are stretching yourself and you are learning to master anxiety instead of avoiding it.

The 'Three Rs' of success: to be helpful, practice has to be:

- **R**egular and frequent enough for the benefits not to be lost
- **R**ewarding – recognize your achievements and learn to praise yourself
- **R**epeated until the anxiety is no longer there

It is a good idea to keep a log of your progress. A log will help you see how you are getting on and it will help you review your progress and learn from it – after all, this is about learning something new. You need to decide what format works best for you, but below (page 259) is an example of a log – you might want to use something like this or you might want to modify it to suit you better. It is always important to tailor your approach to suit you.

Graded practice in action:

Managing a spider phobia

I've always been scared of spiders and I became really worried that I'd pass this on to my children. So, I asked a friend to help me overcome my fears by helping me face spiders. She wasn't spider-phobic and so she was able to catch a really big one and keep it in a jar for me to get used to – then she surprised me one day by putting the thing right in front of me. I say surprised me, but it really terrified me and I burst into tears and my fear was greater than ever. I quickly learnt that it's best for me if I take things gradually. That's why I drew up the graded plan with my partner.

In order to prepare myself I used the relaxation exercises I'd been practising and the 'mantra' that I knew to be true: 'Lots of people are afraid of spiders, it's not weak or weird. But spiders won't hurt me and I can learn to be OK with them.' I also knew that I could use distraction to help me stay in the room with the spider.

The first step went well – I relaxed quite easily and I think I underestimated myself so I moved straight onto step 3 where I sat in the dimmed room alone. No problem! Having the spider in a jar in the room was much more difficult and I had to consciously relax myself and use distraction to stay in the room. I rated my anxiety 9/10. I kept rehearsing this step (once a day) until my anxiety was around 4/10, which for me is very tolerable. Then I moved onto the next step (my anxiety was 8/10) and went through a similar procedure of repeating the step. I achieved my target quite quickly, actually – but I stumbled a bit when I tried to recapture the escaped spider.

258

Facing your fears I: graded practice

Step	Anxiety before	Anxiety after	How it went	What I learnt
1	9/10	4/10	Harder than I thought but with Sue's help I got there and I didn't panic.	I can do this: I can feel nervous without it turning into a panic attack. It's hard, it really is, but feels really good to achieve so I'll keep telling myself it's worth it.
1 (again)	7/10	2/10	Easier this time and we even laughed and joked.	Practice is making things easier. I'm feeling more confident. The distraction of chatting helped, so I'll remember that.
2	9/10	5/10	Hard to do this alone but I used my relaxation exercise and I distracted myself by looking out of the window and studying the countryside. I got to Longtown without panicking.	It's harder on my own and I had to work hard at coping – but I can do things to make it easier for myself (relaxation and distraction). I am learning that I 'can do' rather than 'can't do'.
2 (again)	8/10	5/10	I was nervous again so I did a relaxation exercise while I waited for the minibus. I was tense but the journey went OK – no panicking. I can now remind myself that it's been OK before and I'll be fine. .	Still quite difficult for me but I did it. Well done, me, eh? I am getting more confident but I think that I'll have to practise this step a few more times as it is still a real challenge and I want to get my anxiety down further before I move on. Better safe than sorry!

Despite my growing confidence, trying to catch it shook me up and I had to rehearse it several times. But it was worth it because once I could catch a spider I felt really confident and I was especially pleased that the kids could see me do it. My partner and I went out to celebrate in an outdoor restaurant that was only lit by candles – and I was absolutely fine.

Managing a fear of public speaking

My fears had grown over the years and had reached a point where I worried that it would harm my career chances. So I was motivated to do something about it. I'm a well-organized, systematic person so making a graded plan appealed to me. I made a 'schedule' for myself where I listed the task, how anxious I felt before and after doing it, and I always noted what I'd learnt from doing the task. The first step was easy enough – I opted for an informal presentation as it was not possible to set up a large-scale presentation – but the rest of the steps were not so simple to organize and although I was keen to make progress I couldn't find enough opportunities to present to a dozen people for me to get in the practice. I mentioned this to a friend who had overcome his flying phobia with the help of a therapist. He said that he couldn't keep going up in a plane so his therapist encouraged him to do it in his imagination. If you really get a vivid picture in your mind you can actually get all the anxious feelings and you can mentally rehearse coping. And this is just what I did. Where possible I set up real speaking opportunities, but I also practised in my imagination and used my relaxation skills and my calming self-talk to help me keep control both in real life and in my imagination. I think this made all the difference and I moved up my hierarchy of tasks reasonably quickly. I had one set-back at step 4. I was in the London office and was well prepared for my presentation when I got the message that a team from our overseas office would join us and I would have to modify the presentation to take this into account. I was more nervous when this happened and I think I didn't perform as well as I would have liked. But I realized that it was 'good enough', which is something that I don't usually accept. It was a good learning experience to have presented something less than 'perfect' and to have discovered that it was fine to do so. This made the rest of the tasks easier because I could relax and not worry about getting it absolutely right. I think this need to be perfect was behind my problem. Recently I flew out to Dublin to attend a mini-conference and was asked to stand in for a colleague who was ill: this was my chance to see if I could go 'the extra mile'. I had lunchtime to prepare myself – not long enough really, so it meant that I gave a rather impromptu presentation. I did fluff some of my lines – but I was relaxed enough to make a joke out of it and my audience seemed to appreciate that. That evening my friend (the one who was no longer scared of flying) and I treated ourselves to an 'overcoming anxiety supper' to acknowledge what we'd achieved.

Managing a fear of using public transport

Years ago I had a panic attack on a bus and I couldn't get off. I know it was a panic attack – nothing really threatening – and I know that I probably had it because I was stressed and worried about our finances and my mum's health at the time. Even though I understood this, I just couldn't use the bus any more and as the years went by I completely avoided buses and I got less and less confident. Then my daughter moved to Longtown and I couldn't see her unless I took a taxi or the minibus (as long as Roger was driving because I trusted him to let me sit where I wanted to sit and to stop if I asked him to). The taxi fare was really expensive and Roger worked irregular shifts so it was hard to plan my visits and I had reached the point where I was even scared to use the taxi or minibus without a beta-blocker – so I decided to take the bull by the horns and learn to use the bus again. My daughter helped me to plan to do this in small steps and she supported me where she could. We told Roger what we were doing and he was also really supportive. The first thing I decided was that I'd stop using the odd tranquillizer – and I was pleased with myself for managing this at the outset. I knew a brief relaxation exercise that I could use when I was sitting on the bus; it is a very discreet exercise – no one would know that I was managing my tension and my breathing and thinking of a soothing image as I sat there – but it was very effective. I also used it before I got on to the bus as it gave me a good start. Whenever I'd managed a step I'd say to myself: 'What have you learnt today? I've learnt that I can do this, I'm strong and I might get tense but I don't panic any more. Well done, me.' I really think that this bolstered my confidence. The hardest step was moving from using the minibus to using the regular bus. I had to repeat this step many times before my anxiety came down. I really needed some support and my daughter was not always available so I asked a friend to come with me in return for a cream tea in Longtown. This turned out to be a real bonus as we had a lovely time out together and she also enjoyed seeing my grandchildren. Overall, the plan worked nicely and there was always a reward at the end because I saw my grandchildren and my daughter. It only took about a month for me to be able to use the buses on my own and the only times I've not faced the bus have been when I've not been feeling well. For instance, I took a taxi after I'd had my flu jab because I was feeling under the weather, really didn't want to be in the crush on the bus and I thought I'd spoil myself. I know that I could have taken the bus if I'd really had to, but I chose to not to. That's the difference – I now have a real choice.

Each of these examples illustrates some common themes in graded practice:

- the need to reward yourself for your achievements
- the need to review your progress at each step (it is a particularly good idea to review your progress using a tangible record and to give yourself well-deserved praise and assurances)
- the need to be flexible
- the need to practise and rehearse until you feel confident enough to move on

The examples also remind us that we sometimes have to be creative – like using imagination to help us practise when there isn't the opportunity to do it in real life, or calling on

263

a friend to help. Rehearsing in imagination is a really cheap and effective method of gaining confidence – research shows that practising in imagination can be extremely powerful. For decades, sports and physical therapies have used *imagining* improved movement to actually achieve just that – improvement in using injured limbs and improvement in sports performance. Now we are seeing that mental rehearsal can be just as effective in improving our state of mind. In the chapter on distraction, you have already read that picturing soothing images can be calming, and there is also evidence that imagining coping images can boost confidence and make a difference to our actual performance. It costs nothing – you can do it almost anywhere – and it's worth a try because if it works for you it's another power tool in your coping toolkit.

Difficulties in using graded practice
'I can't keep going: I keep failing'

If you find that a task is too difficult, don't give up or feel that you have failed – you've simply been overambitious. Instead, look for ways of making the task easier – perhaps as two or three smaller steps. Expect set-backs from time to time – this is only natural – and, when it happens, think about your task. Did you overestimate what you could do and make the task too difficult? Did you practise when you were feeling unwell, tired or stressed? Did you have other things on your mind so that you could not put enough effort into your practice? If you keep a record of your practice, you can more easily work out why you have difficulties on certain days. Then you will get a better idea of how to tailor and adapt your practice so that you get the most out of it.

'I'm not getting anywhere'

As you move up your hierarchy of tasks, it is all too easy to dismiss or fail to appreciate your progress. Do you find yourself saying: 'Oh, anyone could do that', or, 'I'm only doing a short journey / using an ordinary lift / looking at a spider . . . that's no big deal'? If you are overcoming your fear, then these *are* big deals. The aim of graded practice is to build your confidence, and to do that you need to acknowledge your achievements and give yourself credit for them. If a step goes easily, give yourself praise; if it doesn't go smoothly, then try to understand why this was and revise your plans in the light of this. Be kind to yourself and be encouraging. Keeping a diary or a log will create a record of your achievements and you can review this to remind yourself of your progress.

In short, give yourself credit for your achievements, no matter how small. Try not to dismiss your successes and try not to criticize yourself: encouragement works best. In this way, you will manage to reach your goals and face your fears with confidence.

Also, make sure that your plans fit your lifestyle. You will get stuck if you make plans that you can't afford or can't carry out because of the limitations of your lifestyle. Always make sure that your plans are realistic.

Summary

- We have to face our fears in order to overcome them. It is that simple!

- This can be done in safe, small steps so that we build on success

- Detailed planning is very important and this needs to incorporate how to cope with set-backs

- Repeated practice is crucial for improved confidence

13

Facing your fears II: problem-solving

I'm still not good at keeping really calm in a difficult situation, but at least I can now do something constructive in a crisis. I have a problem-solving format and I use this to guide my thinking and planning. It takes a lot of pressure off me because I always know what the next step is. Others think that I am calm because I always ask sensible questions, come up with lots of solutions and I am very structured in putting them into action. I'm amazed how much I can achieve, even when I'm upset, by simply following a problem-solving protocol. Knowing that I have this up my sleeve also helps me to keep my anxieties in check: I don't worry so much about being faced with a challenge and then I think I'm better at coping.

Graded practice is the best way of facing your fear if you have the time to organize a programme for yourself. Sometimes this isn't possible because a stressful event is imminent and you don't have time to follow a step-by-step approach. Occasions such as weddings, examinations or holidays tend to be fixed and we can suddenly find them almost upon us. Whatever the situation, being faced with an immediate problem can trigger alarm and then, as you know, it's even more difficult to

267

plan how to cope. The problem-solving approach gives you a framework for organizing your thoughts and plans even when you are stressed and facing a challenge.

You might be confronted by a wholly unexpected event, or you may have to tackle something that you have faced in the past (but now find that you have little time to prepare for it). The problem-solving approach can structure and focus your thinking so that you come up with solutions to your dilemma rather than panic in the face of it. It will help you tap into your creativity and this will give you more ideas, and with that, more hope.

There are six steps in problem-solving:

1. Define your problem(s)
2. Brainstorm solutions
3. Look at your resources
4. Evaluate the pros and cons of each solution and order them
5. Choose a solution and plan to put it into action
6. Review the outcome

Step 1: Define your problem(s)

It is really important to be specific about the task ahead – it is also important that you don't confuse several tasks. Sometimes the problem facing you will be a single challenge – but sometimes it will actually be made up of several difficult things, so take some time to reflect on the situation and tease out different aspects of it, if necessary. If you do identify several different elements to your problem, make a plan for each. For example, an imminent wedding might trigger the following thought in Aesha:

I've got to go to Rebecca's wedding next week and stand beside her as her best friend in the church and at the reception – without panicking!

At first this might look like a single problem, but in fact it reflects several challenges, each of which needs to be described in detail:

1. 'I have to deal with my claustrophobia in the church. This means being able to stand for at least an hour, in a confined space, some distance from the exit and without the support of my partner.'
2. 'I have to cope with being a focus of attention for at least four or five hours – both in the church and at the reception – without getting too self-conscious and panicky.'
3. 'I am expected to attend a reception of about fifty guests. I will be without my partner and in an enclosed space (the marquee) for three or four hours and I will need to stay calm enough to mix and mingle.'

You will notice that Aesha's three challenges are described in detail: what she needs to do, where, with whom, for how long. This will be really helpful in her planning because she knows precisely what she has to deal with – vagueness makes it harder to come up with sound solutions.

If you find that your problem has several challenges to it, only try to problem-solve one task at once – it is a false economy to try to address more than one difficulty at a time because it can confuse the issues. When you have completed the first step in problem-solving, you will have either a single problem-solving plan or two or three plans, which, together, will address all aspects of your difficulty. If you have more than one challenge, you can choose just what you focus on first – sometimes people take the easiest task first because it seems more manageable and gets them off to a good start; sometimes people take the most difficult task as they feel more confident if they have got this out of the way. It's up to you – the important thing is one at a time. So, select your task and state it in very specific terms. Example 1, below, reflects the third aspect of Aesha's problem. She chose to deal with this first because she had experience of coping at a wedding reception before, so she thought that it would be the easiest challenge to tackle. In Example 2 you will meet Dougie, who has a work issue coming up. He had been ignoring this and now he has only two days to tackle it.

Example 1: Aesha – 'I have to go to Rebecca's wedding reception, alone, next Saturday. I will sit with Rebecca for the dinner and then mix with about fifty guests for three or four hours.'

Example 2: Dougie – 'I have to see my boss and put forward my argument for a pay rise within two days or lose the chance of an increase in salary.'

Step 2: Brainstorm solutions

This is an opportunity to be as creative as possible, to come up with as many ways of dealing with the problem as you can. In order to get the most out of Step 2, you need to let your imagination run free and not judge your ideas. At this stage, you are aiming to come up with a wide range of possible courses of action and you will slow down the process if you stop to consider your responses. The more solutions you generate, the better – you can judge them later.

Write down all your ideas, no matter how trivial or outrageous they might seem: some of your 'trivial' or 'outrageous' solutions might turn out to be most useful in the end. It's often helpful to put yourself in someone else's shoes and consider how a friend or your partner or your boss would respond if asked to come up with ideas. If possible, you could actually enlist the help of someone else – two heads are usually better than one.

In the example below, Aesha did the brainstorming by herself and you'll see that she just jotted down solutions as they came into her head – she didn't pause to judge them – so some might seem a bit odd or extreme. The advantage of not pausing is that she did not interrupt a train of thought that was becoming rather productive. You will see that her first thoughts are of avoiding the situation (this is a common starting point), but as she gets into her stride, her solutions become more constructive. If she'd paused and reviewed her first ideas, she would have lost the flow of her brainstorming and she might not have been able to come up with the excellent later solutions.

271

Problem-solving in action: Aesha

Problem: 'I have to go to Rebecca's wedding reception, alone, next Saturday. I will sit with Rebecca for the dinner and then mix with about fifty guests for three or four hours.'

Sitting with Rebecca for the dinner did not pose much of a problem as Aesha knew she'd be distracted by chatting – so she focused her thoughts on the challenge of mixing with guests after dinner.

Solutions

- Stay in bed – get under the duvet and say I'm ill so that I can avoid the whole thing
- Avoid the whole thing by sending my apologies, with an explanation of my problem
- Take a beta-blocker to calm me before the reception
- Send my daughter in my place
- Drink a lot at dinner so that I have 'Dutch courage'
- Recall how I coped the last time I went to a public event and use these strategies again
- Plan 'escape routes' that I could use if I thought I'd panic
- Practise 'small talk' with my partner so I feel I've got something to say to the guests
- Ask Rebecca if I can bring along my daughter for support
- Sit and talk through all my fears with a friend or my partner as this puts things in perspective
- Spend the morning before getting as relaxed as possible

- Take breaks – I can leave the marquee from time to time to compose myself and then go back in
- Listen to calming music when I take a break – I've several good tracks on my phone

Problem-solving in action: Dougie

Problem: 'I have to see my boss and put forward my argument for a pay rise within two days or lose the chance of an increase in salary.

Solutions

- Quit to avoid the confrontation or the embarrassment of not making a good enough argument
- Say I'm sick to buy myself some time
- Ask a colleague how I might phrase my request
- Ask my friend, Ali, to rehearse what I might say – and do some role-play with me
- Go to the pub and get relaxed before the meeting
- Do something else to get as relaxed as possible – I'm quite good at yoga meditation and I can distract myself by reading a good book (I've always got one with me)
- Ask for a time extension so that I can prepare myself better
- Ask if I can submit my argument by email
- Just keep my head down and miss the chance of a rise this year
- Remind myself that it's not the end of the world if I don't get a rise, but at least I can give myself credit for trying.

Step 3: Look at your resources

You are going to look at your ideas with a critical eye in Step 4, but first you need to reflect on the support and resources you have to help you. These resources might be around you (family and friends and a cash flow, for example) or within you (good social skills, a reliable memory, for example). When Aesha did this part of the exercise, she recalled that she had a very supportive partner who would do all he could to help her before the big day, although he would not be there for the wedding; she had a daughter who was always sunny and supportive and distracting in a very helpful way; Rebecca herself was a good and sensitive friend who would understand Aesha's struggles; Aesha had learnt a few stress-management skills that she could call on – distracting herself with soothing music, for example.

When Dougie carried out a similar review, he realized that he had a very good friend in Ali and, at work, his colleague Joanne was particularly trustworthy and kind. He also knew that he had a loving family who would be understanding whatever he did and this took some pressure off him. He knew that even without a pay rise they would be financially comfortable. Finally he recognized that on paper he was a very articulate and clear thinker, more so than many of his colleagues.

Step 4: Evaluate the pros and cons of each solution and order them

Step 2 gives you a list of possible solutions and now you can scrutinize them and decide which to hold on to and which to reject. You need to do this in the light of what you discovered at Step 3. So take a step back and consider the pros and cons of each – this will help you decide which solutions are non-starters, which are really good and which lie somewhere in between. When Dougie considered the pros and cons of: *Quit to avoid the confrontation or the embarrassment of not making a good enough argument*, he decided that there were no advantages to this and that the downside would be enormous – so it was easy to delete it. However, when he considered: *Ask if I can submit my argument by email*, it was less straightforward: the advantages would be that he would be more relaxed and able to make his points more clearly and forcefully in an email; the downside was that he thought he'd seem odd and unassertive if he made his request this way. So he decided to keep this idea, but as a 'last-resort solution'. When he reviewed the possible solutions: *Ask a colleague how I might phrase my request*, and, *Ask my friend, Ali, to rehearse what I might say*, it was clear to him that these were both good ideas with no disadvantage and so they would stay near or at the top of his list. In addition, he now realized that Joanne would be the ideal colleague to consult.

When you have done this exercise for yourself, you will be left with a list of useful ideas that you can rank in order of usefulness. Put the most useful and 'do-able' one at the top of your list and work down from there. By this stage, you might also see that some of the ideas complement each other and they will work well together. For example, Dougie realized that he could first ask Joanne's advice about phrasing his request and then take this forward into a role-play of the meeting with Ali.

Problem-solving in action: Aesha

Problem: 'I have to go to Rebecca's wedding reception, alone, next Saturday and mix with about fifty guests for three or four hours.'

When Aesha looked over her ideas she quickly got rid of three of them because they really had no advantages for her:

Reject these solutions:

- stay in bed – get under the duvet and say I'm ill so that I can avoid the whole thing
- avoid the whole thing by sending my apologies, with an explanation of my problem
- send my daughter in my place

She then considered the remaining ideas and drew up a list. Her number-one solution was to take some time and recall how she'd last coped – she thought that she might be able to calm and reassure herself just by doing this. If not, there were other things she could try – talking through the situation with someone, practising social chat, etc. You can see her list below and you can see what she decided were her 'last-resort solutions', which she again put in order of usefulness. She really hoped that she did not have to resort to taking a beta-blocker so she put this at the bottom of the list, but she kept it there because it was an option if all else failed.

My list of solutions:

- recall how I coped the last time I went to a public event and use these strategies again

- sit and talk through all my fears with a friend or my partner as this puts things in perspective
- practise 'small talk' with my partner so I feel I've got something to say to the guests
- spend the morning before getting as relaxed as possible
- take breaks – I can leave the marquee from time to time to compose myself and then go back in
- listen to calming music when I take a break – I've several good tracks on my phone that will help calm me down

Keep as 'last-resort solutions':

- plan 'escape routes' that I could use if I thought I'd panic
- drink a lot at dinner so that I have 'Dutch courage' (change this to one or two drinks)
- ask Rebecca if I can bring along my daughter for support
- take a beta-blocker to calm me before the reception

Problem-solving in action: Dougie

Problem: I have to see my boss and put forward my argument for a pay rise within two days or lose the chance of an increase in salary.

Dougie looked over his brainstorming list and rejected several ideas. He quickly got rid of the following because he thought that they would only make things worse for him in the long run:

Reject these solutions:

- quit to avoid the confrontation or the embarrassment of not making a good enough argument
- say I'm sick to buy myself some time
- just keep my head down and miss the chance of a rise this year

He then went through the remaining solutions and drew up his final list with a set of 'last-resort solutions'. His preferred solution was to discuss his request with Joanne and then to practise making the request with Ali. If this didn't calm and reassure him enough, he could use relaxation and distraction and self-talk to help him. If all else failed, he had his last-resort list of options.

My list of solutions:

- ask Joanne how I might phrase my request
- ask my friend, Ali, to rehearse what I might say – and do some role-play with me
- do something to get as relaxed as possible – I'm quite good at yoga meditation and I can distract myself by reading a good book (I've always got one with me)
- remind myself that it's not the end of the world if I don't get a rise, but at least I can give myself credit for trying

Keep as 'last-resort solutions':

- ask for a time extension so that I can prepare myself better

- go to the pub and get relaxed before the meeting (but don't drink more than one unit of alcohol)
- ask if I can submit my argument by email

Step 5: Choose a solution and plan to put it into action

When you have your list, simply take your first-choice solution and plan how to put it into action. Be very specific and concrete – remember that vagueness usually makes it harder to follow a plan. Be sure to answer the following questions:

- what will I do?
- how will I do it?
- when will I do it?
- who is involved?
- where will it happen?
- what is my back-up plan?

A back-up plan is one that you can put into operation if your task is more difficult than you anticipated, or something unexpected turns up and stops you from carrying through your original course of action. For example, Aesha might carry the telephone number of a friend whom she could ring if she needed some words of encouragement.

Problem-solving in action: Aesha

Task: Recall how I coped the last time I went to a public event and use these strategies again.

Action: This afternoon, I will sit in my bedroom (which is quiet and comfortable) where I shan't be disturbed. I'll try to recall the details of the last wedding reception I attended and I'll write down all the things I did that made it possible for me to stay there. This will remind me that I can cope. I will keep this list with me to reassure myself. If I struggle to come up with ideas I'll ring my partner – although he's working away from home right now I know that he'll spend some time on the phone with me. If I can't come up with ideas and I can't get hold of my partner, I'll contact one of my good friends. If this solution doesn't work for me, it's not the end of the world because I'll move on to solution 2, which means I'll begin by talking through the whole problem with a friend who will help me get things into perspective.

Problem-solving in action: Dougie

Task: Ask Joanne how I might phrase my request.

Action: Right now I'll text Joanne, explain my situation and ask her if and when she's available to talk with me. I'd like to do this as soon as possible. I'll fit in with her and go over to her place or meet her here in the study – whatever suits her. I'll make notes and try to run through several options so that we can choose the best. I know I'm good with words if I'm not under pressure so I think that we'll come up with some good ideas. If Joanne isn't available then I could try Jude or Chris – or even Joe. If for some reason I don't manage to write a little script with a colleague, I'll write my own and go to option 2, which is role-playing it with Ali.

All this planning might have already taken the edge off Aesha's and Dougie's anxiety – having a clear plan and a back-up strategy can often give us the reassurance we need to gain confidence. Clearly, we still have to put our plans into action and this can be stressful, so, where possible, it's a good idea to rehearse dealing with the task. You can do this either in your imagination (running through the task in your mind's eye until you feel more relaxed about it) or, better still, with someone who could role-play with you. Another good idea is scanning all your solutions to see if you might combine them for better effect. For example, you might find that 'Asking my friend to rehearse with me what I might say' links very well with 'Preparing myself by relaxing before I see my boss'.

Once you've done as much as you can to prepare, the next step is putting this into action: doing it!

Do it

This is your chance to try out your solution, making sure that contingency plans are in place and that you are properly prepared both physically and mentally. You've planned well so things could go smoothly, but in real life there are sometimes unforeseeable obstacles or problems – so be open to different outcomes. We often learn a lot from set-backs, so they are not the end of the world – far from it. Whether or not you regard your action as successful, you then need to review it and see what you can learn.

Step 6: Review the outcome

If your solution works and is sufficient, congratulate yourself and remember this successful experience for the future. Always 'de-brief' thoroughly and ask yourself why it was successful: what did you learn about your strengths and needs? By doing this you can 'tailor' your coping strategies so they reflect your needs and play to your strengths.

If your solution does not solve your problem, try to understand why it didn't – perhaps you were overambitious, perhaps you were not feeling strong that day, perhaps you misjudged someone else's response to you. Whatever conclusion you reach, remember that *you did not fail*. You might have had a set-back, but this is very different from a 'failure'. We can learn and grow from set-backs. Expect some disappointments, but commend yourself for having tried. Learn as much as you can from the experience and go back to your solution list and select the next one.

You can continue to return to your list of solutions as often as you need to. The more solutions you are able to generate, the more options you'll have to go back to.

Difficulties in using problem-solving

'My solution didn't work and I didn't know what to do!'

Remember how important it is to prepare thoroughly. Thorough brainstorming is essential to problem-solving; without this, you will be short of solutions and back-up plans. When you do make specific plans for action, always ask yourself what could go wrong and prepare a back-up solution, have contingency plans. If you do this, you'll have a reserve plan if your first choice doesn't work. Not only is this helpful because you have something to fall back on, but think how much more confident and calm you'll feel knowing that you've got options.

'*I can't possibly include such unhelpful solutions as avoidance and using drugs*'

Why not? Avoidance and taking medication isn't ideal and certainly not a long-term solution, but if you have to face a fear and the time isn't right for you to tackle the problem head-on, then this might be an acceptable compromise. You do need to consider other options first, but if you have tried other ways of coping before resorting to your 'unhelpful' solution, accept that you have tried your best. Sometimes we all have to handle difficulties in ways that aren't entirely satisfactory to us. With time and practice in dealing with problem situations, you will be better able to use strategies with which you are happier.

A final note: problem-solving is a useful technique when you find yourself in a situation that requires prompt action. However, it is always better to plan well in advance if you can; so try not to put off thinking about a difficult task until the last moment.

Summary

- Sometimes there is little time to prepare for facing a fear

- In that case we can use problem-solving steps to generate ideas

- This involves: defining the problem(s) and brain-storming solutions in the context of personal resources and thoroughly reviewing the outcome

- It gives us a framework for structuring our planning and this takes some of the stress out of the situation

14

Being assertive

It was a bit of a joke to the others – I was either a mouse or a raging bull. I couldn't seem to get the balance right in confrontations. I never achieved what I really wanted – it was so frustrating. Assertiveness training helped me to find a position that was neither mouse-like nor bullish, and the more I practised being properly assertive, the easier it became. I even found that I could do this when I was upset – I could be level-headed and fair even in the heat of the moment. My job became more enjoyable and the workers around me relaxed because they could trust me to be reasonable.

Assertiveness is another skill that can help you to manage worry, fear and anxiety. It describes a way of communicating your needs, feelings or rights to others while still being respectful. So it is particularly useful in dealing with stresses arising when we have to tackle something difficult that involves another person – saying 'No', for example, or returning goods to a shop, or keeping one's temper when crossed.

Assertiveness is all about balance: balancing your needs and rights with the needs and rights of others. Contrary to some beliefs, it is not about getting what you want at all costs – that's bullying and that would disrespect others. But simply giving in to the demands of others could be disrespectful of *your* needs and rights. You might think that it is worth it – that it's easier to avoid conflict by giving in to others – and you could be right. However, think about the longer-term consequences, too. If it is of no real disadvantage to you to give in, then fine, but if it means that you get put upon more and more, or if you end up feeling devalued, or if it just gets harder and harder – for example, to control your children or to get your needs met – then you probably need to consider being more assertive.

Although some fortunate people find it easy to be assertive, very many find it difficult – so once again you are not alone if being assertive is a struggle for you. The reasons for struggling range from simply not knowing the basic rules of assertiveness or not being confident about your rights, through to having low self-esteem and not feeling worthy or having difficulties managing anger. Luckily, not knowing the 'top tips' of assertiveness is easily addressed – we'll quickly cover these in this chapter. We will also take a good look at your rights and see how you can express them effectively. However, if you think that you are held back because you have low self-esteem and because of that you find it hard to put your needs first, then you might also find it helpful to read another book in this series: see Further Reading on page 381.

The basic rules

As we've already learnt, being assertive means communicating in a way that is clear and respectful of ourselves and of others.

This means not being passive or aggressive or manipulative, because none of these approaches shows mutual respect. Manipulation is often expressed as a charming form of aggression and it can therefore be hard to spot as being disrespectful: this makes it a powerful form of aggression. The 'charming' manipulator will cajole and flatter: 'I'm only asking you to do this because you're so clever'; 'I'm only thinking of what's good for you when I say "No"'. It's easy to be hoodwinked into assuming that you are not being bullied.

Assertiveness sits somewhere between passivity and aggression or manipulation.

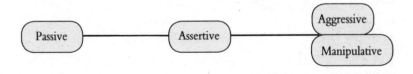

Quite simply, if we are passive, we are not respecting ourselves, and if we are aggressive or manipulative we are not respecting others. The goal of being assertive is to achieve a special kind of interaction that undermines neither party and which involves *balance*. Being passive is not balanced as it means avoiding conflict but disrespecting oneself in the process. Being aggressive or manipulative tips the balance in the other direction – the goal here is to win, irrespective of the other person's rights.

The Passive Person tends to opt out of conflict, can't make decisions and aims always to please others. If this is you then you might well find yourself feeling very frustrated as you are not getting *your* needs met and you might even begin to feel resentful and devalued – neither of which is good for your self-esteem or stress levels.

The Openly Aggressive Type can appear forceful, even bullying, ignoring the rights and needs of others in the quest to win. If you tend towards aggression, then you will get what you want in the short term but you need to ask yourself if the approach really works for you in the longer term. Can your relationships survive? Do you feel good about yourself?

The Manipulator's aggressive attack is cleverly concealed. This person can appear to be considerate but will be using emotional blackmail in the form of charm, or they might be saying things aimed to undermine the confidence of the other person. They do not fight fair. Again, if you tend to take a manipulative position, ask yourself if it works well for you in the long term or if you find that you lose friends and the trust and respect of others.

The Assertive Person takes a broad view of the situation and considers all sides of the argument so that they are able to put forward a good case for what is fair. The goal is to say what they want clearly and respectfully: quite a different picture from the passive and aggressive types.

If you realize that you need to be assertive, your best starting point is thorough preparation: prepare your assertive statement and prepare yourself. With practice you will be able to be more 'spontaneous', but in the early days you'll need to invest in preparation time. There are four steps to follow:

Step 1: Decide what you want
Step 2: State what you want
Step 3: Prepare for refusal and manipulation
Step 4: Prepare to negotiate

Step 1: Decide what you want (. . . and make sure that it is reasonable)

Put yourself centre-stage and ask: *What do I want?* This sounds so obvious, but if you are used to putting others first it can be quite difficult to simply consider *your* needs. So, forget everyone else for a moment and think of your wishes and then state them clearly. For example, you might want a new computer for your work ('I'd like a new work computer'); you might want your children to tidy up their toys each night ('I want you to put away your toys before you go to bed'); you might want to say no to your friend's request to help her move house ('I can't help you move house next week'). You should also think how you feel about the current situation, as this might be relevant to your argument. Do you feel hurt, upset, frustrated?

Now it's time to consider the perspective of others. Balance your wishes with the needs and rights of others by asking yourself: *Am I being reasonable?* This is more of a challenge if you tend towards the aggressive or manipulative end of the spectrum, but try to put yourself in the other person's shoes and see things from their perspective. A balanced argument will be more engaging than an aggressive one, and remember that your aim is not to win at all costs, but to put forward a reasonable and considerate proposition. When you have thought things through, you might conclude that:

- it is reasonable to ask for a new computer as other members of your team have more up-to-date models, although you might be aware that money is tight in the department
- it is reasonable to ask your children to tidy up before bed, because your home is quite small and the living area is easily cluttered, and because they need to learn the habit of tidying after themselves – however, you might also think that they can have more freedom in their own bedrooms
- it is reasonable to refuse your friend's request as she has given you little notice and you already have other commitments

Next, think through your argument and try to put across the consequences of the other person's cooperation. These could be positive – 'It would help me do my work much more efficiently and not waste time because of computer glitches'; 'If you tidy every evening for a week, I'll give you extra pocket money' – or simply practical – 'If you feel that you can't authorize a new computer, then I can go to the Area Head

Office and make the request there' – or there could be a negative message – 'If you keep ringing and asking me to help you move, then I'll have to stop answering my phone because it is disturbing my work'. On the whole, positive consequences are more effective – reward works better than punishment – so, for example, it is better in the long run to reward your children for good behaviour than to punish them for unwanted behaviours.

Step 2: State what you want

Now you have the basis for an assertive statement: you know what you want, you believe that it is reasonable and you have thought through the consequences. It's time to rehearse what you are going to say, and you can make your argument more effective if you follow these rules:

- be positive and understanding
- be objective – no personal attacks
- state the consequences
- be brief

I need a new computer. My old one is unreliable and, although I appreciate that we no longer have a generous budget, I need a new computer in order to do my job properly. If you can do this I will be very grateful but if you are not able to authorize it, I'll make the request through Head Office.

Dad and I are really pleased with the way that you take care of your toys, and now we want you to tidy them up nicely in the living room before you go to bed. I don't mind if your own bedrooms have some toys lying around, but the living room is for all of us and I want it tidy at the end of the day. If you do this, Dad and I will be really pleased and we'll give you a bit more pocket money at the end of the week.

Normally I'd be more than happy to help, especially as I appreciate that moving is a huge stress for you, but I can't be there this time. I have already made commitments for next week. I can spend an hour or two at the weekend helping you pack, but I won't be able to help with the move itself.

You can see that none of these statements is complicated or long, but they are all polite and they all begin quite positively. That's the essence of a good argument. A good argument brings the other person on board, engages them so that they listen to you. If you are critical or negative then you run the risk of losing their attention and any hope of cooperation.

Once you have a good argument, you need to deliver it in the best way possible. Simply by attending to your body language and choice of words, you can send out the message that you are not being timid or aggressive when you make your request. To make this easier, here are some tips for making the most of your presentation:

- **Facial expression**: try to adopt a firm, friendly expression. Avoid a tense, aggressive look, or one that suggests that you are nervous.

- **Posture**: keep your head up (but not so high that you look haughty!) – lowering it will make you look submissive.
- **Distance**: not too close, but close enough to be heard and to make good eye contact.
- **Gestures**: make these relaxed and not intimidating – no finger wagging, for example. But also make sure that you are not making nervous gestures like wringing your hands.
- **Eye contact**: don't stare at the other person, but don't be afraid of looking them in the eye. A comfortable pattern is to shift your focus between the other person's eyes and mouth during a conversation.
- **Voice**: keep the tone, volume and pace of your voice such that it communicates thoughtfulness and calm. Try not to let the pitch or the volume of your voice go up, which it can easily do if we feel stressed.
- **Vocabulary**: use constructive and non-critical words and phrases – your aim is to get the other person on board, not into conflict. Acknowledge the other side of the argument, empathize and never attack.

Possibly the greatest 'top tip' is to **Keep Calm**. As you already know, this is often more easily said than done, but by now you have a good grasp of stress-management strategies and have possibly tailored them to suit you. Nonetheless, below is a brief reminder of the key aspects of keeping calm:

- be prepared: if you can, get the facts to support your case and rehearse what you want to say. Try out your statement on a friend and get some feedback

- be aware of your feelings and try to 'stand back' from them – don't ignore them
- catch nervousness and anger as early as possible – it's easier to deal with them earlier rather than later, and by now you probably have a good set of skills for managing the thoughts behind unhelpful feelings
- have your own 'mantra' to help you keep calm
- use physical relaxation techniques and calm, regular breathing
- distract yourself if necessary
- keep to the point: don't get side-tracked, and repeat yourself as often as you have to

Forgive the repetition, but it is such an important point that it is worth saying again: the aim of being assertive is not to win at all costs, but to reach a solution that is reasonable all round. This can, therefore, involve **negotiation and compromise**. Your strongest position is one where you have already thought through how far you would be prepared to compromise – so:

- decide, in advance, how far you will compromise
- set your limits and be prepared to stick to them unless your negotiations genuinely change your mind
- if you stand your ground, accept that there will be consequences; the other person may be uncooperative or even aggressive – but we will look at ways of dealing with this in Step 3

In the examples above, the compromises might look like this:

To be prepared to wait for a new computer until the next tax year when the department will have a new budget – but not to wait any longer than this.

To allow the children to keep toys out in their own rooms and to help the children to put away toys in the living room if they are particularly tired – but to keep the onus on them.

To be available via text on the day of the move to offer advice if necessary.

Step 3: Prepare for refusal and manipulation

At last you are all set to be assertive. If you have prepared well and feel confident, there is a good chance that you will be listened to. However, you also need to be prepared for the other person not 'playing ball' – not listening to you respectfully. If the other person simply refuses your request or refuses to accept your argument then you can stay calm, knowing that you've thought through the consequences – you will go to a higher authority, you will stop taking phone calls, etc. It is a shame that you are now forced to do this but it's better than simply giving in.

Harder to deal with are the 'manipulators' who will use charm or bullying to get their way. They will try to make you feel flattered or guilty in order to undermine you. But how do we know that we are being manipulated? A tell-tale sign is feeling bad about making our request.

Imagine that you had asserted that your boss gave you too much work to do. You had thought this through and discussed it with a friend, and, although you recognized that the department was very busy, you still felt that you were being unreasonably burdened and that your request to be given less work was fair. Your boss, rather than respecting your statement and considering your point of view, reacts by using manipulative criticism that is intended to make you feel guilty or just stupid. Your boss might use tricks such as:

- *Nagging*: 'Never mind that, haven't you finished yet? Your problem is that you are too slow. Now get on with the job.'
- *Lecturing*: 'Well, quite *obviously* the real problem is that you are not organizing yourself well enough and what you should do is . . .'
- *Insults*: 'Typical woman: can't cope in the real world.'
- *Hurt*: 'You've made me feel terrible . . .'

Your boss might be more subtle than this and use manipulative 'concern', where the goal is to leave you feeling supported and grateful that your request or point of view is not accepted. This is a more powerful strategy because we can initially feel good about the situation and we don't realize that we've been manipulated. Later, the reality might hit us. If your boss was using false concern, you might hear the following:

- *Caring*: 'That's all very well, but I really do think that it is in your best interest to improve your skills by carrying a substantial work load.'
- *Concern:* 'If you are having these problems, are you sure you're right for this job, after all?'

296

- *Advice*: 'Let me tell you what I would do if I were you . . .'

Each of these responses is intended to side-line your needs and your rights and to deflect your argument. To deal with this, you will need to develop the skills and confidence to stand your ground. There are two particularly useful approaches to help you to be more assertive and handle manipulative criticism and false 'concern':

1. the 'broken record'
2. preparing for criticism

It is also useful to refresh your awareness of your basic social rights. Some of us – particularly the more passive – tend to underestimate our rights, and this can get in the way of being truly assertive. Remember that we each have the following rights:

- to be treated respectfully (it is most important that you remember this)
- to say what we want and express an opinion (respectfully, of course)
- to make mistakes (within reason)
- to change our minds when we have reviewed a situation
- to not know / understand something and to ask for more information
- to ask for clarification of an argument so that we know what we are dealing with
- to take the time that you need – you can say, 'Let me think about this', or, 'I'll get back to you on this', or, 'I

can't make a decision right now, I'm going to have to give it more thought'

Keeping in mind your rights will help you to be more firm and confident when you take an assertive position.

Something else that will help is reminding yourself that you have given a lot of thought to your argument and you know that it is fair – and you could always check this out with a friend if you are in doubt. Once you are confident that your statement is reasonable, then stick to it, using the strategy called the 'broken record'.

The 'broken record'

This technique is aptly named because you simply keep repeating your argument. If we are unassertive, we take 'No' for an answer far too easily and we are not persistent in making a point. A basic assertiveness skill is being persistent and repeating what you want – calmly. Remember, you have decided that you are making a fair and reasonable statement, so go ahead and assert it. In the face of unreasonable opposition (that is, when the other person is not listening to your argument), simply repeat your message. Quite often you will find that the other person begins to listen.

This is a particularly useful approach when your rights are clearly in danger of being abused, or when you are likely to be diverted by articulate but irrelevant arguments, or when you feel vulnerable because you know the other person will use criticism to undermine your self-esteem. The great thing is that once you have prepared your 'script', you can relax and repeat your argument, knowing that you are being reasonable and knowing what you are going to say. This means that you are much less likely to be side-tracked, however abusive or manipulative the other person tries to be.

Clearly it can become tedious if you use exactly the same statement over and over again without variation, so you can slightly vary the way you phrase it each time. In the example below you will see how it is possible to stand your ground in the face of aggressive manipulation that is intended to induce guilt and self-doubt.

I need a new computer in order to be able to do my work efficiently

Boss: I'm sorry: you are asking too much

I can only work efficiently if I have a reliable and powerful computer

Boss: *You're making things very difficult for me*

Nonetheless, I need the computer to do my work properly

Boss: *Others aren't asking for new equipment*

Maybe, but I need the computer

Boss: *I'm sure that you are exaggerating*

Not at all – if I am to work efficiently I need a decent computer

In many cases, the person you are dealing with will start to listen to your argument. However, some people might play nasty and use outright insult to try to manipulate you, and if there is a grain of truth in the criticisms, you can find yourself wrong-footed by this. This is the aim of the manipulator, because if they can divert you away from your argument they stand a better chance of undermining your efforts. So, make sure that you have prepared yourself for dealing with criticism.

Preparing for criticism

You can 'stress-proof' yourself enormously by being prepared for criticism. If you are not prepared, then manipulative criticism might leave you feeling so bad about yourself that you agree to do something you would rather not do. Criticism that gets to us often holds a grain of truth – that's why it can be so effective – but it is exaggerated.

For example, a boss might say: *That's typical of you – you're always demanding, nothing is ever good enough!*

It might be true that a person has high standards and has asked for things in the past, but saying that he is 'always' demanding and that 'nothing is ever' good enough might be blatant exaggeration.

A friend might say: *You really don't care about anyone but yourself – you are so selfish!*

Again, it might be true that a person is thinking about her own needs right now, but this doesn't mean that she is 'selfish'; she may have considered what is fair and this criticism is exaggerated.

However, if we are not prepared, these sorts of manipulative comments can so easily trigger guilt – and then we give in.

The crucial thing is not to engage with the criticism – let it wash over you and get back to your argument. This is so much easier to do if you've thought ahead of time just what might be thrown at you. If the man in the first example is aware that he does have high standards, or the woman in the second example is aware that she is asking for something for herself, then they are not going to be taken by surprise when the criticisms are thrown at them. They will then be able to field the criticism calmly by acknowledging that there may be some truth in it, before returning to their argument. For example:

That's typical of you – you're always demanding, nothing is ever good enough!
It is true that I have high standards in my work and that I've asked for things before – however, I've thought this through carefully and I need a new computer.

You really don't care about anyone but yourself – you are so selfish!
You are right that I am thinking about my own situation, but I have given it some thought. I do have other commitments and it is reasonable for me to say that I can't help you out this time.

Fielding criticism in this way also keeps the situation calm and allows you some time to think clearly, which means that your responses can be controlled and reasonable. You can avoid getting into a battle and you can simply return to your 'broken record' technique. For example, imagine the situation where a boss yells: *A typical woman: can't cope in the real world!*

A calm, detached series of responses might look like this:

That's right, I can't cope. And that is why I am asking you to recognize that you give me too much to do.

Never mind that, haven't you finished yet? Your problem is that you are too slow. Now get on with the job.

You are right, I can't keep up, given the amount of work that I have to deal with. That's why I am asking you to recognize that you overload me.

Now you've made me feel terrible!

I am sorry that you feel terrible but I still want you to recognize that you give me a bigger workload than is reasonable.

In fact, just echoing the criticism – 'I agree that I am not tidy. . .'; 'I am sorry that you feel hurt . . .' and so on – can buy you time. You can think about the criticism and think about your response – and then you are so much more able to resist the manipulation.

Your opponent will want you to get side-tracked from your assertive argument. To avoid this, simply acknowledge the criticism, agree calmly with the truth in it and resist arguing against it. Don't get engaged. This can be really difficult, as it is only human to want to defend ourselves, but remember that disengaging from the criticism will keep you calm. Then

int that you don't know how to tidy up properly so
ith you — not for you — for the first few days. That
t the hang of it and you'll find out just what you
get a treat.

the example of the friend who wanted help
u had decided that you could not help her
ere prepared to be available via text on the
to offer advice if necessary. Let's imagine that
th your partner and got confirmation that
e given your other commitments that day,
end asked at short notice and given that she
amily and friends to help her out. You let
cannot physically help on the day of the
be on the end of the phone (via texts) so
dvice. Your response meets with quite a
: 'I'm really surprised that you've let me
lways been there for you. Can't you can-
me and help me?' She looks so dejected
her but you know that you have given
d that you cannot be there on the day.
hize with her plight and, in order to
sible, you try to understand why she
ou there:

e disappointed but I cannot cancel my
ially at short notice. You have lots of
nd I'll be at the end of the phone so
ed me to be there?

---

you can stay in control and you can think more clearly. So, if someone is mean enough to try to distract you by saying: 'Your appearance is a disgrace. You are so untidy and should be ashamed of yourself,' you might reply: 'Yes, I could be neater. However, the point I'm making is . . .'

If you are able to accept yourself with all your faults, then your acknowledgement of them will not distress or distract you and should put an end to your attacker's remarks.

Knowing your Achilles heels: As well as preparing yourself by being aware of what you might be criticized for, you can also strengthen your position by being aware of your 'Achilles heels' – knowing what presses your guilt, shame or insecurity 'buttons'. For example, anyone with the fixed belief: 'I should please other people' has an Achilles heel. This belief would make anyone crumple when faced with the criticism that they were 'selfish'; someone who believes that 'I don't matter and my needs are not important' would have difficulty not accepting 'No' for an answer – another example of an Achilles heel.

If you've worked through the earlier parts of this book you are probably already very aware of the beliefs that might make you an easy target for the manipulator, so think about them carefully.

Step 4: Prepare to negotiate

Given that the aim of being assertive is to reach a solution that is reasonable to all parties, it is quite usual to engage in compromise and negotiation. You need to be ready to do this.

Negotiating is a skill that improves with practice and confidence, and if you are just starting out, it will be easier if you:

- have already decided how far you will compromise
- have done your homework and got the facts to support your case and rehearsed your script
- keep calm
- ask for clarification of the other side of the argument so that you know what you are dealing with
- try to understand the other person's position and needs – you are aiming to be reasonable
- stay respectful, empathic and never attack – this will increase the chances of maintaining good communication
- keep to your point – don't get side-tracked

A good starting point in negotiation is to begin with a phrase like: 'I understand . . .' and then reflect the other person's situation and dissatisfaction as you see it. This achieves three things: it helps you get a sympathetic angle on the other person's viewpoint, it buys you just a moment or two to keep calm, and it tells the other person that you are reasonable. If you do this you are much more likely to set the scene for a genuine conversation rather than an unproductive battle.

Let's return to the example of asking the children to tidy their toys. You have decided how far you will compromise – *to allow the children to keep toys out in their own rooms and to help the children to put away toys in the living room if they are particularly tired* – and you have done your homework in that you've spoken with other parents and found out what the usual expectation is. You get yourself in as calm a state as possible

and you tell the children
that's not fair! – you are
can't do it on our own!'

Still keeping calm, y
fair and they say that r
You have done your
them that they are
children do this tas
because facts are fa
of their second a
on their own. T
what they thin
that they can't
to compromis
asking: '. . . s
to make it
some groar
show then
see the p
them ho
prepare
do this
them

I

take your p
I will do it i
way you'll g
need to do to

There was also
moving and yo
move but you
day of the move
you'd spoken w
this was reasonab
given that your fri
has quite a lot of
her know that you
move but you can
that you can offer
disappointed reactio
down like this. I've a
cel something and co
that you really feel fo
this a lot of thought a
You genuinely sympa
be as reasonable as po
believes that she needs

I understand that you a
other commitments, espe
other friends and family
why do you particularly n

Your friend then says that you are the most practical of her friends and therefore the best in these situations and you are the best at dealing with stroppy delivery workers. She's nervous not having you around. Now you have a better grasp of her perspective and fears and you can do a bit of problem-solving with her:

I realize that not having me there in person leaves you feeling nervous so I'll prioritize your texts and get back to you as quickly as I can so that I can give you advice over the phone. But I think that you can deal with a lot of things yourself if you've done some good planning. If you make a list of all the things that you think will be stressful for you, I'm happy to come over the night before and go through them with you.

In both these examples there is give and take – and that's the basis of negotiation.

To sum up:

1. Decide what you want, decide what is fair. Rehearse your statement if you can, check out your thoughts with a friend. Make yourself as confident as possible
2. Keep as calm as you can
3. Make your point clearly, briefly and respectfully
4. Have a contingency plan and be prepared to compromise and negotiate
5. Be ready to deal with manipulation and outright aggression

You will find it easier to be assertive if you draw on your other stress-management skills – this will help you to keep physically and mentally calm.

Being assertive isn't so very difficult once you are aware of, *and have practised*, the strategies. However, while you are new to asserting yourself, it is crucial to plan and rehearse; otherwise you will slip too easily into the position of aggressor, manipulator or passive avoider.

Remember that assertiveness is a skill and it improves with training and practice. You might find that it can be most effectively learnt in a class. See if there are assertiveness training classes in your area.

Assertiveness in action: Managing social fears

I stopped being able to mix with others after a bus driver humiliated me because I didn't have the right money for my ticket. I was already feeling fragile after a row with my husband and I was completely unprepared for a hostile driver. Right in front of twenty passengers, he called me names and finally yelled: 'Get the right money or get off the bus. Now!' I just stood by the side of the road silently sobbing as the bus drove away.

The next day, I avoided using the bus and I walked into town. I was still upset and anxious, so when an assistant in the delicatessen was a bit sharp with me, I simply fled without finishing my shopping. After that I stopped going out alone and little by little I withdrew because I was so sure that people would humiliate me if I expressed myself. I even began to avoid friends.

Fortunately, I found a local assertiveness training class where I learnt that I could regain my confidence – as long as I remembered to prepare myself. I made a list of difficult situations, decided what I wanted from them and how to ask for this. I started with the easiest (contacting a friend I'd been avoiding and daring to say that I'd like to meet her for a coffee) and I worked my way up to taking a bus into town. On the day that I tackled that task, I really did not have the correct money for the fare. I thought about it and decided that it was reasonable for me to ask for a ticket anyway. I prepared a speech so that if the driver complained about the fact I didn't have the right change I would be able to respond: 'I realize that you ask passengers to have the correct money for the fare, but I've been unable to find it today. I appreciate that you might not be able to give me change, but if you could, I'd be very grateful.'

I had also prepared myself in case the driver was hostile; I had planned to say: 'I made a reasonable request and I'm sorry that you haven't respected that. I'm perfectly prepared to walk but I'm going to report your conduct to your manager.'

I practised and practised these phrases until I felt confident with them. In the end it all went smoothly and the driver let me travel without a fuss! Once I'd tackled that situation my old confidence started to return, and by using this assertive approach, I was more able to speak up in shops or restaurants or with friends.

309

Difficulties in being assertive

'I get too nervous at the last minute'

It is not unusual to feel anxious when you are about to tackle a difficult situation, but there are steps you can take in order to minimize your fear. It always helps to start with the least threatening task and work up to the most difficult challenges. By doing this you'll build on successes and develop your confidence as you go. It is absolutely essential that you prepare yourself, rehearse and have a contingency plan for coping if things do not go smoothly – simply by preparing thoroughly you can reduce your anxieties enormously.

'I have to back down: I can't achieve my goal'

Remember that you are aiming to reach a reasonable conclusion – don't get hung up on 'winning'. Make sure that you've thought about compromise and have a back-up plan. Good planning and practice will increase your chances of achieving the outcome you desire, but you should always be ready to settle for less as long as it is still reasonable. Remember that you can walk away rather than give in. If someone does not agree to your request you can say something like: 'It looks as though we'll have to agree to differ right now. I'm going to have to give this some more thought and I'll get back to you.' You have the right to take the time you need.

'I can't get people to do what I want them to do'

This will happen from time to time – being assertive is about doing your best to engage and persuade someone else. You are in control of what you do but not how they react. No matter how well you put forward your case, sometimes the other person will choose not to listen to you, or choose to be disrespectful. You can only do your best to be reasonable and respectful and if you achieve that then you have been assertive, and you should give yourself credit.

Summary

- Being assertive can help us manage stress

- Assertive communication is clear and respectful of all parties

- It requires learning the skills of communication and developing the confidence to be assertive

- Assertiveness means standing your ground when necessary but knowing how and when to negotiate and compromise

15

Anxiety management: it's not just for anxiety disorders

I was really pleased with the way I managed to learn to deal with my fears and my worrying. It made a real difference to my life, as I could face up to things and not get overwhelmed by anxieties – but I found that learning to cope with fears and stress helped me do so much more. I'd always struggled with my weight and then it dawned on me that I ate when I was stressed – learning to manage my stress helped me to stick to a diet. I was also able to sleep better because I became good at relaxing and I discovered that I was more 'chilled' at work and I think I get on better with people as a result.

As you can see, once you've mastered stress or anxiety management skills you can almost certainly cope better with all sorts of other difficulties. You might find that you can use your new-found understanding of the stress response to help you deal with problems such as:

- under- or over-eating (or drinking, or smoking)
- sleep problems
- depression
- sexual difficulties

- anger
- Pain
- Memory problems

By now you are probably becoming quite good at understanding your difficulties – keeping notes and finding patterns, identifying those vicious cycles that keep problems alive. If you identify anxiety, stress or worry playing a part in your difficulties you can take a constructive step and aim to break the cycle by managing your anxieties. You might need additional support, and you might well find other books in the 'Overcoming' series as well as other self-help books that offer this, but just learning to take anxiety out of the equation can ease things enormously and sometimes it actually resolves the problem.

Under- or over-eating (or drinking or smoking)

Stress affects our appetites. High levels of stress can easily spoil our appetite and we can be too tense to eat. If you are one of those people who struggle to keep up your weight because stress stops you from feeling hungry, or even makes you feel sick, then you probably find that losing your appetite just adds to your stress and makes eating even more difficult. You can see where this pattern is going – a vicious cycle of stress, loss of appetite, worry and more loss of appetite.

Alternatively, you might be someone who has difficulty keeping your weight down and who comfort eats in the face of stress. If you are, you will be all too aware that comfort eating (or drinking, or smoking, for that matter) works in the short term: in fact, in the short term it's a very effective 'quick fix' and it's no wonder that we get hooked on it. The problem comes later when we are left feeling worse about ourselves and even more stressed – and even more vulnerable to comfort eating, drinking or smoking. So, overindulging has two driving forces: the short-term fix and the longer-term additional stress. And it's all too easy to get caught up in these problem patterns.

By now you know that once you've worked out just what your vicious cycle looks like, you can break the cycle by managing the stress that drives it. You can identify your personal cycles of under-eating or over-eating, drinking or smoking simply by monitoring your feelings and behaviours for a while. It probably won't take long. Then you can see when you are at risk, you can pinpoint the tell-tale signs of your stress and you can identify your own patterns of behaviour. After that, you can start to manage the stress and anxiety that fuels them. Max and Jodi's stories will give you an idea of how you can do this for yourself.

Max: Since I left college I've nearly always struggled with my weight. Once I stopped exercising the weight crept on and I keep meaning to diet but every time I'd fail – and then I get miserable and then I eat for comfort. Everyone tells me that this is common – but that doesn't stop it being a problem for me. So I decided to keep track of my eating using a simple diary that helped me see just why I struggled and also how I could cope better:

Anxiety management: it's not just for anxiety disorders

Urge to eat: when and where	How I felt	What I did	How I felt
Thursday: 6.00 p.m. when I was leaving work	I hadn't eaten all day and I was hungry and I didn't care what I ate	Bought chocolate at the garage and ate it in the car (ate a lot of it!)	After the initial relief I felt really upset that I'd eaten so much and so much junk – I felt anxious about my weight
Thursday: 6.30 p.m. at home	Still feeling worried about never getting in control of my weight. So wanted to have a glass of wine and not care and not worry	I poured a large glass of wine and then I didn't care and I comfort ate all evening	At first I felt calmed but next morning I felt ill and even more worried that I'll never conquer my weight problem
Friday: 11.00 a.m. at work – my computer is playing up again and I'm worried that I could start losing work	Tense, anxious, frustrated – I've got chocolate biscuits in my drawer and I want to eat them	I walked away from my desk and went into the courtyard. I sat in the sun for fifteen minutes and did a quick relaxation exercise	I felt calmer and my head cleared. I could make a plan – I decided to call the IT helpdesk and ask for help before I do lose any important work. Felt better and not hungry at all

I kept this sort of log for about a week and then I could clearly see my patterns: if I got over-hungry or over-anxious I would over-eat (and drink). I learnt to do two things:

1. avoid getting over-hungry
2. take two minutes to relax each time I get anxious and began to crave food or alcohol

The brief relaxation really worked because not only did it calm me, but it helped me decide whether or not I really needed to eat. On many occasions, if I was calm the so-called hunger went away. At first this helped me regulate my eating and I stopped snacking and bingeing when I wasn't really hungry. Later, when I felt more in control I began to try to lose weight and the relaxation, along with distraction, helped me get through. It's not always easy to stick to my diet but it is a lot easier if I use my stress-management strategies.

Jodi: So many times I was determined to give up smoking. You know what it's like – start off with good intentions and then give in to the craving and promise yourself that you'll 'give up smoking tomorrow'. My problem was that every time I got nervous I would really, really want a cigarette. I mean, I couldn't think of anything else – I was always convinced that this was the only way to get on top of my nerves. So I'd have a smoke (always promising myself that today was my last smoking day) and then I'd feel OK – and this just seemed to prove to me that the only way I could handle myself was if I smoked. The last time I visited my doctor about my bad chest, she gave me a very stern message – she said that I wouldn't be around to see my children grow up if I didn't stop smoking. Maybe she was exaggerating, I don't know, but what she said made me stop and think that I had to do something. I literally sat down and thought about my smoking habit and what I could do. I remembered that we'd had a bit of stress-management training at work and although I hadn't paid much attention at the time, I did have my notes. When I'd reflected on things and reread my stress notes, I came up with this conclusion:

- **I'm at risk:** when I'm tense and anxious or when I'm with smoking friends
- **What I feel is:** agitation and a really strong urge, a craving really, to smoke (so no wonder I give in)
- **What I usually do is:** give in to the urge and smoke either on my own or with friends
- **What I'll do instead:** (i) remind myself that it is understandable that I have this craving after years of smoking but also remind myself that I want to be as healthy as possible for my family – they are the most important thing in my life; (ii) I'll try some of the stress-management strategies like distraction and brief relaxation; (iii) I'll reduce my risk by saying no to going outside with the smokers and I'm going to put a ban on smoking in the house (that will please my husband!)

It was really tough to begin with – but I was lucky to have a lot of support from my husband who gave me a little reward every day that I did not smoke. I found that I couldn't just 'switch on' the relaxation and distraction exercises – they didn't come that easily – so I had to find time to practise them. Again, I was lucky as a friend of mine had a relaxation recording and she lent it to me and I got into the routine of spending a few minutes in the morning and in the evening doing the exercise. I wish I'd paid attention to the stress-management training at work because I discovered that I love relaxation times and I got really good at simply letting go of the tensions, slowing my breathing and clearing my mind. Armed with my 'toolkit' of strategies and my determination, I have been able to stop smoking. I think I'll always be 'a smoker' at heart, but now I've got the skills and the confidence not to give in to cravings.

Sleep

The most common sleep problem is probably not being able to fall asleep easily. This is often called insomnia and everyone will have experienced it at one time or another. It is really only a problem if it goes on for long periods and if you are not getting enough sleep to function well the next day. It's worth noting that not everyone needs eight hours' sleep; our needs vary enormously and people like Margaret Thatcher and Napoleon are said to have only needed three hours a night. So, if you only sleep for a few hours, there is a chance that you don't need more sleep – if you feel rested the next day, then you will have had enough.

If you are struggling, though, there are lots of practical things you can do to make it more likely that you'll have a better night's sleep. The usual tips are:

- try to have a bed-time routine where you wind down before going to bed
- keep your bedroom dark and quiet and make sure your bed is comfortable
- avoid napping during the day
- don't overdo eating and drinking alcohol or caffeine before bed and try not to smoke before going to sleep
- get enough exercise during the day
- if you wake and can't get back to sleep, get up and do something until you feel tired – don't stay in bed tossing and turning
- avoid watching TV or using the internet in bed

These guidelines are worth considering. Something as simple as cutting out caffeine can make a huge difference.

However, the one thing that drives insomnia more than anything is psychological – it's worrying about not being able to sleep. The most common vicious cycle is the one where worrying about not sleeping stops us from sleeping – this then makes us more worried about not sleeping and the cycle continues. If you have already read through this book, you can see where this is going – managing the worries about sleep can often break the cycle. Your most powerful strategy is learning not to worry. If you think back over what you have covered in this book, you'll realize that you have learnt many techniques to curb worry: problem-solving to address the worry, self-talk to reassure yourself, and distraction to take your mind off the nagging thoughts that won't go away. You have also learnt how to relax yourself, and at night this can be very helpful. Rik – in the example below – managed to put all of these strategies into action, although you might find that just one or two of them is enough to break your worry cycle.

Rik: It began with me spending just a bit longer on the computer or in front of the TV or with my nose in a book each night – it seemed easy to stay awake and so I didn't think I was ready to go to sleep but then it got harder to get up in the morning. This was OK until I overslept and missed the beginning of an important meeting, and not long after that I made a stupid mistake at work – which was probably because I was still feeling sleepy and not on the ball. I realized that I needed my sleep after all, and that night I had my worst night's sleep ever. I just worried that I wouldn't sleep properly, and I didn't. I was stuck with the thoughts that I wouldn't be able to drop off and then I wouldn't be able to function at work and then I'd make mistakes and I'd get into trouble. I got more and more tense, both physically and mentally, and then I grew more wakeful. After that it became an ongoing problem and I'd lie awake at night worrying about things. I saw my doctor who said that she could prescribe a sleeping pill but she'd rather not, so I tried to learn how to calm myself and get a good night's sleep that way.

I knew something about overcoming fears as I'd had a phobia as a teenager and I'd learnt ways of dealing with my scary thoughts and feelings using balanced thinking, problem-solving, distraction and relaxation. So I decided to see if they would help with my sleep.

I kept track of what was going through my mind when I was restless and then I made a plan for dealing with my worries. First I came up with a two-part solution: once I had named my night-time worries I would try to problem-solve, and if I couldn't solve the problem, then I'd distract myself by thinking of a walk through my favourite woodland. I quickly discovered that this wasn't a bad solution but that I could do better. I'm a great one for trial and error and I expect to have to give something a few goes. I soon realized that although problem-solving was a good, structured approach to real challenges, at night I had more of those vague 'what if . . . ?' questions going round in my head, and at 2 a.m. I couldn't shift them, so I turned to distraction more often than not. My soothing image was a good one and I made it even more effective by giving it a 'soundtrack' of my favourite, restful music and by putting my dog into the picture. So far so good, but I then came up with another good idea – full body relaxation. When I got into bed, I'd do a full body relaxation, working up through my legs and arms and body. This meant that I was physically relaxed and that made me mentally relaxed. Usually I'd fall asleep before I'd even finished the exercise and if I woke in the night I'd either go back to my image of walking the dog or start another relaxation exercise. This was all so helpful that my confidence about sleeping improved and I was genuinely able to reassure myself if I had a period of wakefulness: 'Rik,' I'd say, 'don't worry – you know that worry only makes it worse. If you can't solve the problem right now, then take your mind off it and get a decent night's sleep. You know you can do it and you'll feel better for it in the morning.'

Depression

It is very common for anxiety to be part of being depressed – in fact, one type of depression is called 'agitated depression' because it is experienced as low mood coupled with tensions and anxiety. Although managing anxiety won't necessarily resolve the depression, it can make coping with depression a lot easier.

Below are two examples. Dominic's story is about using stress-management strategies to help cope with long-standing depression, and Viv's account shows how assertiveness and distraction helped her cope with her first bout of depressed mood.

Dominic: I've always been what my friend calls 'a bit of a glass-half-empty bloke' and I often feel really down. I worry that I'll never enjoy life and I worry that things will get worse – then I feel even more low in my spirits. My doctor and I have talked about medication but I've always preferred not to go down that route – after all, I can still work and have a social life so surely I don't need medicine. About a year ago I was talking to my friend about how I always felt down and on edge and he told me about a stress-management group he had attended at his local GP practice. He thought that some of the things that had helped him to calm himself and get into a better frame of mind could help me. There wasn't a group running at my GP's surgery but I did find a book that helped me. What I learnt was that I could catch the worrying thoughts (and sometimes images) that went through my mind and I could do two things:

1. I could switch them off by thinking of something more positive: because my worries are all about not coping with my depression and getting into messes at work and at home, I developed some positive images of doing the things I could do and that I like doing. For example, I made myself remember an afternoon at work when I'd run a training event that went smoothly and I was given a lot of credit for it; I recalled knocking a football around with friends in my local park and driving to the beach on a sunny day last summer. These images gave me a good feeling just by thinking of them and they also represented coping and being well in the future – which gives me hope. I could also switch off my worries by just doing something distracting like taking a walk or reading a magazine.

2. I could reassure myself, too. I learnt to stand back from the worrying thoughts and remind myself that, although I tended to be 'a glass half-empty bloke' I still had friends I loved and who cared about me and a job that gave me some pleasure. I had achieved a lot really and I had also learnt that I could make myself feel a bit better by learning how to switch off the worries – this helped me feel in control for the first time and made me feel more hopeful that I could do something about it and the future became less scary.

My friend was really helpful and he encouraged me to hang in even when I had low, hopeless days, and it was worth the effort. I feel calmer and so much more optimistic about being able to take control of the way I think and feel, so the next book I buy will be about how to manage my depression.

Viv: My depression came on quite suddenly when I was in my mid-thirties. My work at the centre had always been stressful, but I enjoyed the challenge of helping people. Then along came my own children, but I seemed to be able to juggle home and work life, although the pressure was greater, of course. Then came the cutbacks in my service and we all seemed to have to do twice as much work. I think I reached breaking point – I didn't feel that I was doing a good job at work or at home. I got agitated about things, about forgetting important stuff or about doing a bad job. I woke at night and in the mornings with a dread of the day to come – what might I do wrong? How was I going to cope? Thoughts just going round and round. I lost sleep, I felt worse and worse about myself and it got me down. My memory was bad, I couldn't concentrate, I didn't look forward to things – I got depressed.

My partner noticed the change. He's a very practical person and he sat down with me so that we could talk about what was happening. He helped me to see what things were real problems and what things were problems because I was feeling depressed. There were real problems, there is no doubt – I had to do the job of two people now and this was impossible. Then there were the problems that stemmed from my depression and worry. One of the most disabling things for me was the night-time ruminations – they left me tired and ragged in the morning and this meant that every day got off to a bad start. My partner pointed out that I could try to do something about both of these things. He said that I could approach my boss and be assertive in explaining that I was overworked, but to be honest I didn't feel up to the challenge so I said that I'd start by trying to tackle the ruminations in order to get a good night's sleep. I used relaxation exercises to get me off to sleep at night and to take my mind off my worries. If I woke in the night, I had a soothing image that I kept returning to and I had a little mantra: 'Leave it until the morning – you think better then.' This helped and I began to get a better night's sleep. Then I was actually better at problem-solving in the morning and I got a bit of my old confidence back. But the big problem of being overworked was still a reality and things would be difficult until I addressed it. With some better sleep behind me and with the support of my partner I was able to prepare an assertive speech and I went to see my boss and explained my impossible situation. I was lucky in having a boss who listened. She had not realized that I was struggling because I had never complained; she assumed that I was coping and so she just piled on the work, but now that she appreciated that I wasn't coping, she was happy to redefine my responsibilities. Without the stress of overwork, my mood began to lift.

Sexual difficulties

There are many reasons why sexual difficulties arise for couples or singles. If you are finding that you have problems within a relationship, then you may need to consider couples' counselling but there are also things you can try yourself. Many factors impact on sexual well-being: ageing, depression, medications, histories of abuse and so on, but anxiety about sexual performance and enjoyment often plays its **part**. Jenna, in the excerpt below, was not in a permanent relationship but she knew from previous disappointing experiences that whenever she did become sexually intimate, she found penetration painful. This had made her quite scared of having penetrative sex and this, in turn, affected how relaxed she was in a relationship with someone. She had become tense and she anticipated physical problems. This physical tension simply made the problem worse.

Jacob, in contrast, was in a very loving relationship but he found that his libido had weakened when he had been very stressed at work and had other things on his mind. It was during this time that he had not been able to maintain an erection and this stressed him further. Now he worried about this happening and the worry seemed to sap his sexual interest and stopped him from being able to have an erection.

Jenna: As a college student, I was looking forward to discovering sex but my first experience was not good. It was rather fumbled and painful and I didn't see the boy again after that date, and I didn't have sex again for some time. I hadn't expected it to hurt or to be so embarrassing and this was very much on my mind when I did get into a relationship later in the term – and a similar thing happened. I really liked my boyfriend and he was affectionate, but I was very self-conscious and again I found penetration painful. Then I started to anticipate the pain and it put me off sex. I liked the cuddling and closeness but was worried that this would lead to sex so I became less affectionate and I think that took its toll on the relationship and it ended. I saw the college counsellor and she helped me to see that I'd got caught up in an unhelpful cycle that began with anticipating pain.

Anticipation . . .

becoming tense and unable to relax . . .

making sex painful . . .

anticipating pain. . .

She suggested that the next time I was in a relationship I should be assertive about my needs – I should say that I wanted to take things slowly and to have non-penetrative sex to begin with – just caressing and stroking. She told me that it was really important that I began to link sexual acts with being relaxed and feeling safe – she said that it was OK for me to say no if I was in pain and that I could approach sex by taking things one step at a time. We practised what I might say to my next boyfriend until I felt comfortable asserting my sexual needs. When I did meet someone, I felt OK about telling him what I did and didn't want, and the fact that he listened to me strengthened our relationship. We discovered lots of creative ways of being intimate and, again, I think this helped our relationship. I began to relax and look forward to our physical contact. Often I would ask my boyfriend just to pause a moment so that I could properly relax and he did this and I grew even more confident. For the first time I was enjoying myself and when we did have full intercourse I was ready, I was relaxed, I felt safe and I enjoyed it. If I was to say what had been most helpful it was learning that I could be assertive about my needs, and also learning to relax was crucial.

Jacob: I love my partner and at first we had a great sexual relationship but then the whole thing became so fraught and stressful that in the end I preferred not to bother. When we went to bed it felt like a burden and the thoughts that went around my mind were not about loving and sex but they were worries: will I have to perform? What if I can't? What if Chris has enough of this and leaves me? Often I made the excuse that I wanted to stay up late and watch TV. I'm lucky – I have a wonderful partner and eventually we sat down and talked things through and I explained my problem. Chris was great and said: 'Let's forget sex – let's just agree to cuddle and kiss as that's what I miss most. Then you won't feel under pressure and we'll still feel close. You need to learn to relax again and you need to get pleasure from our relationship again.' So we agreed that we would just cuddle and kiss for the time being, and to make our relationship even better, we reintroduced 'date nights', when we'd really make the effort to dress up for each other and have an evening out.

It worked and my worries gradually faded – and if they did come back, I tried to be calm and rational: 'It's understandable that I worry about Chris leaving me because I've always been an insecure person, but everything we've spoken about reassures me that we are a strong and loving couple and we can get through this.'

Anger

Anger is normal and quite justified when we feel exploited and mistreated. Up to a point it gives us the sense of having a right to something better and it gives us courage. We need to be able to recognize when anger is justified and when we handle it well.

Problems arise when we don't handle our anger well, when we 'explode' or are mean or we take it out on innocent people. Poorly controlled anger like this can get in the way of relating to others in a constructive way and it can take its toll on relationships with family, friends and colleagues. Anger towards ourselves can make us very self-critical and this just eats away at self-confidence.

If anger is a problem for you, you will be pleased to learn that very many of the anxiety-management strategies you now know will also work for anger management.

- **Keeping a log** of your angry feelings and outbursts, so that you understand just why and when you get angry, will help you spot problem patterns
- **Learning to stand back** and reflect rather than reacting too soon is key
- **Using distraction and relaxation** to combat angry thoughts and feelings will help
- **Learning to think in a balanced, fair way** will stand you in good stead
- **Assertiveness** training will help combat angry behaviours – reread that chapter

Rachel: I recently attended an anger-management group, and although I was sceptical at first, I've changed my view completely. It was really helpful – and not just for people like me who have always been a bit outspoken and 'fiery' but for people like Abe who are usually quiet but bottle things up and then explode. The approach helped us all. We started by keeping diaries of our angry outbursts: we noted when they happened and the thoughts, feelings and behaviours that went with them. Then we looked for patterns to help us predict when we would lose our tempers. I didn't lose my temper that often, but the pattern I saw was that when I did feel annoyed, I just let rip without thinking about the other person's feelings or the consequences. As a result, I scared my kids and got myself a bad reputation at work. Abe was quite different – he felt angry from time to time but he controlled it – or rather he over-controlled it. He'd bottle it up and get more and more stressed by this and more and more tense. Then he'd 'blow' – often when he got home so his poor partner was the 'cat that got kicked'. Like me, he always felt bad afterwards when he realized that he'd hurt the person he loved most.

We both had to learn to be assertive – which meant that we both had to learn to stand back and get a balance: be respectful to others and ourselves. My problem was that as soon as I got mad I didn't respect other people, while Abe didn't respect himself enough to say when he was hurt or upset and then it all got too much for him. The assertiveness training, which involved lots of role-play and practice, made a big difference, and then we added other skills – we learnt how to calm ourselves by using a brief relaxation exercise and distraction. I learnt to count down from ten before I reacted and this bought me time to use the relaxation and 'talk' to myself in a constructive way. For example, I'd say: 'Come on, Rachel – you know he's only nine and nine-year-olds do this. If you explain to him why it's not a good idea, he'll learn far better than if you just yell at him and scare him.' Or I'd say: 'She's being pushy and unreasonable and disrespectful, that's true – but I can be better than that and earn my team's respect by setting an example.' Abe learnt to say to himself: 'My feelings matter – if I feel angry I can say so and I can do it in a respectful way now.' He stopped bottling up his anger and stopped 'kicking the cat' when he got home. Very soon the anger management paid off and for me the key had been the practice and role-play of learning to be assertive.

Pain

There is a lot of research that shows that, no matter what the source of pain, getting tense only makes it feel worse. This is true even for pain that the doctors call 'psychosomatic' and your stress–management strategies might be even more effect-ive with this type of pain. Psychosomatic doesn't mean that the pain is all in your mind – it simply means that the pain is probably driven by a psychological rather than a physical cause. A good example would be tension headache – the cause is psychological but the pain is very real.

Again, vicious cycles drive the pain or increase the pain and you need to identify your own patterns of tension. Some years ago I saw a patient who had heart problems and very severe angina pains: the origin of his pain was physical. There was nothing we could do to improve his heart condition but we did do something to help him manage the stress that the pain caused him and the extra pain and disability that the stress caused. He was afraid of the painful attacks and was in a constant state of worried anticipation – a state that would make any of us more sensitive to pain. In addition, he'd stopped going out in case he had an angina attack and so he stayed at home where he wasn't really distracted so he had more time to dwell on the pain. The first thing we did was learn how to relax. This was difficult for my patient so we started with a lengthy relaxation exercise and over time and with much practice, he adapted this and developed a short routine that he could use almost anywhere. This wasn't quite enough, though, and we added to his skills by creating a very soothing mental image that he really enjoyed replaying in his mind. It was an image of going fishing – his long-abandoned hobby; he filled the mental picture with details of how the early-morning light fell on the river, of the sounds and smells of the scene, and he followed a detailed procedure of preparing his hooks and line for fishing. This image not only gave him relief from pain by distracting him but it inspired him to take up the hobby again now he was becoming more confident about pain management. The more he got out and about, the more distracted he was and the less scared of his pain. When I discharged him from the clinic he said: 'I've learnt to live alongside my pain. When it comes I don't fight it any more, I just accept that it's part of my life and that I can do things to soothe myself and move on through it.'

Maggie had a different experience of pain – she was referred to me because she had 'irritable bowel syndrome' (IBS) for which no medical cause could be found. She had changed her diet but to little effect – she was still regularly troubled by severe stomach cramps. There was a pattern to her pain – stress seemed to make her more vulnerable, but she had many sources of stress in her busy life and it wasn't possible to eliminate them all. So, like my other patient, she needed to learn to live alongside it and to develop some strategies for easing it when it occurred.

Maggie: I wasn't optimistic about managing my IBS; it had been part of my life for so long and nothing had helped. However, I learnt to relax regularly throughout the day and this kept my general stress levels down and that alone helped reduce the number of attacks I had. I also learnt to relax in response to having an attack – so instead of tensing up, I told myself: 'Here it comes – it's just a pain and you can get through it, relax your body, control your breathing and let it pass.' Relaxing when I was in pain did not come easily – it's counter-intuitive – but I remembered that my friend had been told to do just this in childbirth when she was having contractions, so I knew that there was a medical reason for it and that spurred me on. Sure enough, it helped. Now, I have fewer attacks and I can get through them without too much bother because they don't make me so tense. Also I began to see that my IBS is my 'stress-o-meter'. I get more attacks when I'm stressed and I now think of IBS as my body's way of telling me to take it easy.

Memory

We've known for over a hundred years that stress affects memory. When I worked in a neurological unit carrying out memory tests, the majority of the patients I saw had anxieties about their memory rather than true memory losses. Their stress and worry interfered with their memory, and once they had learnt some anxiety-management techniques their memories improved. Most people I saw were very worried that they had dementia, and what we all have to accept is that our memories do get worse as we get older – it's a sad fact, but it does not necessarily mean that we are developing dementia. So check with your friends – do they have similar 'senior moments'? If so, then your difficulties remembering names or recalling where you put your car keys or going upstairs only to forget what you went for are probably normal.

In order to remember, we need to be able to do three mental tasks:

- pay good enough attention to take on board information. If we don't, then we'll never form a memory
- hold onto information long enough to store it as a memory
- be able to recall it when we need to

As we learnt right at the beginning of this book, stress and anxiety affect the way we think and this means it affects our ability to carry out these three mental tasks. So it's understandable that anxiety and stress can, and do, interfere with remembering. Just being aware that this happens might help put your mind at ease the next time you struggle to recall something. Another reassuring fact is that lack of sleep interferes with memory: there is a wealth of research showing this, and we've already seen that stress and worry affect sleep. So if you are not sleeping well, take this into account when you worry about your memory.

If we take the three mental tasks one at a time, we can see how the process of remembering can get derailed.

Paying attention

When we are stressed, we are often distracted by our worries and catastrophic thoughts so we can easily fail to attend to information well enough to form a memory – we have not forgotten, we simply didn't make a memory.

I remember going into my interview but I can't remember half of what we talked about. I was too nervous to take it all on board.

Everything that happened after I had the car crash is muddled – there are bits of memory missing. I think that I was so scared that I just didn't process things.

Work kept piling up and I got more and more stressed over the weeks, if not months. It affected my attention and I missed things that I should have noticed. Lucky for me I have a good secretary who kept pointing out the things I'd not noticed.

Holding onto information

We don't form a memory just because we pay attention to something – we need to hold it long enough for it to get etched in our minds. We've all had the experience of forgetting a new person's name or the new key code for the door, even though we might have repeated it once or twice. This is particularly so if we are distracted by something else, and the something else can be worry. You know that stress affects how well the brain works – we talked about this at the beginning of the book. Stress seems to disrupt the functioning of the bit of the brain that helps us hold onto new information (the hippocampus), so it makes sense that when we are stressed we don't form memories quite so well. As our stress levels reduce, the hippocampus starts to work better and our memory can recover.

Recalling a memory

Even if we've formed memories, stress and worry can get in the way of accessing them. You might have had this experience in an interview or an exam when you know that you have the answer to a question but you simply can't bring it to mind when you need it. It's frustrating and even more so when we remember the answer as soon as we leave the room. We remember it because our stress levels have dropped: when we are over-anxious, we don't perform well, but as our tensions reduce we do better (you might remember this from the introductory chapters of this book).

Conrad: I was terrible in exams – I would revise really hard and then my mind would go blank in the exam. My best friend said that this had happened to her once or twice, so she used a trick, which was to spend the five or ten minutes before a test relaxing. She was a great yoga student and she used some of the visualizing exercises from her class. In the actual test, if her mind went blank, she would say to herself: 'I know that I know this and if I'm calmer it will come back to me.' Then she either tried to relax herself again or moved to a different question for the time being. She said this helped her recall things. I'm going to try this from now on.

Magda: Part of my job is explaining things to visitors or new staff – I used to be able to do this with confidence but then my memory started to play up and I became nervous about it. My boyfriend said that it was no wonder my memory played up because we had a small child who kept us awake at night and I had returned to a very stressful job. I think that he was right, but by then I was caught up in a cycle of nervousness that affected my memory and this made me more nervous. My boss sent me to see our occupational counsellor who agreed with my boyfriend's explanation, and he then taught me a brief relaxation exercise that I could do before presentations. He also gave me some advice on getting a better night's sleep and he suggested that I use simple notes to remind me of the key points I needed to remember. All this really helped – and the notes put me at ease so much that I found that I wasn't nervous and then I didn't actually need them!

This chapter will have shown you that worries, fears and anxieties can play a part in other difficulties, so learning the techniques in this book can help you head off or manage much more than just anxiety. But other books in the 'Overcoming' range can help too – see Further Reading on page 381.

Summary

- Managing stress and anxiety can benefit us in many ways

- It can help us keep our appetites under control, sleep better, manage our moods, improve our relationships and even cope with memory problems and pain

- Managing the stress and anxieties that non-anxiety problems cause requires the same dedication to understanding patterns that need to change and to practising new ways of tackling the problem

16

Coping in the long term

At first I thought that stress management was like taking anti-biotics: take the course and feel better. Well, I did feel better, but I've come to appreciate that stress management and keeping on top of my worries is a long-term commitment. It's a bit like exercise: you need to keep it up, but the more you practise, the better you feel. I've also learnt that it won't always be plain sailing – stress and worry don't simply go away, I just manage it better. I've learnt how to make stress management part of my life and I've learnt how to predict and handle the occasional set-back. This might sound like an onerous task, but really it isn't; it's enjoyable to get on top of my troubles and feel that I'm in control. And I always feel that it is a wise investment of my time and effort.

If you have got this far, I hope that you have changed your view of stress and anxiety and that you have begun to develop the coping skills that you need. I also hope that you are beginning to feel optimistic about the future and pretty good about yourself. This final chapter aims to help you to hang on to optimism and success by explaining how you can maintain your achievements so that worry, fear and anxiety need not be a problem in the future.

Key to coping in the long term are:

- practising
- 'blueprinting', or planning ahead
- using set-backs to move forward
- changing your lifestyle to minimize stress

Practising

At the risk of sounding like a broken record, this is absolutely fundamental to coping in the long term. Enough has been said in the earlier chapters, so this is just a reminder that practice and rehearsal are your best allies. The skills that you have now learnt will become easier to use and more effective with practice, but you must keep on practising.

'Blueprinting'

This is also known as 'troubleshooting'. To do it, you need to set aside some time for thinking about:

1. Your future challenges (try to describe them very specifically), such as: 'Giving a brief presentation to colleagues about my work', or 'Taking this faulty iron back to the shop before the end of the month', or 'Going into the garden shed (spiders!) sometime in the next week or two'.

What are your upcoming challenges?

....

....

....

2. Your times of vulnerability, such as: 'When I get tired or ill', 'When work gets overwhelming', 'When I'm put on the spot to talk in public'.

What are your times of vulnerability?

....

....

....

Once you have predicted the situations that will be stressful for you, you can take a step back and plan how you will deal with each challenge. Keep in mind your entire coping toolkit – by now you will probably have a set of skills that will stand you in good stead in a number of situations. Which of your coping techniques will help you? Write down your management plan – our memories are not at their best when we are stressed and you might forget some very good ideas. Do this for every situation that will present a challenge.

What are my best strategies?
Situation: ....
How I'll cope: ....

....

Your approach to coping might look something like this:

What are my best strategies?
Situation 1: Taking this faulty iron back to the shop before the end of the month

How I'll cope: Remind myself that it only gets harder if I put it off. Rehearse my assertive request with my friend. Relax before I go to the shop. Reward myself with a latte afterwards.

Situation 2: When work gets overwhelming
How I'll cope: Keep my stress log so that I am aware when the workload is getting too much – better to catch it early. If I am overstretched I can delegate at home and at work (I'll practise being assertive with my staff so that it's easier to delegate at work). Be assertive and say 'no' to more work. Make sure that I jog each evening – it only takes half an hour and it makes me feel so much better. Stay away from alcohol – that always makes me feel worse in the long run.

Some additional top tips for you:

- Make a back-up plan: consider how you will deal with the situation if things do not go according to plan; have a fall-back scheme.
- Try to blueprint when you are in a more relaxed frame of mind or when you have a buddy to help you – that way you'll be able to be more creative and productive.
- Anticipate difficult times and predict your needs, then you can organize your life to minimize your distress at these times. For example, if you know that Christmas pressures always cause stress and leave you feeling miserable and likely to turn to chocolate and alcohol for comfort, you could rethink your Christmas activities to limit your stress: do some delegating, plan to shop

earlier than usual, make sure that you don't have easy access to alcohol and chocolate; schedule time to yourself, practise saying 'No'.

Using set-backs to move forward

Even the best-laid plans can come unstuck, and on occasion you'll be disappointed in your performance. It is only to be expected but it is a time of vulnerability to relapse. If you view a set-back or a disappointment as a 'failure', you'll feel demoralized and this will begin to sap the confidence you've been building over the course of this programme. If, however, you use a set-back as an opportunity for learning more about your strengths and needs, you can turn a disappointment to your advantage.

Each set-back tells you something about yourself and your 'Achilles heels' and you can learn from this, as Coleen did. Coleen had had a disappointing shopping expedition. She now had a choice: she could leave it at that or she could try to find explanations for the set-back. In reviewing the outing, she realized that it was the first time she had tried shopping alone in a long time, that the crowds were so dense that she felt that she couldn't breathe, that the shop did not have what she wanted so she grew frustrated. She also remembered that her period began the next day. This all helped her reach a compassionate conclusion: 'It's no wonder that it was tough, I had a lot going against me!' This understanding stopped Coleen from being over-critical and it armed her with useful knowledge that she could take into account when she planned a future shopping trip – that way she'd make it easier for herself. For example, she might decide not to take on a major challenge when she was premenstrual; she might now appreciate the importance of not taking too big a step at once and arrange for a friend to accompany her; she could shop at a quieter time; and she might decide to telephone the shop to check that they had what she wanted so that she could avoid frustration. In a nutshell, she had learnt how to learn from having a set-back and that is the essence of long-term coping.

So, if you have a set-back, it is important to accept that slips and lapses will happen. First ask yourself:

- 'Why is this understandable?' Then ask yourself:
- 'What can I learn from this?' and
- 'How will I do things differently from now on?'

By running through those three questions, you will be helping yourself to use set-backs to move forward.

Changing your lifestyle to minimize stress

There are some very simple changes you can make to your day-to-day routines that will further 'stress-proof' you in the future. You will find some suggestions below – read through them and consider how many of these things you could do.

- Build a 'relaxation slot' into your daily routine. This might only take a few minutes but it will be a valuable use of your time. Try to develop the habit of relaxing.
- Do as many pleasurable things as possible: if your

pleasurable activities release tension too, so much the better. You might try physical exercise and yoga.

- Don't let stress build up. If something is worrying you, seek advice from friends or professionals. Find out now where you might seek help – have a list of useful telephone numbers that will include friends and organizations such as the Samaritans.

- Organize yourself at home and at work. If you need professional help, find a time management course in your area.

- Assert yourself at home and at work. Avoid the unnecessary stress of being a doormat or being exploited. Look out for local assertiveness training classes or search the library for books on this topic.

- Avoid getting overtired or taking on too much work. Recognize when you have reached your limit and stop. Take a break and try to do something relaxing and/or pleasurable.

- Don't avoid what you fear. If you find something is becoming difficult for you to face up to, don't back away – if you do, that situation will only grow more frightening. Instead, set yourself a series of small and safe steps to help you meet the challenge.

- Remember to recognize your achievements and to praise yourself. Never downgrade yourself and don't dwell on past difficulties. Give yourself credit for what you do achieve, plan and look ahead.

Summary

Once you have mastered anxiety and stress management you need to invest in the future by:

- practising your skills regularly
- planning ahead thoroughly
- using set-backs as learning opportunities
- changing your lifestyle to minimize stress

17

Postscript: A final word about overcoming anxieties: from the people who know

I want to finish this book by telling you the story of my first anxiety management group and the crucial message that I learnt from the members of that group.

It was over twenty-five years ago, I was an enthusiastic, newly qualified clinical psychologist and I did what many enthusiastic, newly qualified clinicians do – I set up an anxiety management group. I worked extremely hard researching the content of the course, writing hand-outs, supporting group members. The course ran for three months and by the end everyone had done very well and I was really pleased. Now, all good clinicians evaluate their interventions and so I devised a rather long questionnaire to find out what group members had found most helpful. In my questionnaire I detailed all the strategies that we'd covered – strategies with which you are now familiar.

The group members decided that they didn't want to complete my questionnaire individually because they would rather give group feedback. So they went off in a huddle to share their thoughts. I waited quite excitedly – were they going to tell me that the well-researched psycho education had been most helpful? Or the very systematic relaxation training? Or the painstaking coaching in learning to test negative thoughts? Or the practical problem-solving strategies? There were so many possibilities and I wanted detailed feedback on the impact of each of these interventions. At last, the group spokesperson said that they were all in agreement about what had been most helpful to them over the past three months.

Imagine my disappointment when they had clearly abandoned my questionnaire because she gave only a simple summary: 'By far the most helpful thing we've learnt is to say, "Sod it!"' All that hard and meticulous work and this was the conclusion – a simple blasphemy! I was really taken aback. But they were right – this is at the heart of overcoming anxiety. The strategies and techniques are a means to an end and the end point in overcoming anxiety is a change of attitude that frees you. All the guidelines in this book will, I hope, get you to a place where you will be skilled enough to respond to stresses and worries by taking a confident step back and saying to yourself, 'I can do it, let it go, move on.'

So I remain grateful to that original group of patients for educating me in the essence of managing anxieties.

Finally, remember what we said at the start of this book: this self-help guide might be all that you need, but some of you might find that a bit more guidance is called for. If parts are unclear, if the exercises in Part Three are not sufficient, don't regard this as a failure. You just need a little more help and your family doctor should be able to offer support and/or a specialist referral if necessary. Needing more support is not unusual and we often experience it when we try to learn a foreign language for ourselves or follow a diet alone – the teach-yourself books sometimes only take us so far. If our lifestyle or learning style isn't suited to self-teaching, we might need to join an evening class or find a tutor. If you enlisted help with your language or your diet, you probably wouldn't view yourself as having failed. Nor have you 'failed' if you find that this programme is more helpful to you if it is supplemented by a support group or some individual work with a specialist. Whether you go solo or use the help of a friend or professional support, the important thing is that you develop your confidence in yourself and there is no single way to do that – you need to tailor this programme to meet your needs. I wish you every success in gaining that confidence.

Time management in a nutshell

Time management reduced my stress and my worries by helping me to find enough time in the day to do what was necessary. At first, I had to invest some time in planning and organizing myself, but now things run smoothly and I find that I am less pressured and frustrated with my work and I can enjoy my family more. I feel as though I have a good balance in my life and that helps me to relax and to keep things in perspective.

Putting things off and being poorly organized usually makes us more stressed, so learning to manage time efficiently can be really helpful. Time management follows very straightforward principles, but it does require quite a lot of effort as it is based on very thorough preparation. That is where the challenge lies, in making the time to do good groundwork. Difficulties usually arise when this is neglected.

The groundwork

You need to gather some basic information about yourself and your routine before you can begin to reorganize your time. This is because you are going to review how you can balance your strengths, needs, priorities and goals with the demands on your time. You have to start from an honest base and be realistic about what you can achieve. To do this, you will need to reflect on:

- the way you work
- your routine
- your priorities
- your [reasonable] goals

The way you work

First, stand back and give some thought to the way in which you work. Consider your strengths and your needs. For example, are you the sort of person who:

Plans ahead? Prioritizes? Is able to focus your concentration? Is punctual? Puts things off? Is obsessional? Makes lists? Works on a cluttered desk? Can say 'No'? Conforms? Innovates? Is able to delegate? Prefers to work alone?

You need to be honest in your summing-up of yourself – don't be over-modest and don't avoid saying what you are not so pleased with either. Jot down your thoughts under two headings: **strengths** (which you'll make the most of) and **needs** (where you know you'll have to do some compensating). You can use a grid like the one overleaf, and you should also consider how you can make the best of your strengths and how you can meet your needs.

Strengths	Needs
How I can use my strengths	What I need to do about my needs

When you have done this, you'll be in a much better position to draw conclusions about the way you work. When Nina, a single mother who helped in a charity organization, did this exercise she concluded:

My strengths are that I am an 'ideas person', an innovator and forward planner, and I have a lot of energy and drive that could benefit the charity. However, if I'm honest I have to say that I'm untidy and I can be disorganized. This reminds me that I'll need to have diaries and wall charts around to keep me mentally organized. I also realize that, in order to work well, I need others around me to bounce ideas off and to give me inspiration.

Strengths	Needs
Ideas person: have 'vision' Innovator Forward planner Energy and drive Work well with people	To be more organized To finish the things I've started To be tidier To have people around me
How I can use my strengths	**What I need to do about my needs**
Write down my thoughts so I don't forget my good ideas Be assertive in sharing my ideas and taking things forward Work in the mornings when I'm at my best Go into the office rather than work at home so I'm bouncing ideas off my colleagues	Ask my friend to show me how to use my smartphone to keep notes and a planner (if the technology is too confounding, I'll buy a notebook / organizer and use that) Get a wall planner for my study Buy box files to keep my papers sorted Go into the office – or at least phone or Skype my fellow workers Ask Simon to help me follow through with my ideas and plans and he's really good at finishing tasks

Your routine

In order to manage your time effectively you'll also need to know how you currently use it. The best way to find out is by keeping a 'time diary', a record that you can then analyse. By reviewing this, you will get an idea of where and when you use time productively, when you waste time and where you can make savings. No one form of diary will suit everyone, so you'll need to devise one to suit you.

Having read this book, you probably have a good idea how you might monitor your activities, but if you need a few ideas, here are three basic time diaries:

(a) Listing activities over a set period of time: collecting hourly information

9.00 a.m.	Cleared away breakfast dishes, washed them and sat with cup of coffee, making a shopping list. Began to read a new novel.
10.00 a.m.	Reading the novel instead of getting on with chores!
11.00 a.m.	Went into town to pick up the groceries and some wallpaper stripper.
12.00 noon	At home. Start to strip wallpaper in the spare room but changed mind and began to wash and rub down the paintwork instead. Ran out of sandpaper so went into town again to buy some more.
1.00 p.m.	Ran into my friend Sheila and had lunch in the café instead of going home.

Time management in a nutshell

(b) Listing all you do and noting times

Task	Time began	Time finished	Time taken
Answer phone when I arrive in office	8.30	8.45	15 mins
Make coffee	8.45	8.50	5 mins
Talk with Suzie about her day's work (interrupted by secretary: 5 mins)	8.50	9.30	40 mins
Meeting with line manager	9.30	11.00	90 mins

(c) Listing usual activities and tasks and noting times

My usual task	Total time taken on: Tuesday
1 Sorting bills	30 mins
2 Gardening	6 hours
3 Shopping	2 hours
4 Preparing meals	3 hours

The amount of detail that you put into your diary and whether or not you combine these formats depends on you and what you need. As a rough guide, the worse your problem with time management, the more information you need in order to regain control. If you have a job outside your home, don't forget to log the time you spend on work when you are at home or the times when you slip into work at weekends or in the evenings.

This sort of record keeping is hard work, but you only need to do it for a week or two. So remind yourself that it's a temporary activity and a wise investment of your time. Once you have your log, stand back and review it with a critical eye. Ask questions like:

- do I have a healthy balance of work tasks so that there is always something pleasurable and always something that stretches me? That way I can avoid unnecessary stress and boredom.
- am I doing tasks at the best time for me? Am I doing my 'thinking' when I'm most alert and the physical tasks when I'm less sharp?
- am I taking enough breaks? Every ninety minutes or so I should at least stretch my legs and I should take time out for lunch.
- have I made sure that I have time to plan, to discuss my work, to take into account crises? Have I got 'wriggle room', because without it I'm sure to get stressed?

Now go back to your daily schedule and look where you could make useful changes to your routine. If you find it difficult to review your own record objectively, ask a friend for comments.

Nina concluded:

I can see that I have quite a good balance of tasks: there is always something physical to do in the shop and there is always something more administrative for me to think about and there are things that need me to work with others and jobs that I need to do alone. However, I see that I put off doing the tasks that I don't like so much – like the paperwork that I need to do alone. Then I get increasingly frustrated because they hang over me all day. I also take far too many breaks because I love chatting and sharing ideas about how we can make the charity work better. What this means is that at the end of my day I have things that still need to be done and so I go home late (and resentful). I see that I need to make a few changes:

- *I need to list my tasks and make sure that I get the ones I dislike out of the way as soon as I can. I've discovered that I rather like the experience of physically crossing them off my list – so this might motivate me!*
- *Instead of coming in mid-morning, I could do an earlier shift and come in before the shop opens. It's quiet then and I could get some of the paperwork out of the way before others arrive and distract me. I'm also much clearer in my thinking in the morning, and in the afternoon I can help with more physical and practical things and mix with the others more.*
- *I will suggest that we have a weekly 'ideas meeting' so that we have a place to share ideas and make plans for the charity. By doing this I hope I'll be less tempted to chat about my ideas during the day – I will know that there will be a chance to do this at another time.*

Your priorities

If you've followed the guidelines so far, you will be familiar with your best way of working and ways in which you can make the most of your working time. Now you need to consider how to allocate your time. This means yet another review – sorry – but you do need to think of all the important areas of your life: career, health, friendships, social life, family, money, and so on, and how important each is to you. For example, you might rank your family above health and health above money and career. In the light of this, you can begin to get tasks in perspective and try to allocate a reasonable amount of time to each, so that you respect your priorities and make quality time for your family. If you don't do this, you risk being poorly motivated, overstretched, resentful. If your family is more important to you than your business but you spend long hours in the office, you might feel frustrated because you are not spending time with your loved ones and are overstretched when you do try to be with them.

It all sounds so obvious and yet it is not unusual to allocate time to tasks that we don't prioritize, perhaps because we are not assertive enough to say 'No' to the next-door neighbour who keeps putting on us, or to the children who badger us; perhaps because we are driven by 'shoulds and oughts' and fears rather than by our personal needs. There can be many reasons but the consequences are usually the same: we feel disappointed or frustrated and that means stressed. It might be helpful to review the chapter on assertiveness to help you limit the tasks you undertake to those that are reasonable or to those that you genuinely choose.

Once again, be honest with yourself. Don't think what you 'should' and 'ought' to do but recognize what you feel. If you do not really prioritize tidiness and it is more important to you develop your interests or career, you are not going to be motivated to be tidy so you might as well devise ways around this – if you can afford a cleaner, delegate the task, or enlist the help of your partner or children.

With all this in mind, identify all the areas that are important to you and rank them in order of personal priority: then consider just how much time you are able to give to the things that matter the most to you. You might not be able to give the majority of time to the thing that you prioritize most highly, as life doesn't always allow us to do this – if you have to work full time, then you might not be able to dedicate the majority of your hours to your hobbies or your relationship or whatever you prioritized – but you can see if you are at least giving yourself time to pursue what matters to you outside the hours that you have to work or carry out chores.

Look at your list: do you allocate realistic amounts of time to your priorities? If not, perhaps you need to rethink and reorganize and plan so that you give priority time to priority values. There's no doubt that it's a real challenge to get this balance between 'things I have to do' and 'things I want to do', but if you don't do it you are creating a source of stress for yourself.

	My priorities	How much time I give this priority
1		
2		
3		
4		
5		
6		
7		

Goal Setting

Now you have a 'snap shot' of your strengths, needs and priorities you can use this knowledge for planning. It's time to focus on your immediate and long-term goals to make sure that they are realistic, given what you know about your general characteristics, priorities and responsibilities. When revising your plans you have to take into account your *responsibilities* because you have to plan realistically. You might not enjoy aspects of your tasks but you can't ignore them – children and pets have to be fed, paperwork has to be done, relatives need to be visited, exercise has to be taken, and so on. You can't be reckless and simply do the things you want to do, as this would only give you more stress in the long run. Again, it's all about balance and being realistic.

Goal setting requires you to have some vision of what you want to achieve – what do you want to be doing in the next month, the next year, in five years' time? When you have an idea of what you want, then plan realistically while remaining open to the prospect of adapting your plans as your needs change. For example, if your plan to get regular work is your first priority and you know that it is important for you to establish yourself within the next two years, do not undermine this by getting side-tracked into social commitments in order to please your friends. Later your goal might be to widen your social circle and spend more time with friends. Alternatively, you might want to get a part-time job, but if your immediate priority is to focus on your ageing parents' needs, postpone taking a job until care-taking is no longer your priority, but maintain contacts with people who could help you get back into work at a later date. More immediate goals might revolve around getting to a regular social meeting, being on time and making sure that you have a session at the gym. So – be ready to rethink and re-evaluate your goals regularly and be prepared to update them.

When defining your goal, remember that you need to:

- **Be concrete**: a vague or ambiguous notion of what you hope to achieve is a poor motivator. Also, if the goal is not clearly defined, it is difficult to appreciate when you have achieved it and you might not even realize that you have achieved it!

- **Be specific**: who, what, when, how much, must be spelt out clearly. For example, the goal 'to be a better timekeeper' is too vague. A more useful definition would be: *to arrive at the school, with the children, no later than 8.30 a.m. on quiet days and not later than 8.50 a.m. when I'm busy; to take a lunch break between 12.30 and 1 p.m., which should last at least 30 minutes; to leave work by 3 p.m. when I have a quiet day, but never later than 3.15 p.m., even when we are busy; to collect the children by 3.30 p.m. so that we can be home by 4 p.m.*

This goal is absolutely clear, so it is difficult to bend the rules and easy to appreciate when it's been achieved. The goal also recognizes personal needs for flexibility – it's realistic.

Sometimes goals can be achieved in a single step: for example, revising a diary can achieve several time-management goals at once: one telephone call might enable you to delegate a series of tasks; a single interview can find you the home help that will make a big difference to your stress levels. When this happens it's a real bonus. However, some goals need more planning, and achieving them might involve several steps. For example, the goal of swimming for an hour three times a week for someone who is not fit might best be approached in a graded way, perhaps starting with a fifteen-minute session twice a week with a gradual build-up to the three hour-long sessions. So try to recognize when achieving a goal will demand more than one step, because if you misjudge and expect to reach your target by a single action you risk being disappointed. If a target seems overwhelming, you are very likely to keep putting it off unless you reduce the goal to several manageable steps (the guidelines for graded practice on page 242 will remind you how to reduce major challenges to a series of manageable steps).

Now would be a good point to think about your goals. List them, look at them and decided which are:

- **Long term** (e.g., getting a part-time job, taking a college course)
- **Medium term** (e.g., joining an evening class, joining a gym and swimming three times a week)
- **Short term** (e.g., running for an hour twice a week)
- **Simple** and quickly achievable: (e.g., making one phone call to delegate a task)
- **More demanding** and will need a graded approach (e.g., getting fit enough to build up to going running for an hour twice a week)

Be realistic and work towards your more demanding and your long-term goals at a pace that is reasonable for you. Remember – stretch yourself but don't overstress yourself. Spell out your goals and be prepared to review and revise regularly. Make proper review dates for your goals, particularly the medium- and short-term ones, as they can get forgotten.

Scheduling your time

At last, you have done all the groundwork! You've clarified your preferences, your strengths, your needs, your responsibilities and your goals: you are in the best position to reschedule your diary for greater efficiency.

First, get yourself an organizer such as a desk diary, a wall chart, a smartphone – whatever is affordable and best meets your requirements and personal style. Then the very first commitment to put in your new organizer is 'time for reviewing my plans'. Make sure that you have time at the beginning or the end of the day for reviewing and revising. This will ensure that you have time for proper planning and will also give you the chance to look over recent mistakes and learn from them.

Once you have a system like this in operation you will find that it takes little time to organize – but you *must* make available organization time each day. And you *must* budget your time for a monthly review. If you don't, the system breaks down. Don't be too rigid in your forward planning, because from time to time you will have to act in response to a crisis or a sudden opportunity.

Daily time management

Certain aspects of time analysis should be carried out each day, and with practice this can become part of your daily routine. Each day you will need to generate a 'To do' list of tasks that have been prioritized (A–D) according to the criteria.

A: Do today!

B: Should do today
C: Could be put off
D: Delegate

This involves scheduling time and making more lists but is worthwhile because it can save you so much time in the long run. Delegation is fundamental to time management because it really pays off, and we will deal with delegation next.

Make sure to review how effectively you managed time at the end of each day (or at least at the beginning of the next day), because you will learn such a lot. If you didn't achieve your objectives for the day, you can ask yourself why and then ask yourself what can be learnt from this. Did you fall short of your objective because you underestimated your workload? If so, how might you re-plan? Did you not meet your day's goals because you were not able to say 'No' to interruptions? If so, you might try an assertiveness training course. Did you lose time because your work environment is badly organized and you can't get hold of things as you need them? If so, try rearranging your office.

You can further increase your efficiency by learning to plan and problem-solve (see Part Three, page 267) and by learning to delegate.

Delegation

None of us can manage to do everything ourselves, so we shouldn't expect it. Many tasks can be delegated and this really is fundamental to using time wisely. It might mean giving up some enjoyable jobs, but to be effective under time pressure you have to limit yourself to appropriate work. It *isn't* faster to do everything yourself, and although training someone might take up time right now, it will pay off in the future. In brief, delegating requires you to:

- identify the task to be delegated
- identify to whom it should be given. The task must be suitable for the person who is to take it on: it is no good asking your five-year-old son to wash and dress himself in his school uniform if he is not yet able to button buttons and tie laces; it might be unwise to entrust your secretary with the task of typing your business letters in French if she does not know the language
- brief the relevant person/people and train them by close supervision, with gradual withdrawal ending with monitoring of progress

Training, gradual withdrawal and monitoring are a vital investment of time, because delegation will fail if it is not supervised and paced appropriately, and the standard of performance can deteriorate if progress is not monitored. So you need to budget for review time with the person to whom you delegate, whether this is a colleague, a spouse, a child or a student.

Delegation is different from simply telling someone what to do, and it will not go well if the person to whom you delegate is not also given the authority to carry out the task with minimum need for your intervention. If you delegate a job to your small son, you will have to accept his mistakes; and if you give a co-worker a task, you will have to be able to stand back and risk that person making errors. Error can be minimized by good training and supervision; but in delegating you should be handing over *responsibility with authority*, even if you still keep overall legal responsibility or accountability.

It is also important to remember that delegation is not an excuse for passing on all the boring or unrewarding tasks! Others need fulfilment and challenge if they are to cooperate and to develop in their own right. Don't just delegate stacking the dishes to your children; also delegate things they might enjoy, like choosing their own breakfast cereals and school biscuits during the supermarket shop. Don't just give your staff more admin; make sure that you delegate more interesting and challenging work too. And always, always give verbal or tangible rewards.

If you find that there is resistance to your delegation plans, revisit the chapter on being assertive as you will be reminded of effective ways of putting forward your needs.

Time management in action: Managing burn-out

The stress crept up on me over several months. My department received more and more requests and I was really excited by this. I realized at the time that I was working at the expense of my personal life, but I thought that this was only temporary and I really loved being in such demand. The reputation of my department was so important to me that I made sure that I was involved in every project and I even revised colleagues' work because I didn't feel that it was up to my standards. My partner warned me that I was working too hard but I didn't pay too much attention. Then I got the chest pains. They were so severe that I thought that I was having a heart attack. My doctor said that they were stress-related, and, if I didn't change my work hours, I would put the quality of my life at risk.

I had no choice but to review how I worked. The first step was accepting that I must work less than a ten- or twelve-hour day. I was worried that I'd find life dull without my work projects, so my partner and I planned to do much more together when I came home (so I was able to revive some of the hobbies that I'd been neglecting). Working fewer hours meant that I did need to use my time more effectively and so I asked our HR department to send me on one of the firm's time management courses. It was a few hours well spent. Within the week, I had reorganized my work day so that I no longer wasted time doing jobs that others could manage better and I stopped floating from project to project in an unproductive way, focusing my energy instead on the most important ones for me. I had to overcome my reservations about delegating – but my quality of life and my relationship were more important and delegating turned out to be the most useful thing I did.

I learnt, to my surprise, that I produced more in less time once I became better organized, and I also discovered that there is more to life than work – for which I am very grateful.

Difficulties in using time management

'I haven't the time!'

This must be the most common stumbling block to using time-management strategies. It's true that it does take time to organize yourself, but this is an investment for later. You could try time management just for a trial period – three months, let's say – and see if it does return the investment for you.

'It's no good: it doesn't work for me'

This is most likely to reflect poor planning and not giving enough time to the task of analysis and reorganization. Don't compromise by reorganizing your use of time half-heartedly. Also, you need to allow time for your new system to become accepted by those around you. Others may have to make adjustments as you delegate or as you give less attention to them; and some might even rebel. Accept that there might be a period of settling in.

'I can't delegate'

Among the most common objections to delegating are: 'It's easier/faster to do it myself'; 'If you want a good job doing, do it yourself'; 'I haven't the time to show her how to do it'; 'He couldn't manage it'; 'She wouldn't do it properly'; 'At the end of the day, I'm responsible'. Think now about ways in which you can counter such statements, and when you find yourself using them, consider how justifiable your objections really are. Also, revisit the chapter on being assertive as this will help you frame your requests in the most acceptable way you can.

Scripts for making your own relaxation recordings

Although many discover that relaxation training is an invaluable exercise in stress management, some people find it difficult to remember all the elements of each exercise and to pace the exercises properly. If you find that this is so, you can either buy pre-recorded instructions – there are many on the market – or make your own instructions by recording the scripts below. You can use your mobile phone, or a digital recorder if you have one. The aim of making the recording is to provide you with soothing instructions, so choose a time when you are feeling reasonably relaxed and your voice is not strained and you are not hurried. If you prefer the sound of a friend's voice, ask her or him to make the recording for you.

Exercise 1: Progressive muscular relaxation or deep relaxation

This exercise will help you to distinguish between tension and relaxation in your muscles, and teach you how to relax at will by working through various muscle groups, first tensing and then relaxing them. Starting with your feet, you will work up through your body slowly and smoothly, letting the sensation of relaxation deepen at its own pace: you will be instructed to tense your muscles – but don't overdo this. You are aiming to tighten them but not to get pain or cramps.

First, get as comfortable as you can . . . Lie flat on the floor with a pillow under your head, or snuggle in your chair . . . If you wear glasses, remove them . . . Kick off your shoes and loosen any tight clothing . . . Relax your arms by your sides and have your legs uncrossed. Close your eyes, and don't worry if they flicker – this is quite usual.

Instructions

'You are beginning to relax . . . Breathe out slowly . . . Now, breathe in smoothly and deeply . . . Now, breathe out slowly again, imagining yourself becoming heavier and heavier, sinking into the floor (or your chair) . . . Keep breathing rhythmically, and feel a sense of relief and of letting go . . . Try saying "relax" to yourself as you breathe out . . . Breathe like this for a few moments more . . .

(READ ONCE)

'Now, begin to tense and relax the muscles of your body . . . Think of your feet . . . Tense the muscles in your feet and ankles, curling your toes towards your head . . . Gently stretch your muscles . . . Feel the tension in your feet and ankles . . . Hold it . . . Now let go . . . Let your feet go limp and floppy . . . Feel the difference . . . Feel the tension draining away from your feet . . . Let your feet roll outwards and grow heavier and heavier . . . Imagine that they are so heavy that they are sinking into the floor . . . More and more relaxed . . . Growing heavier and more relaxed . . .

371

(REPEAT)

'Now, think about your calves . . . Begin to tense the muscles in your lower legs . . . If you are sitting, lift your legs up and hold them in front of you, feeling the tension . . . Gently stretch the muscles . . . Feel that tension . . . Hold it . . . Now release . . . Let your feet touch the floor and let your legs go floppy and heavy . . . Feel the difference . . . Feel the tension leaving your legs, draining away from your calves . . . Leaving your calves feeling heavy . . . Draining away from your feet . . . Leaving them feeling heavy and limp . . . Imagine that your legs and feet are so heavy that they are sinking into the floor . . . They feel limp and relaxed . . . Growing more and more heavy and relaxed . . .

(REPEAT)

'Think about your thigh muscles . . . Tense them by pushing the tops of your legs together as hard as you can . . . Feel the tension building . . . Hold it . . . Now, let your legs fall apart . . . Feel the difference . . . Feel the tension draining away from your legs . . . They feel limp and heavy . . . Your thighs feel heavy . . . Your calves feel heavy . . . Your feet feel heavy . . . Imagine the tension draining away . . . Leaving your legs . . . Leaving them feeling limp and relaxed . . . Leaving them feeling so heavy that they are sinking into the floor or your chair . . . Let the feelings of relaxation spread up from your feet . . . Up through your legs . . . Relaxing your hips and lower back . . .

(REPEAT)

'Now tense the muscles of your hips and lower back by

squeezing your buttocks together . . . Arch your back, gently . . . Feel the tension . . . Hold the tension . . . Now let it go . . . Let your muscles relax . . . Feel your spine supported again . . . Feel the muscles relax . . . Deeper and deeper . . . More and more relaxed . . . Growing heavier and heavier . . . Your hips are relaxed . . . Your legs are relaxed . . . Your feet are heavy . . . Tension is draining away from your body . . .

(REPEAT)

'Tense your stomach and chest muscles, imagine that you are expecting a punch in the stomach and prepare yourself for the impact . . . Take in a breath, and as you do, pull in your stomach and feel the muscles tighten . . . Feel your chest muscles tighten and become rigid . . . Hold the tension . . . Now slowly breathe out and let go of the tension . . . Feel your stomach muscles relax . . . Feel the tightness leave your chest . . . As you breathe evenly and calmly, your chest and stomach should gently rise and fall . . . Allow your breathing to become rhythmic and relaxed . . .

(REPEAT)

'Now think about your hands and arms . . . Slowly curl your fingers into two tight fists . . . Feel the tension . . . Now hold your arms straight out in front of you, still clenching your fists . . . Feel the tension in your hands, your forearms and your upper arms . . . Hold it . . . Now, let go . . . Gently drop your arms by your sides and imagine the tension draining away from your arms . . . Leaving your upper arms . . .

373

Leaving your forearms . . . Draining away from your hands
. . .Your arms feel heavy and floppy . . . Your arms **feel** limp
and relaxed . . .

(REPEAT)

'Think about the muscles in your shoulders . . . Tense them
by drawing up your shoulders towards your ears and pull
them in towards your spine . . . Feel the tension across your
shoulders and in your neck . . . Tense the muscles in your
neck further by tipping your head back slightly . . . Hold the
tension . . . Now relax . . . Let your head drop forward . . .
Let your shoulders drop . . . Let them drop even further . . .
Feel the tension easing away from your neck and shoulders
. . . Feel your muscles relaxing more and more deeply . . .
Your neck is limp and your shoulders feel heavy . . .

(REPEAT)

'Think about your face muscles . . . Focus on the muscles
running across your forehead . . . Tense them by frowning as
hard as you can . . . Hold that tension and focus on your jaw
muscles . . . Tense the muscles by biting hard . . . Feel your jaw
muscles tighten . . . Feel the tension in your face . . . Across
your forehead . . . Behind your eyes . . . In your jaw . . . Now
let go . . . Relax your forehead and drop your jaw . . . Feel
the strain easing . . . Feel the tension draining away from your
face . . . Your forehead feels smooth and relaxed . . . Your jaw
is heavy and loose . . . Imagine the tension leaving your face
. . . Leaving your neck . . . Draining away from your shoulders
. . .Your head, neck, and shoulders feel heavy and relaxed.

(REPEAT)

'Think of your whole body now . . . Your entire body feels heavy and relaxed . . . Let go of any tension . . . Imagine the tension flowing out of your body . . . Listen to the sound of your calm, even breathing . . . Your arms, legs and head feel pleasantly heavy . . . Too heavy to move . . . You may feel as though you are floating . . . Let it happen . . . It is part of being relaxed . . .

'When images drift into your mind, don't fight them . . . Just acknowledge them and let them pass . . . You are a bystander: interested but not involved . . . Enjoy the feelings of relaxation for a few more moments . . . If you like, picture something that gives you pleasure and a sense of calm . . .

'In a moment, I will count backwards from four to one . . . When I reach one, open your eyes and lie still for a little while before you begin to move around again . . . You will feel pleasantly relaxed and refreshed . . . Four: beginning to feel more alert . . . Three: getting ready to start moving again . . . Two: aware of your surroundings . . . One: eyes open, feeling relaxed and alert.'

Exercise 2: Shortened progressive muscular relaxation

When you can use the first exercise successfully, you can shorten the routine by missing out the tensing stage.

Instructions

'You are relaxing . . . Breathe out slowly . . . Now, breathe in smoothly and deeply . . . Now, breathe out slowly again, imagining yourself becoming heavier and heavier, sinking into the floor (or your chair) . . . Keep breathing rhythmically, and feel a sense of relief and of letting go . . . Try saying "relax" to yourself as you breathe out . . . Breathe like this for a few moments more . . .

(READ ONCE)
'Now, begin to relax the muscles of your body . . . Think of your feet . . . Let your feet go limp and floppy . . . Feel the tension draining away from your feet . . . Let your feet roll outwards and grow heavier and heavier . . . Imagine that they are so heavy that they are sinking into the floor . . . More and more relaxed . . . Growing heavier and more relaxed . . .

(REPEAT)
'Now, think about your calves . . . Let your feet touch the floor and let your legs go floppy and heavy . . . Feel the tension leaving your legs, draining away from your calves . . . Leaving your calves feeling heavy . . . Draining away from your feet . . . Leaving them feeling heavy and limp . . . Imagine that your legs and feet are so heavy that they are sinking into the floor . . . They feel limp and relaxed . . . Growing more and more heavy and relaxed . . .

(REPEAT)
'Think about your thigh muscles . . . Feel the tension draining away from your legs . . . They feel limp and heavy . . . Your thighs feel heavy . . . Your calves feel heavy . . . Your

feet feel heavy . . . Imagine the tension draining away . . . Leaving your legs . . . Leaving them feeling limp and relaxed . . . Leaving them feeling so heavy that they are sinking into the floor (or your chair) . . . Let the feelings of relaxation spread up from your feet . . . Up through your legs . . . Relaxing your hips and lower back . . .

(REPEAT)

'Now relax the muscles of your hips and lower back . . . If you feel tension, let it go . . . Let your muscles relax . . . Feel your spine supported . . . Feel the muscles relax . . . Deeper and deeper . . . More and more relaxed . . . Growing heavier and heavier . . . Your hips are relaxed . . . Your legs are relaxed . . . Your feet are heavy . . . Tension is draining away from your body. . .

(REPEAT)

'Relax your stomach and chest muscles . . . As you breathe out, let go of your tension . . . Feel your stomach muscles relax . . . Feel the tightness leave your chest . . . As you breathe evenly and calmly, your chest and stomach should gently rise and fall . . . Allow your breathing to become rhythmic and relaxed . . .

(REPEAT)

'Now think about your hands and arms . . . Gently drop your arms by your sides and imagine the tension draining away from your arms . . . Leaving your upper arms . . . Leaving your forearms . . . Draining away from your hands . . . Your arms feel heavy and floppy . . . Your arms feel limp and relaxed . . .

(REPEAT)
'Think about the muscles in your shoulders . . . Now relax
. . . Let your head drop forward . . . Let your shoulders drop
. . . Let them drop even further . . . Feel the tension easing
away from your neck and shoulders . . . Feel your muscles
relaxing more and more deeply . . . Your neck is limp and
your shoulders feel heavy . . .

(REPEAT)
'Think about your face muscles . . . Focus on the muscles
running across your forehead . . . Relax your forehead and
drop your jaw . . . Feel the strain easing . . . Feel the tension
draining away from your face . . . Your forehead feels smooth
and relaxed . . . Your jaw is heavy and loose . . . Imagine the
tension leaving your face . . . Leaving your neck . . . Draining
away from your shoulders . . . Your head, neck and shoulders
feel heavy and relaxed . . .

(REPEAT)
'Think of your whole body now . . . Your entire body feels
heavy and relaxed . . . Let go of any tension . . . Imagine the
tension flowing out of your body . . . Listen to the sound of
your calm, even breathing . . . Your arms, legs and head feel
pleasantly heavy . . . Too heavy to move . . . You may feel
as though you are floating . . . Let it happen . . . It is part of
being relaxed . . . When images drift into your mind, don't
fight them . . . Just acknowledge them and let them pass . . .
You are a bystander: interested but not involved . . . Enjoy
the feelings of relaxation for a few more moments . . . If you

like, picture something that gives you pleasure and a sense of calm . . .

'In a moment, I will count backwards from four to one . . . When I reach one, open your eyes and lie still for a little while before you begin to move around again . . .You will feel pleasantly relaxed and refreshed . . . Four: beginning to feel more alert . . . Three: getting ready to start moving again . . . Two: aware of your surroundings . . . One: eyes open, feeling relaxed and alert.'

Exercise 3: Simple relaxation routine

You can use an even shorter exercise, which you can prac- tise at almost any time you need to. For the shorter routine, you have to imagine a mental image or mental device to use during the relaxation exercise. This can be a pleasant, calming scene, such as a deserted beach; a particularly relaxing pic- ture or object; or a sound or word that you find soothing, like the sound of the sea or the word 'serene'. The important thing is that you should find a mental device that is calming for you.

From time to time, distracting thoughts will come into your mind – this is quite usual. Don't dwell on them, simply return to thinking about your soothing image or sound. Once you have started the exercise, carry on for a few minutes or more (it's up to you to decide how much time you need to achieve a sense of relaxation). When you have finished, sit quietly with your eyes closed for a few moments. When you open your eyes, take it easy and don't begin moving around too quickly.

To start the exercise, sit in a comfortable position. First, focus on your breathing. Take a slow, deep breath in . . . Feel the muscle beneath your rib cage move . . . Now let it out – slowly . . . Aim for a smooth pattern of breathing.

Instructions

'Close your eyes, and, while you continue to breathe slowly, imagine your body becoming more heavy . . . Scan your body for tension . . . Start at your feet and move up through your body to your shoulders and head . . . If you find any tension, try to relax that part of your body . . . Now, while your body is feeling as heavy and comfortable as possible, become aware of your breathing again . . . Breathe in through your nose, and fill your lungs fully . . . Now, breathe out again and bring to mind your tranquil image or sound . . . Breathe easily and naturally as you do this . . . Again, breathe in through your nose, filling your lungs, right down to your diaphragm . . . and out, thinking of your soothing picture or sound . . . When you are ready to breathe in again, repeat the cycle . . . Keep repeating this cycle until you feel relaxed and calm and refreshed . . . When you have finished this exercise, sit quietly for a few moments, and enjoy the feeling of relaxation.'

Further reading

Other books in this series

William Davies, *Overcoming Anger and Irritability*, London, Robinson, 2000

Frances Cole, Helen Macdonald, Catherine Carus and Hazel Howden-Leach, *Overcoming Chronic Pain*, London, Robinson, 2005

Dawn Baker, Elaine Hunter, Emma Lawrence and Anthony David, *Overcoming Depersonalization and Feelings of Unreality*, London, Robinson, 2007

Paul Gilbert, *Overcoming Depression*, London, Robinson, 2009

Sue Morris, *Overcoming Grief*, London, Robinson, 2008

David Veale and Rob Willson, *Overcoming Health Anxiety*, London, Robinson, 2009

Colin Espie, *Overcoming Insomnia and Sleep Problems*, London, Robinson, 2006

Melanie Fennell, *Overcoming Low Self-Esteem*, London, Robinson, 1999

David Veale and Rob Willson, *Overcoming Obsessive Compulsive Disorder*, London, Robinson, 2005

Derrick Silove and Vijaya Manicavasagar, *Overcoming Panic and Agoraphobia*, London, Robinson, 1997

Marcantonio Spada, *Overcoming Problem Drinking*, London, Robinson, 2005

Gillian Butler, *Overcoming Social Anxiety and Shyness*, London, Robinson, 1999

Lee Brosan and Gillian Todd, *Overcoming Stress*, London, Robinson, 2009

Kevin Meares and Mark Freeston, *Overcoming Worry*, Robinson, London, 2008

Roz Shafran, Lee Brosan and Peter Cooper, *The Complete CBT Guide for Anxiety*, Robinson, London, 2013

General CBT self-help

David Burns, *The Feeling Good Handbook*, London, Plume, 1990

Gillian Butler and Anthony Hope, *Manage Your Mind: The Mental Fitness Guide*, Oxford, Oxford University Press, 2007

Dennis Greenberger and Christine Padesky, *Mind over Mood*, London, Guilford Books, 1995

Useful organizations

British Association for Behavioural and Cognitive
Pyschotherapies (BABCP)

www.babcp.com

Tel: 0161 705 4304

The BABCP can provide you with information on how to
find an accredited CBT therapist in your area.

Anxiety UK

www.anxietyuk.org.uk

Helpline: 08444 775 774
(open Mon – Fri 9.30 a.m. – 5.30 p.m.)

User-led charity providing information, support and other
services, including moderated chat rooms and special events.
They also offer one-to-one therapy.

No Panic

www.nopanic.org.uk

Helpline: 0800 138 8889 (open 10 a.m. – 10 p.m. daily)

Voluntary charity that helps people who suffer from panic
attacks, phobias, OCD and other related anxiety disorders.
Specializes in self-help through recovery groups and
one-to-one mentoring over the telephone using
CBT methods.

OCD UK

www.ocduk.org

Advice line: 0845 120 3778 (open Mon – Fri 9 a.m. – 5 p.m.)

Self-help charity offering videos and other useful resources for people with OCD. Holds an annual conference in the UK for OCD sufferers and their families.

Depression Alliance

www.depressionalliance.org

Tel: 0845 123 2320

UK charity that provides information and support services for those suffering from depression.

Index

Page numbers in *italic* refer to figures

Index

Index

Index

Index

Index

Index

Extra diary sheets

Extra diary sheets

Diary 1.

Where and when?	How did I feel?	What was it like?	What did I do?
When did I feel anxious? Where was I and what was I doing?	**What emotion(s) did I feel?** **How strong were they?** 1 (calm) – 10 (worst possible)	**How did it feel in my body?** **What thoughts or pictures did I have in my mind?**	**How did I try to cope?** **How did I feel when I'd done this?** 1 (calm) – 10 (worst feelings possible)

Diary 2: Relaxation Diary

Where and when?	How I felt before the exercise	What exercise I did	How I felt after the exercise	Notes
Note the time and place	How relaxed were you? 1 (not at all) – 10 (deeply relaxed)		How relaxed were you? 1 (not at all) – 10 (deeply relaxed)	What did you notice about the exercise and its effects?

Diary 3: Catching what goes through our minds

Where and when?	How did I feel?	What went through my mind?
When and where was I and what was I doing?	What emotion(s) did I feel? How strong was it? 1 (none at all) – 10 (the strongest possible)	What thoughts or pictures did I have in my mind? How much did I believe them? 1 (did not believe at all) – 10 (absolutely sure they were true)

Diary 4: Catching thinking biases

Where and when?	How did I feel?	What went through my mind?	Can I spot any thinking biases?	Is there another way of looking at things?
When and where was I and what was I doing?	What emotion(s) did I feel? How strong was it? 1 (none at all) – 10 (the strongest possible)	What thoughts or pictures did I have in my mind? How much did I believe them? 1 (did not believe at all) – 10 (absolutely sure they were true)	• Extreme thinking • Selective attention • Relying on intuition • Self-reproach • Worrying	Is there a less alarming way to view things? Can I think of a more balanced possibility? How much do I believe the new possibility? 1 (not believe at all) – 10 (absolutely sure it is true)

Diary 5 : Catching and testing what goes through our minds

When and where	How did I feel?	What went through my mind?	Why is it understandable that I have this worrying thought / image?
When did I feel anxious? Where was I and what was I doing?	What emotion(s) did I feel? How strong was it? 1 (none at all) – 10 (the strongest possible)	What thoughts or pictures did I have in my mind? How much did I believe them? 1 (not believe at all) – 10 (absolutely sure they were true)	What have I experienced that makes sense of my fears or worries?

Extra diary sheets

Are there reasons not to worry or be afraid?	What's the worst thing that could happen? How would I cope?	Is there another way of looking at things?	How can I check this out?
What have I experienced that doesn't fit with my fears or worries? What do I know that might reassure me?	What skills and support do I have to help me deal with my fear?	Can I think of a more balanced possibility? How much do I believe the new possibility? 1 (not believe at all) − 10 (absolutely sure it is true)	How can I put my new idea into action? What do I need to do to see if I'm right?